Home Works – A Cooking Book:

Recipes for Organising with Art and Domestic Work

I0808100

Editors
Jenny Richards and Jens Strandberg

The Home Works programme and this Cooking Book was made possible by many people. Many whom we never met or spoke to, or who appear in this book. People who have been carrying out the necessary work of cooking, cleaning and caring that we all rely on. People who have been investigating the politics of domestic work and the home for literally centuries. This book is dedicated to, and in solidarity with their work and struggle.

How To Read This Book

Home Works – A Cooking Book is a recipe book of artistic and curatorial recipes and reflections. They have been mixed and cooked together during the various exhibitions, workshops and experiments that were developed as part of Home Works, a two-year programme at the art space Konsthall C in Stockholm, 2015–2017. Home Works departed from Konsthall C's location within a communal laundry and investigated questions around domestic labour and the politics of the home.

Central to Home Works was a lot of eating and cooking together, and so the book expands on cooking and eating as a place for collectivity, for coming together, and a space for discussing domestic labour, collaborative practices and feminist politics.

Now, some time after these activities, we have had a chance to consider, draw out and think through what we have learnt. Rather than documenting the things we did as things past, we wanted to share with you the traces of the programme that continue to live and grow. Here, we gather this knowledge and the methods we learnt in the form of recipes, so you can try to cook up your own situations of collectivity today.

We mix together commissioned texts, interviews and DIT (do-it-together) recipes. These recipes span from cooking instructions for feeding over fifty people, to how to make political theatre, to how to build a balloon bass. Their variety hopes to emphasise the importance and value of all the different types of work we engaged in and learnt from.

The different parts zoom into the *hidden* side of the exhibition programme, concerning what funds and resources we had, who washed the dishes and how we took care of guests. In short, the reproductive labour of Home Works. A labour that is often cleaned away, forgotten, or hidden from public view, but is necessary for maintaining ourselves, Home Works, the art space and the life of the workers involved in the programme.

The book is not chronologically organised, instead it is arranged in four interlinked parts: the first, *Preparing the Kitchen*, lays out the working conditions for the research. The second, *Cooking*, focuses on workshops and events; the process-based and collaborative approaches to the production of the programme. The third, *Eating*, outlines the politics and methods for how we worked publicly. The final part, *Cleaning Up*, looks at the waste products, or the traces left behind, and how to compost some of the findings that were produced. Each part introduces the themes and questions through recipes and reflections from an array of different voices and collaborators.

The recipes should be read as tools. Tools that allow us to gather experiences but also unpack some of the challenges that the programme and the different collaborations faced. Rather than reading the recipes as sets of instructions to be meticulously followed and tied to our experiences at Konsthall C, we share the recipes as starting points for your own rethinking, to be embellished, re-written and re-cooked with your own ideas and context.

We tried to keep the development of the Home Works programme open ended in order for it to follow its own path of learning, and allow us to be spontaneous in how we grew in different directions according to the needs and desires of those involved and of those in our wider neighbourhood. As such, many of the recipes are interlinked and can be prepared and discussed in parallel to one another. Skipping between recipes and criss-crossing among the different parts, as a way of restructuring the structure, is therefore encouraged.

We hope you find this book a companion in your own work of collective cooking and organising, so without further ado...
Let's cook!

– Jenny Richards and Jens Strandberg

Contents

Part 1. Preparing the Kitchen

(Labour conditions and art production)

Part 2. Cooking

(Collective processes)

Contents

Kitchen Utensils

Kitchen Utensils

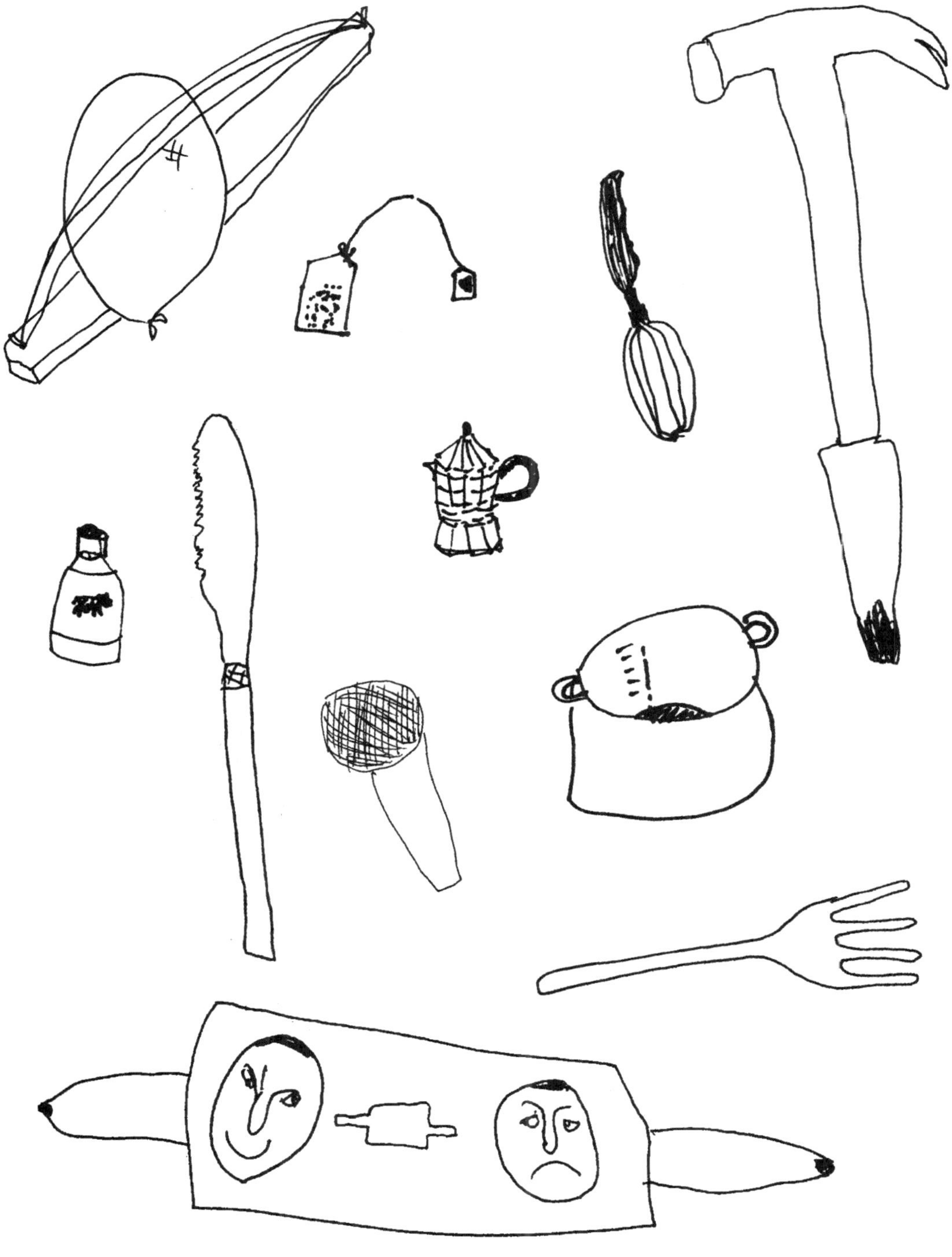

Neighbours –
the art space is located in a densely populated suburb. The neighbours were our closest audience. Their interests and concerns helped shape the programme.

Hökarängens stadsdelsråd is a self-organised neighbourhood council that helps to raise issues and respond to concerns and interests in the neighbourhood.

Artists – we believed that artists should be involved in all aspects of society. They can help us speculate on, imagine and construct other ways of living and being together. The artists and their work was what guided the Home Works programme forward.

Martinskolan is a local Rudolf Steiner school who were keen to collaborate, including working with artists Toncirkeln and Joanna Lombard.

Farsta stadsdelsförvaltning is a division of Stockholm's City Council. They were a key collaborator and supporter in our activities and connected us to other local associations.

Hyresgästföreningen vävstolen is the local tenants association who we collaborated with on the monthly film screening programme – Surr surr.

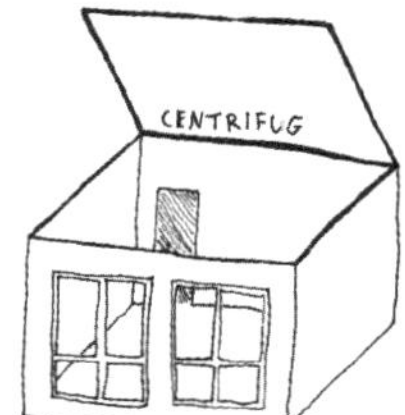

Centrifug was founded in 2005 and is a free exhibition space at Konsthall C, located in the staff room of the former laundry room, where people used to book laundry time. Centrifug functions as a self-organised micro-institution within the institution, where people book to use the space through an open register.

School children – we wanted art to be accessible to all. Hence, collaborating with schools and sharing artistic methods and tools with children from a young age was key to the programme.

Archive – history offers important lessons for rethinking today. For Home Works, we used the archive of the local area – Hökarängsarkivet, MayDay Rooms in London and the Women's History Archives in Iceland, as starting points for the programme.

Stockholmshem is Konsthall C's landlord.

The Siblings Network is a network of art spaces located in residential suburbs in Stockholm, including Tensta konsthall, Marabouparken and Botkyrka konsthall.

Entering Home Works
Jenny Richards and Jens Strandberg

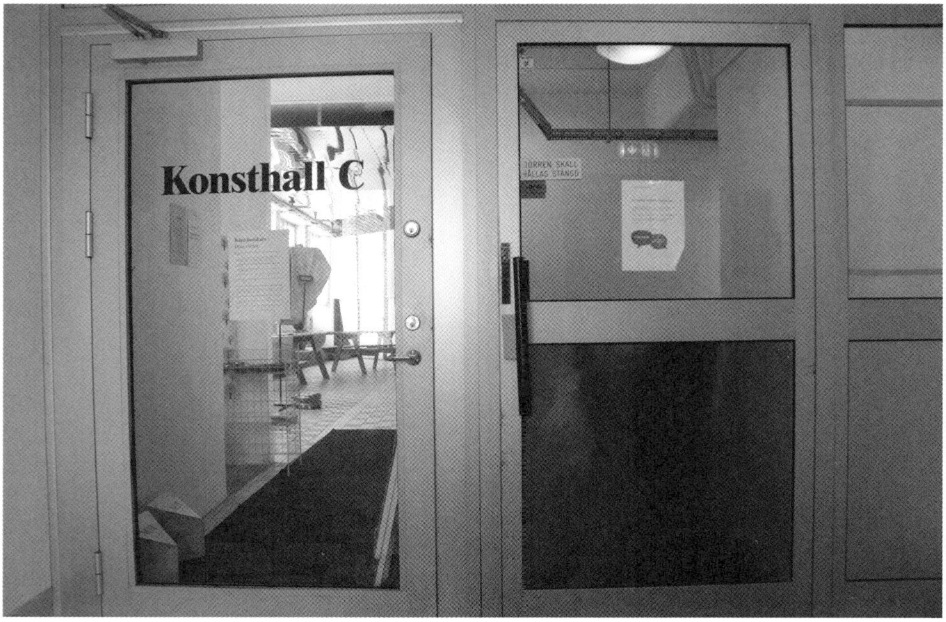

You are faced with an interesting choice when entering Konsthall C. As you cross the threshold of the main entrance there are two more doors to choose from. The door to the right leads to the communal laundry, where you can wash and dry your clothes. The door to the left leads to the art space, Konsthall C, where the majority of the activities presented in this book took place.

This architectural split presents a number of pertinent questions. Does one turn right and do domestic work, or does one turn left and do artwork? What is the relation between artwork and domestic work? How do they differ? And what can this architectural division teach us about the gendered and racialised division of labour within a capitalist society? Why is domestic work often unpaid, devalued, isolated, hidden, and invariably carried out by people who identify as women?[1] How can art be a tool for investigating domestic labour and the home? And, equally, how can we learn from domestic work in order to practice art differently?

All these questions are foregrounded upon entering the building, present when your fingers reach for the door handle and you are hit by the warm aroma from a tumble dryer. It was this physical experience that gave birth to the Home Works programme. For two years we developed exhibitions and events that scratched the surface of this architectural and social division, investigating through artistic methods, domestic labour and the politics of the home.

The way different types of labour are valued within a capitalist system connected to our

1 Please note where the authors use the term 'woman/women' it is trans inclusive.

long-running interest in the International Wages for Housework Campaign, which began in the early 1970s and focused on the devaluation of so-called women's work, arguing that the largely unpaid labour of cooking, cleaning and caring was the foundation upon which all other work was possible. The Campaign successfully challenged the idea that work only takes place in the factory or a workplace outside the home. Instead, it showed that the *factory* was a society-wide construct and that the often unpaid labour in the home was integral to the functioning of this mass factory and the broader production of capital, as one of their campaign posters states:

> The women of the world are serving notice. We clean your homes and factories. We raise the next generation of workers for you. ...In return for our work, you have only asked us to work harder. We are serving notice to you that we intend to be paid for the work we do. We want wages for every dirty toilet, every painful childbirth, every indecent assault, every cup of coffee and every smile. And if we do not get what we want, then we will simply refuse to work any longer.
>
> – The International Wages for Housework Campaign, Poster[1]

As wages are the general means of signifying what is seen and valued as work, the Campaign demanded a wage for the unpaid work carried out in the home. The International Wages for Housework Campaign used the wage as a political tool to recognise and value the labour that had been isolated, marginalised and made invisible by capital.

During our time researching the Campaign with the help of the MayDay Rooms archive in London,[2] we had come across a video featuring one of the campaign's founders, Silvia Federici, who described a mass mobilisation of women in Iceland in 1975.

> Recognising that the lack of a wage and the lack of a social contract does not signify the lack of work; has also meant, demystifying the idea that you are nothing; and recognising that in fact you have a tremendous amount of power in relation to capital. In the case of women; reproductive work, and reproduction of the workforce, has been the pillar to every form of work. In October in 1975 women of Iceland went on strike and the country came to a halt.
>
> – Silvia Federici[3]

Through our research we learnt that the mobilisation was called the Women's Day Off and that it had brought together ninety percent of all women in Iceland on 24 October 1975, forcing the country and its everyday operations to come to a complete stop. The year 2015 marked the 40th anniversary of this mobilisation and provided a timely point of departure for the Home Works programme. How was the Women's Day Off made possible? What can we learn from this significant event of feminist collectivity? How might this kind of collectivity be possible today, when the categories of work have expanded? What does it mean to organise under the term 'woman' which perpetuates an essentialist gender binary regime? And what lessons could the programme learn from this mobilisation in order to develop an intersectional feminist politics?

1 The International Wages for Housework Campaign, Poster, 1976, Courtesy of MayDay Rooms, London.
2 MayDay Rooms is an educational charity founded in 2012/13 in London, United Kingdom. It describes itself as a safe haven for historical material linked to social movements, experimental culture and the radical expression of marginalised figures and groups. See https://maydayrooms.org for more information.
3 Silvia Federici, 18 November 2013, MayDay Rooms. See https://vimeo.com/57818731.

WOMEN´S DAY OFF
OCTOBER 24th 1975.

WHY A DAY OFF FOR WOMEN?

The Women´s Congress, held in Reykjavík, June 20th and 21st 1975, urges women to take a day off on October 24th, the United Nations´ Day, in order to demonstrate the importance of their work.

Why was a motion like that put forward and carried at a congress where women of all ages and political parties were assembled?

The reasons are many and here are but a few:

--Because when someone is needed for a badly paid low-status job the advertisement specifies a woman.

--Because average wages of women in trade and commerce are only 75% of the average wages of men doing the same jobs.

--Because the principal negotiation body of the Icelandic Trades Union Congress has no woman representative.

--Because the difference between the average monthly earnings of women and men laborers is icel. kr. 30.000.- (approx. £100.- or $200.-)

--Because farmers wives are not accepted as full members of the Farmer´s Union.

--Because it is commonly said about a housewife "she isn´t working - just keeping house".

--Because there are men in authority unable or unwilling to understand that day nurseries are a necessary part of modern society.

--Because the work contribution of farmers wives on the farms is not valued at more than icel.kr. 175.000.- (approx. £500.- or $1100.-) a year.

--Because whether an applicant for a job is male or female is often considered more important than education or competence.

--Because the work experience of a housewife is not considered of any value on the labor market.

The general conclusion is that women´s contribution to the community is underestimated.

Let us demonstrate to ourselves and to others the importance of our role in society by stopping work on October 24th.

Let us unite in making the day a memorable one under the theme of the International Women´s Year:

EQUALITY - DEVELOPMENT - PEACE

Executive commitee for women´s day off.

Women's Day Off demands. Photo: Women's History Archives, Iceland, 2016.

Women's Day Off. Photo: Women's History Archives, Iceland, 2016.

Concerned by the lack of public awareness regarding the Women's Day Off, Home Works provided a way for us to discuss this marginalised history. It became a starting point for artists and visitors involved in the programme to discuss different mobilisations against the gender division of labour, and histories of how the politics of the home has been critiqued and ruptured.

During the programme, we visited Iceland twice, learning about the event and the women involved in it. In 2015, we met with Auður Styrkársdóttir at the Women's History Archives in Reykjavik,[4] which holds most of the material from the event. She told us about her memories of the day, 'I remember going with my mother and grandmother to the strike. It was incredible. So many women'. The day was more than an isolated event for Styrkársdóttir. Over time it became a pivotal event for her and her friends as it showed the collective power of women. She explained, 'from that day, we knew that if we wanted to turn something on, we could'.

We also met with the artist Hildur Hákonardóttir who explained how her involvement in the organisation of the event had taught her about the role art can play in social movements, as well as what her practice of weaving had taught her about political organising.

> When organising a loom, one needs to know how the threads work together, the difference between warp and weft, how to keep the tension even and visualise the outcome before you start. The same goes for politics. In that way weaving taught me how to organise and how to mobilise.
>
> – Hildur Hákonardóttir[5]

Later, Hákonardóttir wanted to share her pedagogical experience of being involved in the Women's Day Off, and she produced

[4] The mission of The Women's History Archives in Iceland is to 'collect, register and preserve records of the history of Icelandic women as well as women in Iceland, past and present'. Published online at: https://kvennasogusafn.is/index.php?page=english. (Accessed 30 January 2020).

[5] Hildur Hákonardóttir, in conversation with authors, 2015, Reykjavik, Iceland.

a comic, *Ég þori, get og vil* (Yes, I dare, can and will), which shares her views on how the event was made possible.

While the Women's Day Off can be seen as a strike, and was called a strike by Federici, we learnt through our conversations that it was never termed as such by those involved. Calling it a strike would have positioned it within the legacy of resistance of the political Left which might have alienated some women. For many women, working in jobs with precarious contracts, a strike would have meant stopping work without the consent of their employer; carrying out such an act would have left them at risk of losing their jobs and jeopardising their income. Thus, an agreement was made between the unions and the workplaces to allow women to take a 'day off', which enabled the organisations to mobilise as many people as possible and encouraged all those who wished to participate to join.

Despite this, many people still today refer to the event as a strike. For us this indicates the incredible impact the mobilisation had on individuals, families, relationships and the country's political system. In our research we found that the event raised awareness of the importance of so-called women's work and has continued to effect politics and feminist groups in Iceland to the present day.

During one of our trips to Iceland we met with Brynhildur Heiðar- og Ómarsdóttir, managing director of the Icelandic Women's Rights Association (IWRA) to discuss how the effects of the Women's Day Off are felt today.[6] Heiðar- og Ómarsdóttir, who was born after 1975, discussed some of the current feminist mobilisations and their connection to the Women's Day Off, which had showed the power women can have when collectively coming together.

In 2008, during the so-called credit crunch and 33 years after the original day off, the three main commercial banks in Iceland collapsed, causing one of the largest economic crises in the history of the country. As in 1975, people took to the streets to protest and make their voices heard. Inspiration was drawn from the kitchen in the now famous Pots and Pans Revolution, a series of large-scale anti-government protests in which crowds were banging pots and pans outside the Icelandic parliament. Not settling for compromises, these mobilisations initiated the fall of the government. The Pots and Pans Revolution speaks to a legacy of protest that has dramatically changed the running of the country. Heiðar- og Ómarsdóttir discussed with us how activism after the financial crash reminds her of one of the strategies learnt from the Women's Day Off.

> After the financial crash, young people, especially young women, are realising that they cannot make society a better place for themselves by only operating on the individual level ... Women are coming together and doing it in an old-fashioned manner, an age-old tool that we lost for a couple of decades while we were meant to be all independent, meant to work alone, as individuals.
>
> – Brynhildur Heiðar - og Ómarsdóttir[7]

With the Home Works programme we wanted to take this lesson forward and create a communal space for people to come together, face to face, to fight societal injustices. We learnt that the collective potential to change society and working conditions is at its most effective and transformative when bodies mobilise together in space. These

[6] We met Brynhildur Heiðar - og Ómarsdóttir at the home of the IWRA. The building hosts many organisations that fight for gender equality and is an important space for groups to organise. The work of the IWRA includes increasing women's representation in politics, working to eradicate gender income inequality and lobbying to make gender studies a mandatory subject in secondary schools. http://kvenrettindafelag.is/en.

[7] Brynhildur Heiðar - og Ómarsdóttir, in conversations with the authors, 2015, Reykjavik, Iceland.

discussions and experiences in Iceland influenced how we thought about our work at Konsthall C and what direction we wanted the Home Works programme to take. Instead of limiting our time at the art space to individualised artistic experiments, we saw our two years there as a chance to learn from the Women's Day Off and create moments of collectivity where we could feel connected with others.

For example, during the programme we developed a collective reading group as a way to explore the isolation and individualisation not only of domestic labour but also, as Heiðar- og Ómarsdóttir had reminded us, of the individualisation of the home in contemporary Western societies. The series was called the *Airbnb Reading Group*[8] and took place in homes that rented out rooms via the home rental platform Airbnb. Airbnb is often used as a way for occupants to help pay the rent or contribute to the family income. During our gatherings we read texts related to the commercialisation of the home and discussed the intensification of a compartmentalised society.

Our discussions led us to the work of urban geographer David Harvey, who has written extensively on the social and political implications of privatising public space. He returns to the philosopher Henri Lefebvre's idea of the 'right to the city', insisting on the vital importance of a communal right to accessing and contributing to the way in which, and for whom, the urban space is developed. According to Harvey:

> the right to the city is far more than the individual liberty to access urban resources: it is a right to change ourselves by changing the city. It is, moreover, a common rather than an individual right, since this transformation inevitably depends upon the exercise of a collective power to reshape the processes of urbanisation. The freedom to make and remake our cities and ourselves is, I want to argue, one of the most precious yet most neglected of our human rights.
>
> – David Harvey[9]

Harvey critically describes the process of privatisation, delivered through neoliberal housing and social policies, as an 'accumulation by dispossession',[10] highlighting how ownership connects with colonial and imperial processes. While accumulation by dispossession is commonly referred to as an 'original' or 'primitive' concept during the rise of capitalism,[11] he shows that, on the contrary, it is an ongoing process within capitalism that continuously transforms the collective and communal to

8 Developed in collaboration with the Stockholm based curator Emily Fahlén.
9 David Harvey, "The right to the city", *New Left Review* 53 (2008): 23.
10 David Harvey, *Spaces of Global Capitalism*, (London: Verso 2006), p. 43.
11 Ibid. p. 43.

the private and individual. A process that connects the land enclosures of the 16th century to Airbnb today.

The idea of creating spaces where people can come together and communally confront injustices became a key thread throughout a lot of the Home Works programme's activities. Events and commissions often contained collective strategies for producing art that were centred around pedagogical discussion and sharing. A method to ground and situate the effects of a divisive and exploitative society within our own experiences.

This notion was also evident in our organising of the many workshops that were centred around collaboration and worked closely with the community and neighbours of Konsthall C. Often these situations created intimate environments where participants would come together and challenge their own ideas and viewpoints. For us, these intimate and sometimes conflictual discussions were also connected to the legacy of the communal laundry that Home Works found itself a part of – a discursive practice embedded in the walls of the building.

Learning about the history of the communal laundry was an important part of our beginnings at the art space. The communal laundry is a key component of the Swedish housing project *Folkhemmet* (People's Home), begun in the 1920s and based on the idea that everyone should have access to a good home regardless of their economic situation. This project was implemented through the modernisation of living conditions, including the construction of the communal laundry where citizens could carry out some of their domestic work. While an efficient hub for residents to take care of their domestic chores, it was also a place where people would bump into each other and chat about changes and challenges in the neighbourhood. Therefore, it became known as a site not just for sharing labour, but indirectly as a place for conflicts and democratic conversations. People would air their ideas and viewpoints, and inadvertently construct a space for public debate, not far from Harvey's ideas of how people might reclaim their right to the city and its development.

Over the years, the communal parts of the People's Home project, such as the communal laundry, have undergone major changes and cutbacks. When the communal laundry connected to Konsthall C began there were two full-time staff employed to help manage and run it. They were an important part of the neighbourhood, as they were the ones who recognised every member of the community and could take part in, and manage the discussions that took place. Like a human conduit, they connected people in the community with each other and refereed conflictual conversations between neighbours. This role existed until 1995, after which the laundry staff were replaced by an automatic booking system, and later the washing machines were separated and reorganised into individual booths. Like with many similar cutbacks, what the decision makers fail to recognise is the additional, critical work of community relations and social connection that workers such as the communal laundry staff perform.

As the community laundry was a key meeting place for the area, its compartmentalisation marked a moment in which the democratic ideas of the People's Home were starting to erode. Thereafter other changes began. While the communal laundry had provided a space for creating and managing conversations, meetings and conflicts between neighbours, it has, over time, grown into a barren environment in which neighbours are strangers to one another and greetings are rare. One might now find passive-aggressive complaints and tumble-dryer-trolling notes on the notice board. Disagreements between neighbours, without a staffed space to share thoughts and opinions, has ended up in arguments, uncontrolled conflicts and even physical fights. If the communal laundry was once a symbol of local democracy in Sweden, it is now also a symbol of a lost era, and the erosion of democratic ideas and policies.[12]

While the reorganisation of the communal laundry took place in the 1990s, another reorganisation, this time architectural, took place in the neighbourhood in the 1940s, at the start of the People's Home project. When the architects Ernst Grönwall and Georg Varhelyi were designing the area, Veckodagsområdet, close to Konsthall C, they were forced to split the originally planned three-bedroom apartments in half, thereby creating an additional 500 single bedroom homes for families in the area. Rooms that were planned as bathrooms were transformed into temporary kitchens and communal toilets were installed in the basements. The split was meant to solve the sudden housing demand and was only planned as a temporary solution. However, it ended up lasting for eight years. The overpopulated homes and cramped living conditions led to social problems, particularly around poor health. The increased number of families living in the area at that time resulted in a much larger community than the planned infrastructure was built for.

For us, the splitting of the apartments echoed the way the communal laundry had been divided in half in order to accommodate Konsthall C. However, rather than reproducing practices that led to the separation of spaces and people, we aimed to question the concept of division itself, whether implemented through architecture or work. We worked to create a programme that brought people together with a focus that was able to explore how art could instead be embedded in the community, support local concerns and bridge the physical and conceptual walls that had been erected in the neighbourhood. Could it be that spaces for culture become more urgently needed in an era of privatisation? If so, how could Home Works help build a space that would address these concerns? In a way, we wanted to see how the walls of Konsthall C could become more porous, or in the words of the architect Jane Rendell, to 'undo the architecture' and the spatial divisions and social relations it produces.[13]

The People's Home project has been both praised and criticised over the years. Arguably, it paved the way for the constitution of the Swedish welfare state and the citizens' right to education, housing and healthcare. At the same time, it should be criticised as part of a nationalist agenda that aimed to construct a particular type of

[12] Other social city planning aspects of the People's Home project near Konsthall C is a series of small woodlands that separate the buildings into 'neighbourhood units'. These areas are described as 'green lungs' and were planned as public living rooms, where the community could come together, rest and escape the stress of everyday life. During our time at Konsthall C, these spaces started to become subject to private development and the land was earmarked for the construction of expensive apartments. For us, this continued to make evident Harvey's idea that accumulation by dispossession is an ongoing process, taking place in our very neighbourhood, transforming the communal into the private. The layout of the apartments in the area was also researched and planned in minute detail. For example, to counter the overcrowded homes that had grown problematic in Stockholm's city centre, the kitchens were kept small so as to avoid residents from using them as a sleeping place. The planning of the area was in many ways at the forefront of the development of dwellings that were to alleviate not only the housing problem, but also social problems, including addiction, poor health and domestic abuse. However, the issues that were originally addressed through the People's Home project continue today, with extreme lack of affordable housing in Stockholm and many support structures for vulnerable people privatised or removed.

[13] Jane Rendell, "Undoing Architecture", (2012). Published online at: http://www.janerendell.co.uk/chapters/undoing-architecture (Accessed 20 March 2020).

citizen, all the while excluding those who did not fit into this vision.

Today, the People's Home project has resurfaced in the rhetoric of nationalist, fascist parties such as Sverigedemokraterna (Sweden Democrats). The party often distorts and romanticises the time of its inception in order to mobilise people to take on their nationalist and racist agenda. We felt an urgent need to address this within the Home Works programme, as the community laundry is, in many ways, a symbol of the People's Home project, and, shockingly, many people in the area had begun to vote for the Sweden Democrats. Through the programme, we wanted to critically reflect on how the legacy of the People's Home project continues to inform us today. What latent oppressive ideas might be embedded within the walls of the surrounding apartments and the art space? And how could we undo the architecture of these walls in order to hold debates and discussions which build social and political relations not based on the exclusion of others? How could the Home Works programme actively challenge current racist ideology, politics and methods?

This book discusses and reflects on some of this work, considering the way the home relates to both personal and global issues, whether they be political, economic, cultural, scientific or emotional. A home is needed in order to survive, and yet, the accessibility to safe shelter is never disconnected from structural injustices.

The first part, *Preparing the Kitchen*, begins in the middle of a cluttered kitchen and discusses the underlying structures of the Home Works programme. Through the different texts and recipes we try to peel back the surface of Konsthall C and share the conditions the space and its staff were working under. Who did the space connect with? Who did not know it was there? Without prior knowledge of the area, we wanted to learn about the context and so began the programme with a series of housewarming dinners to which neighbours and members of the public were invited. Through our dinners we quickly learnt about the area and its challenges, and we began to think about how this could influence the making of the Home Works programme but also our own working conditions. How would we like to work? And how would we like to collaborate with others?

The recipes range from the Home Works programme's curatorial structure to an economic potluck and how to write manifestos, (including our own). *Preparing the Kitchen* is, in many ways, inspired by the artist Kristina Schultz's research *100 days of need and greed*, which is here reworked into a recipe. Her work began when she cleared out all of her belongings from her apartment in an attempt to deconstruct her home, relearn from everyday life and understand what constituted her home and why.

Preparing the Kitchen includes a new text, by our long-term collaborator Gunilla Lundahl, which outlines a series of questions she posed to us at the beginning of the programme and a reflection on our collaboration and work. Temi Odumosu's essay "Race-proofing at home" focuses on the racial pollutants that are hidden at home and how we might discover them and look at our homes with renewed critical rigour. Also included is a conversation with Silvia Federici that was made in 2016 when she visited us, and an interview between ourselves and the art magazine Kunstkritikk, that we conducted before the programme began. The interview offers a brief account of our previous work and interests.

The second part, *Cooking*, highlights some of the collective processes within Home Works: the workshops, conversations and experiments that can be viewed as the *hidden* work of the programme, as they often were not seen by a wider public. This consists of recipe contributions from some of the commissioned artists and makers, including Stephan Dillemuth's recipes for political theatre and Joanna Lombard and Gunilla Lundahl's outlines for different educational approaches. Joanna Lombard has also produced an artwork that reflects on her artistic methods during the Home Works Programme. Local council culture secretary Marie Ehrenbåge, shares a recipe for art in preschools, which shows how art spaces like Konsthall C can create meaningful collaboration with children's education. Other recipes are written in direct relation to the work we carried out. This includes the artist collective Toncirkeln,[14] who share their DIY (do-it-yourself) music instrument workshop, and Khasrow Hamid Othman who taught us how to render a wall when we were constructing Hiwa K's *One Room Apartment* and who contributes a recipe with a short text on the importance of solidarity and how it played a central role in his involvement in the Home Works programme. Following this, we have also included some food recipes that were cooked during the programme. The recipes are for meals that can feed larger groups of people and put collectivity, learning by doing and solidarity into practice. Also included is documentation of research made by the artist collective Bolaget, one of the key commissions of Home Works, and an interview with the philosopher Jonna Bornemark who helps us understand some of the thematics of Home Works through the medieval philosopher and theologian Nicholas of Cusa.

The third part, *Eating*, focuses on how Home Works aimed to support communal ways of experiencing art and the role eating together played in this effort. Here we try to think through how we mobilised a semi-public kitchen as part of the programme and the things this facilitated and responded to. Central to this part of the book is an exploration of the politics of hosting. Hosting was an important part of Home Works, our jobs and the running of Konsthall C, and was part of a desire to find meaningful ways to support collaborators, neighbours and visitors. We wanted them to feel at home, while questioning what we understand by *home* in the first place. *Eating* includes DIT (do-it-together) recipes for how to set up communal housewarming dinners in your neighbourhood, how to communicate and speak about Home Works, and the importance of having fun, or a karaoke night, when working with art that is connected to social struggles. It also includes an artistic recipe by Ciara Phillips, *Macaroni with veggie sausages, peas and optional ketchup* which is not just a delicious meal, but also contains suggestions for how to lead a collaborative workshop which builds on her exhibition *Warm Friends, Cold Cash*. Dady de Maximo's text "What if the sea could talk?" pays tribute to the refugees whose voices were violently silenced by the sea when escaping their homes in hope of a decent life in Europe. The text is followed by a recipe in the form of an exercise, which was performed during a seminar in 2015. The recipe helps us navigate migration politics and what it means to leave your home when forced to migrate. Silvia Federici's voice returns to speak about the importance of 'commoning' and discusses eating with others as a form of politics. Also included is a new text by the architect Sandi Hilal, which examines 'hosting' and the role of hosts and guests in different contexts.

The final part, *Cleaning Up*, maps out some of the reflections that have marinated in our bodies after we finished the Home Works programme some years ago. It consists of the leftovers and bread crumbs that were discovered when cleaning up and clearing out of Konsthall C. This part includes our experiences of working with art and social organising, setting up a public home, and the organisation of storage when working with issues related to the home and domestic labour. The artist Nathalie Wuerth has produced an artwork for this book, *To compose the compost*, which is accompanied by a recipe from her investigation into the sounds of domestic labour. We have also included a conversation between Halla Þórlaug Óskarsdóttir and the artist Hildur Hákonardóttir that reflects on the political potential of arts involvement in social movements. Samira Ariadad shares her research into the working conditions of

[14] Swedish for tone circle.

domestic workers in Sweden. While Gunilla Lundahl returns to share some of her notes and reflections on our close collaboration. This part concludes with our reflection on the ongoing maintenance of Home Works and some of the leftovers that ended up in our bodies and homes.

Through this book, we hope to share our views on the importance of process-based art working and the centrality of this practice within the Home Works programme. Our attempt was rarely to produce beautiful exhibitions (delicious meals), but to focus on the mixture, a forum for generating conversations and unexpected results.

ÞJÓÐVILJINN

Föstudagur 24. október 1975 — 40. árg. 242. tbl.

KVENNAVERKFALL

Nær 100% þátttaka

Í dag sýna íslenskar konur samstöðu og sanna mikilvægi sitt í atvinnulífinu með því að leggja niður vinnu um allt land. Nær 100% þátttaka er í verkfallinu. Stöðvast öll atvinna kvenna í framleiðslugreinum, auk þess margskonar þjónusta eins og talsímaþjónustan við útlönd, skiptiborðum stórra fyrirtækja og stjórnarráðsins verður lokað — og blöðin koma ekki út.

Á þriðju síðu blaðsins er greint ítarlega frá atburðum dagsins víðsvegar um landið. Á opnu eru viðtöl við hóp fólks um kvennaverkfallið, jafnréttissíður Vilborgar Harðardóttur, frásögn af ráðstefnu BSRB og ASÍ í Munaðarnesi, forustugrein um verkfallið, birtir eru söngtextar dagsins og sagt frá upptöku kvennalagaplötu.

Þjóðviljinn flytur íslenskum konum baráttukveðjur í tilefni dagsins, en næsta blað kemur út síðdegis á morgun, sunnudagsblaðið.

Undirbúningur kvennaverkfallsins í dag hefur krafist mikillar undirbúningsvinnu, enda eru konur ákveðnar í að gera þennan baráttudag sinn slíkan að eftir verði munað — og tekst það án nokkurs vafa. Þessi mynd var tekin í Myndlista- og handíðaskólanum í gær, þegar verið var að leggja síðustu hönd á … (Mynd: Haukur Már)

Sigríður Sigurðardóttir,

LEIKFÉLAG VESTMANNAEYJA
ERTU NÚ ÁNÆGÐ KERLING

A Typical Home Works' Day

This document is inspired by Mierle Laderman Ukeles' long-term research *Touch Sanitation* (1977–1980), a collaborative work with the New York City Department of Sanitation. The research involved shaking hands and thanking every sanitation worker for the essential work they do in keeping New York City alive. In a *Typical Performance Day* (1979), one of the documents in *Touch Sanitation*, she meticulously notes all of her activities during a day with the sanitation department. In 2015, during our exhibition with her, we wrote our own version to depict the activities involved in a typical Home Works' day.

- 6:50 Alarm rings, tired, tired, tired, snooze snooze, up. Forcing myself into shower, wash in order to wake up, in order to clean, shave. Breakfast, tea, reading news, listening to the news, brushing teeth, getting dressed. Yet still tired.
- 8:00-9:00 Out, coffee to wake up, catching up on emails that should have been answered last week, writing new emails, setting up meetings.
- 9:00-9:45 Late, running. Meeting the auditor of Konsthall C to maintain accounts, no money, no news.
- 9:45-10:00 Travelling to the art space, getting on the wrong route, getting on the right route.
- 10:00-11:00 Shopping for tonight (using my own money).
- 11:15- 12:00 Making soup for lunch, while answering emails, making funding and production strategy.
- 12:00-13:00 Lunch. Making a strategy for an application to Stockholm city. Also checking out the funding guidelines of Nordic Culture Point and when the next application is due. Running to check the storage to make sure we have tables, buying limes that we had forgotten.
- 13:00-14:00 Cooking food for dinner, writing emails, planning meetings, finding tablecloths.
- 14:00-15:00 Catching up on emails, burning food, throwing away food, going back to the shop for peppers we had forgotten. Fixing tables. Washing up. Someone comes to see the show, putting the show on, introducing the show, discussing the issues raised in the show. Emailing, setting up meetings, cutting myself, cleaning myself.

- 15:00-16:00 Unfolding the tables, cleaning tables, cleaning the toilet, cleaning the floor.
- 16:00-17:00 Still cooking, trying to work out how to make the space more homely. Playing Tetris with the tables.
- 17:00-18:00 Meeting with Gunilla Lundahl to talk about how we will develop the next exhibition.
- 18:15 Running out to buy more coconut milk. Doubting if we have enough food. Setting up a projector.
- 18:30 Getting changed, smelling the cooking. Trying to work out how the bloody printer works. smelling myself.
- 18:45 Writing this list, writing a series of questions we wanted to ask tonight during the workshop.
- 19:00 Welcoming guests.
- 19:15- 21:00 Hosting and making a workshop.

And again tomorrow...

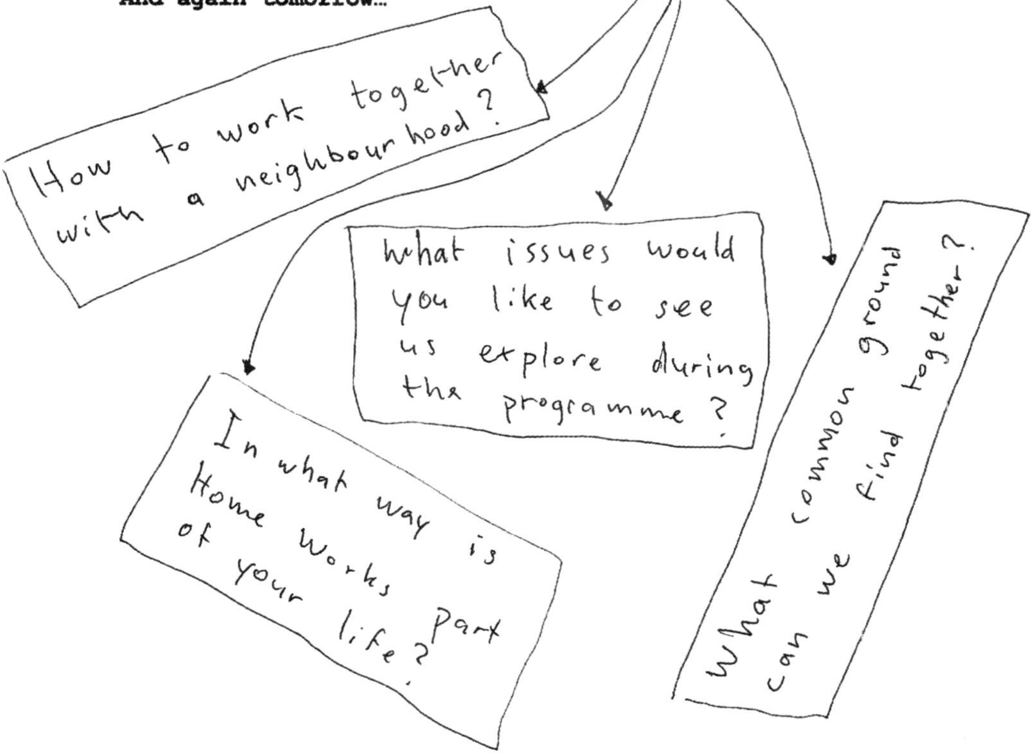

Part 1. Preparing the Kitchen

(Labour conditions and art production)

> **Since the left has accepted the wage as the dividing line between work and non-work, production and parasitism, potential power and absolute powerlessness, the enormous amount of wageless work women perform for capital within the home has totally escaped their analysis and strategy.**
>
> **— Nicole Cox and Silvia Federici[1]**

Central to Home Works was understanding the relationship between the home, the labour performed there and how this connected to wider feminist and anti-capitalist struggles. The programme wanted to explore the politics of domestic labour and challenge the general understanding that domestic work was separate to the reproduction of capital, and how that could inform the workings and running of an art space. In line with Nicole Cox's and Silvia Federici's essay quoted above, the programme aimed to show how our intimate environments – our homes, kitchens and bedrooms – are not suffering from capital, but instead are suffering 'precisely from the absence of it'. Capital will never be dismantled if we accept the view that

1 Nicole Cox and Silvia Federici, "Counterplanning from the Kitchen", in *Revolution at Point Zero: Housework, Reproduction, and Feminist Struggle*, (Oakland: PM Press, 1975), p. 28.

our kitchens and bedrooms are separate from the reproduction of capital.

Preparing the Kitchen focuses on the organisation of labour during Home Works in an attempt to shape and change our working conditions both at home and at work. How has the struggle for the recognition of domestic labour influenced the way we value our work? What role does the home play and what role has it played in different social movements? How are collectivity and communality strategies to counter the individualisation and compartmentalisation of labour both in the home and at work? How can the kitchen be a site for counter-planning and organising?

The curatorial recipe of Home Works

The framework for Home Works was structured around two long-term collaborations with Gunilla Lundahl and Joanna Lombard. At the beginning of the programme, a workshop was held in which Gunilla Lundahl outlined six questions that the programme would work through during the two years. The questions were intentionally broad and were not meant to provide any clear answers. Each question became a starting point for an exhibition or was discussed through the public programme. The questions were also used as starting points for invited artists to speculate or reflect on through their practice. Curatorially, this was a way of letting the artists' practices guide the direction of the programme, and for the organisers it facilitated discussions that allowed us to learn together.

The curatorial approach of the Home Works programme was also underpinned by the Women's Day Off, an event that took place in Iceland on 24 October 1975, which sought to mobilise a nationwide 'day off' for all women in Iceland.

This recipe outlines the curatorial approach of the Home Works programme. It was cooked in a rather cold art space, as the heating was on strike for a large part of the winter. At times, this recipe caused us a lot of stress. A warmer climate, a strict time schedule and reasonable working hours are therefore encouraged when attempting this recipe. Allow time for the cooking process and stay alert to its many as yet unknown outcomes.

Ingredients

- Friendships
- Strict working hours (8 hours a day max.)
- Time
- An interest in the home
- A specific context (in our case the art space located in a community laundry)
- A resourcefulness with materials to hand
- 6 unanswered questions to be investigated *(see This is how it began* ⤳ *p. 39)*
- History, learn from the past in order to rethink today
- Trust and openness
- A desire to learn
- An active connection to the local community (requires a lot of work, but you can do it!)
- An emphasis on process rather than known outcomes
- Experimentation
- A few unknown ingredients, leftovers from previous work and matters that are left at the back of the fridge or cupboard
- An idea of who your work is for
- A salary, to support your essential living expenses
- Workshops, as a way of organising *(see Storage matters* ⤳ *p. 237)*
- An openness to climbing ladders, building walls, rendering surfaces and using your hands *(see How to render a house?* ⤳ *p. 121)*

Method

Domestic work is predominantly taking place within a private dwelling, hidden, individualised and isolated from other types of work. Hence one of the key aspects of Home Works was to find communal ways of collaborating, highlighting how this isolated labour is part of a shared struggle. Collaboration and the often hard work of collaborating *(see Col-labor-ation* ⤳ *p. 53)* can be a central aspect in overcoming the individualisation and isolation of domestic labour.

The key to this recipe is that there is no way of knowing the outcome. Pay attention to the details and use all your senses. Listening is an active activity, do not try to hear what you want to hear, but listen to the process and allow it to grow and unfold beyond your expectation. Who will take part in the work? Who is it for? Invite collaborators at an early stage so you can develop the process collectively, learn from each other and establish a shared language and desire.

Study the context. What are the historical connections to the question you are trying to explore. Home Works wanted to understand the historical construction of domestic labour as a task largely performed by women, either unpaid or poorly paid. Why was the home organised in this way? What sexist, racist and class-based logic was this labour predicated on? The Women's Day Off offered Home Works a toolbox of experiences and knowledge for organising around domestic work. Home Works began forty years after the Day Off in 1975. Two visits to Iceland during Home Works meant that the programme became informed by those involved in the movement, and we learnt how one of the most significant examples of feminist organising came to be.

Make sure to listen and learn from the context you are working in. Gather material. Rather than labelling the material as primary or secondary, consider all materials as equally important and as needing to be reworked into the main mixture at different times, or thrown on the compost to nourish the soil and help new ideas germinate *(see Choral cleaning p. 244)*. Due to the long-term nature of this recipe, leftovers created on the way can often find a new purpose in other recipes, allowing already established collaborations and artistic relationships to evolve and be included in different parts of the research.

Your unanswered questions are key to the start of this recipe. They provide the point from which the wider public, participants and artists can begin to respond. Using questions as tools for speculation is similar to the way an egg acts as a binding medium in cooking; it offers a point at which ideas, the local community and a public can come together, where a common ground can be found and mutual concerns voiced.

An extended time period is necessary for the ingredients to find out how they can work together and what they might become or develop into. When they are mixed, you should be able to smell a distinct odour of the unknown. Allowing the ideas to marinate and grow by themselves is important for the active ingredient in this recipe, it will enrich the potential impact of the experiment on its locality and on a wider audience.

The equity of the ingredients creates a flow between them and a shared sense of responsibility, so that no part of the programme is more significant than another. These ingredients are found by gathering resources and building relationships, getting to know people, spaces and interests in your locality.

Another vital factor for this curatorial recipe is the reproductive work involved. The duration of this recipe means that it needs considerable care and attention in order to establish how things are working together and in what other ways the ingredients can be combined. Work such as making coffee, cooking large amounts of food for guests, cleaning the house, spending time together talking, are all crucial to protecting the openness of this recipe and offering a chance to listen to that which we do not yet know.

Some of the things that this recipe has developed in the past

- Friendships
- Exhibitions
- New relationships within your neighbourhood
- New perspectives on the gendered division of labour
- Political discussions on issues that matter to people
- Bridging experiences between the historical and contemporary
- An appreciation for the hard work involved in domestic chores
- An emphasis on making things together, particularly food
- An embodied sense of unknowing

Leftovers

Leftovers from this recipe are key nutrients that an organisation can absorb, learn from and boil down into new contexts. The leftovers become important traces of activity and will play a part in shaping the inner workings of the organisation in the future.

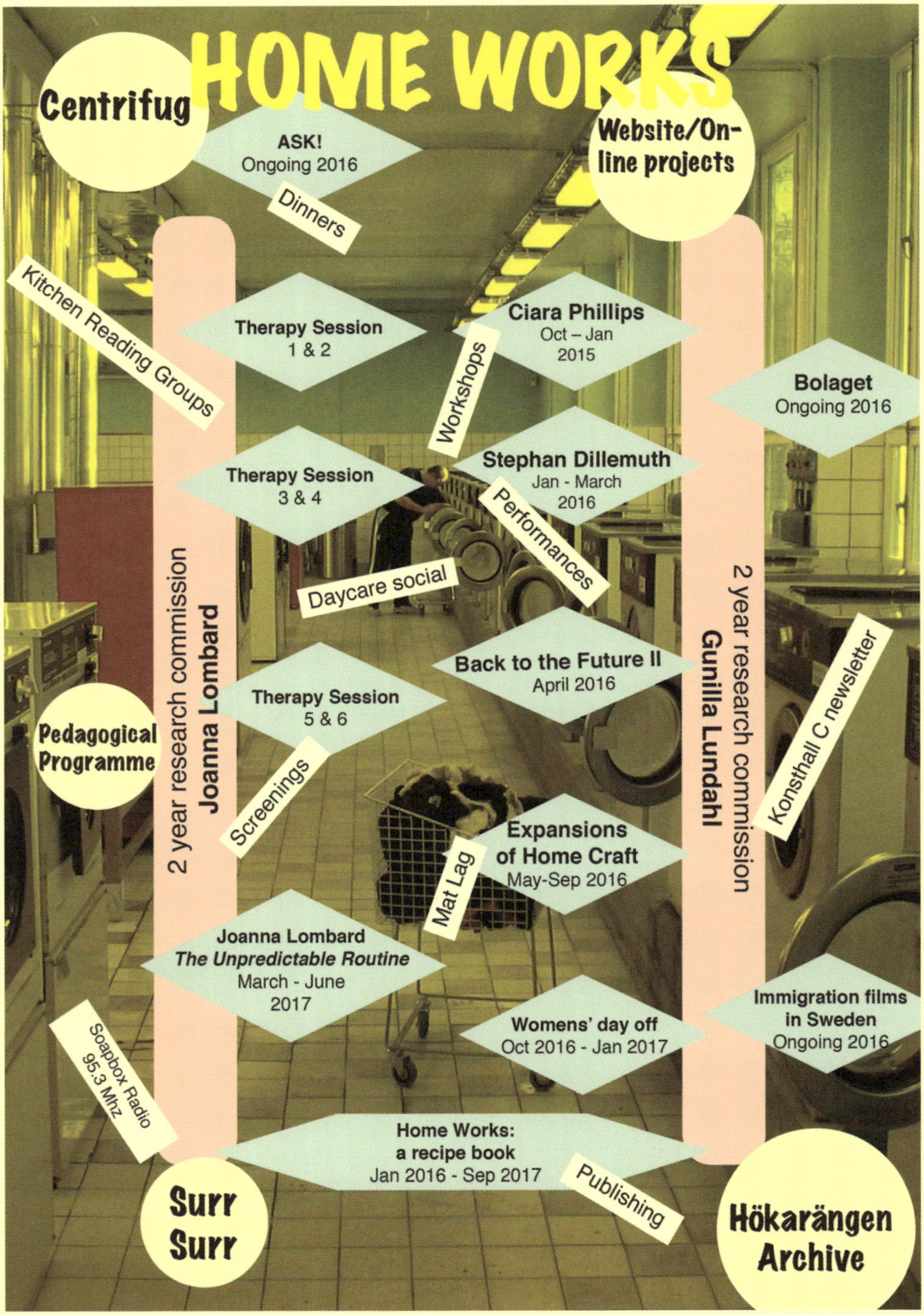

A diagram of Home Works' curatorial structure.

This is how it began — *Gunilla Lundahl*

Jenny Richards and I had met at the art space Tensta konsthall and started a conversation about domestic labour. We talked about the way industrial economics and industrial organisation – and thereby the logic of capital – had penetrated ever further beyond the threshold of the home. At the same time, work in the home became increasingly invisible, unpaid and deprived of its value.

A few months later, Jenny Richards and Jens Strandberg invited Joanna Lombard and myself to discuss a two-year programme they were responsible for developing at Konsthall C. From that conversation came the question of whether I wanted to be part of an ongoing discussion during that period, and whether I would be interested in drafting a series of questions within the overall theme of Home Works. To follow along as a kind of advisor; a role I would share with Joanna Lombard.

What an adventure! I did not know what to expect. I knew quite a bit about Konsthall C. But did Konsthall C know me?

The collaboration relied on openness and trust. Through the Home Works programme I encountered a professional world that I had previously seen mostly from the outside and whose working methods differed a lot from those I was used to. The offer was to establish a dialogue with members of an artistic generation with a completely different approach to the questions I had asked myself in various forms throughout my working life, as a journalist, critic, writer, teacher, lecturer and a curator. It was irresistible. A bit magical. How would it go?

The questions that would inform the starting point for Home Works had to be both wide in scope and basic. We live in a time when imagination is necessary in order to change our ways of living. We need to reverse our thinking, use our imagination, and our expectations need to be completely different from the expectations of those that seek to harness and promote the destructive European world view of today. These questions need to be answered in a very personal way and new doors must constantly be opened. These questions can be perceived as the start of a conversation.

A small art space with limited financial resources, but all the more an affection for the task of using art as a tool for change and reflection – was that not the place where large questions could come to life?

This is how my questions were formulated:

1. What is a home?
2. What is work?
3. Play. Who is playing?
4. What does collectivity offer as a way of working?
5. How to create a sustainable household?
6. How can you connect the bigger societal structures with the smaller ones within the home?

1. It is 2015 and a terrible war in Syria has begun. Many flee to try and find safety in Europe. The Swedish government decides to accept approximately 160 000 refugees. This was the context for the first conversation we had. I had images of women and children who had escaped the fighting in Syria and were now uprooted, living on crowded streets in Istanbul, stuck in my mind. An image of a woman with a small child sitting on a rug that she had spread out on the street particularly struck me.

The rug was like a symbol of a home, of a private sphere. It acted as a sort of protective circle; an inviolable marking.

So, what constitutes a home? The right to housing was formulated in the Swedish housing policy programme. Now, has it been lost? What then are we to ask of society and ourselves? What is a home? An emotion, a strategy, a creation of the self? A social project? A framework for growing? A community? Or a rug spread out on the street?

2. The second question, of work within the home, tears apart the whole question of what should be called work and if it is only about paid production. If so, what is reproduction? Just a question of terminology in today's society? Or, a question of how the conditions for work in a capitalist society are made possible and reproduced? Is work for money or is work for life? How to question what work is needed to sustain life? And who will perform it and under what kind of working conditions? Questions around emotional, intellectual and artistic work are raised. What work remains in the home when the work there is increasingly exposed to outsourcing? Who is affected?

3. My concern with the third question was around play as a way to consider the child's role in the home and how this is rarely open to negotiation. Child labour is largely prohibited, but at the same time children are expected to work to become adults. Is work play or play work? What do childrens' rights look like in the home? Do children have rights in a home? What is their responsibility at home? What happens if children become empowered? What barriers are in the way of this empowerment? Is the home a protective nest that protects a child's freedom to develop? Institutions for children, such as preschools – should they be homely? Do parents need to be raised? What could we learn from children if they were given more freedom at home?

4. Collective housing. Is it a solution to facilitate the collective maintenance work that everyday life requires, or an altogether different way of living, one that broadens the community and the ability to question how we live? But, if the home were to grow outside the door of the private home, what is then our joint responsibility? Can we see the city as a home? How will our maintenance work be carried out? By duty, by agreement, or through living collectively?

How is empathy and friendship created within this work? Would it be a practical solution to create tools for formulating new goals for the common good? Working this out on your own is not possible.

5. Peak oil. Does it matter how we behave at home? How to create a sustainable household? The death of the housewife was proclaimed a long time ago.[1] But what can we learn from the housewife? What knowledge has now been lost? What is there to learn practically and ideologically by exploring the concept of the housewife? What is the knowledge she silently formed, and that is now forgotten? How can we regain and bring innovation to knowledge concerned with utilising, reusing, and employing one's hands and senses, sharpening one's eyes in order to see how we relate to nature and our consuming needs? Is the housewife's knowledge the basis for how this transition can become more ecologically sustainable? The transition we have ahead of us, does it entail stepping forward, towards a greater sensitivity to the mutual dependencies that are revealed in everyday life at home?

6. What can we ask from the city as a collective home? More access to meeting places in order to transform the city into a social organism? Where is there a place for self-organising within the city? What can the city offer that cannot be fitted into a home? When is the city sufficient as a home, and when does it become more than just a sleeping space? Do we need the commons to expand homes in the city? The city as a contrast to the home – another rhythm that pulses through life, a breathing place outside the home. The feeling of relief at home, when living in a megacity or refugee camp. The home as an atom in the social body of the city?

1 In 2014 Sara Danius published a collection of essays. One was a review of Bonniers Cooking Book, which was originally released 1960 and updated three times in 1983, 2002 and 2010. Her essay analyses how the role of the housewife changed through time, until its final demise in 2010. Sara Danius, *Husmoderns död och andra texter*, (Sweden, Albert Bonniers förlag, 2014).

Home economics: a potluck

The term home economics was originally coined in the United States by Catherine Beecher and Ellen Swallow Richards in the late 19th century. The term was used to refer to the education that prepared young women for their duties at home. Later, in the European high school system, this developed into an education in managing a home where one would learn how to bake cakes and wash dishes. Practising and learning about home economics was central to developing and running the Home Works programme. If the art space ought to be a public home *(see How to create a public home → p. 239)*, what kind of home economics would we learn and practice there? How can we share and collectivise the duties of the home? And in what way is the economy of the home linked to larger societal structures?

While home economies are often not publicly discussed, the aim of the programme was to question and be transparent towards Home Works' collaborators by sharing organisational budgets in order to be clear about what conditions collaborators were agreeing to while working within the programme. The relationship between home and economy can be found in the Greek root of the word economy, *oikonomikos*, which means home and management. Home Works wanted to explicitly explore this connection and confront the myth of the home as an unproductive space, or a space outside the boundaries of paid production and the economy.

In an attempt to be a resourceful 'home', Home Works tried to make use of various sources of income in order to make ends meet. The aim of the programme was to put 'food on the table', or, in other words, make available resources transparent so that it was possible to find creative ways of nourishing and sustaining the art space's existing community. By being transparent with the Home Works' economy, it hoped to create more reasonable expectations around work and thus better working and living conditions for artists.

Another key ingredient for the Home Works programme's home economics was the inherited wage structure, set up for Konsthall C by Kim Einarsson and Anna Ahlstrand, which strived to reproduce an art space that opposed a hierarchy of labour by paying all employees the same salary, regardless of their role.

Similar to domestic labour, art is often understood as a labour of love. Looking back now, artists could have been further encouraged to pay closer attention to the amount of time that was involved in their collaboration within Home Works, in order to avoid an excess of overtime. The flat wage system was unfortunately not extended to the artists' own labour; they instead received a fixed fee. The programme also failed to be fully transparent about the budget, which would have required more time and a better system for making the programme's financial transactions comprehensible to the public.

This recipe displays the variety and combination of different monetary sources for the creation of Home Works, an at times precarious funding recipe, but one that sustained the reproduction of the basic means of the programme.

Ingredients

- A flat wage structure
- A smell of transparency
- A pinch of playful administrative tools
- Collaborative networks
- A plethora of monetary resources:
  - Swedish Arts Council
  - Stockholm City Council
  - Region Stockholm
  - ABF Stockholm
  - Swedish Arts Grants Committee/Iaspis
  - Office for Contemporary Art, Norway
  - Nordic Culture Point
  - Nordic Culture Fund
  - Goethe-Institut, Schweden
  - Stockholm konst
  - Norwegian Embassy
  - Nordic Culture Fund
  - Nämnden för hemslöjdsfrågor
  - Nordic Art Association
  - Farsta stadsdelsförvaltning
  - Konstfrämjandet
  - Kommunal
- A sponsor for a rent-free space
  - Stockholmshem (landlord)
- Teaching incomes that were transformed into monetary income for Home Works:
  - Dance and Circus University
  - Royal Academy of Art
  - Konstfack University of Arts, Craft, and Design
  - Stockholm University of the Arts
  - Stockholmsskolan (Konstfrämjandet)
- Collaborations that generated revenue for the programme:
  - Nordic Art Association
  - Film i samtidskonsten
  - Inter Cult
- Home Works operated with free entrance to the art space

Method

A potluck is a dish that consists of a lot of small plates from many contributors. To recook the home economics of Home Works you will need financial support from a variety of sources. While this can be good in some cases – for instance by providing a good overview of various funding bodies and a sense of security in not being at the whim of one funder – it can also create a massive amount of administrative work. Applying for funding and reporting back to funding bodies is a time-consuming process. Another strategy that was employed in funding Home Works was putting income that was received from teaching back into the programme. While teaching did not provide an additional wage for us, (so perhaps it was more like the labour of love described above), it was a great way to season our existing resources and allow ideas to marinate and be discussed in an educational setting. It was a way of finding additional funds for the survival of a small arts organisation.

- Do not be afraid of collaboration. In today's individualised and competitive society, institutions fight for their survival. Hence, the importance of collaborating and creating mutual alliances are more urgent than ever. The Home Works programme began as a collaborative effort with the art space Marabouparken through an exhibition of the work of Mierle Laderman Ukeles, which was split across the two spaces.

- Setting up alliances between art spaces was essential for the Home Works programme's existence and it allowed it to develop in new ways and be served with care and love. Another collaborative network was the *Siblings Network* – an independent Stockholm-based network *(see Collaborators and other chefs p. 10)*. The network had an important impact on Home Works home economics as it allowed for solidarity and sharing of resources, materials and ideas, as well as the formation of an advocacy group that empowered each space when communicating with funding institutions.

- It is helpful to be transparent about your resources, eat the potluck with as many people as possible, and enjoy the company. Instead of spreading the resources thin, aim to make sure that everyone gets paid, as much as possible. Fewer commissions mean better pay for those involved. Ideally, the flat wage structure can guide you in this.

- Sustainability was central to the home economics of the Home Works programme. As maintenance is an essential part of the programme, it was important to leave the art space with a sound economy for its continued survival, and with healthy relationships and alliances to support its further reproduction.

Leftovers

How can leftover resources be reused? Who needs them? How can the crumbs be recooked? What other organisations would you like to support with your resources? For example, Home Works, when possible, during openings and dinners, collected funds to donate to the association Föreningen HEM that supports migrants from the European Union in finding a home.

What recipe is needed for a Home Works manifesto?

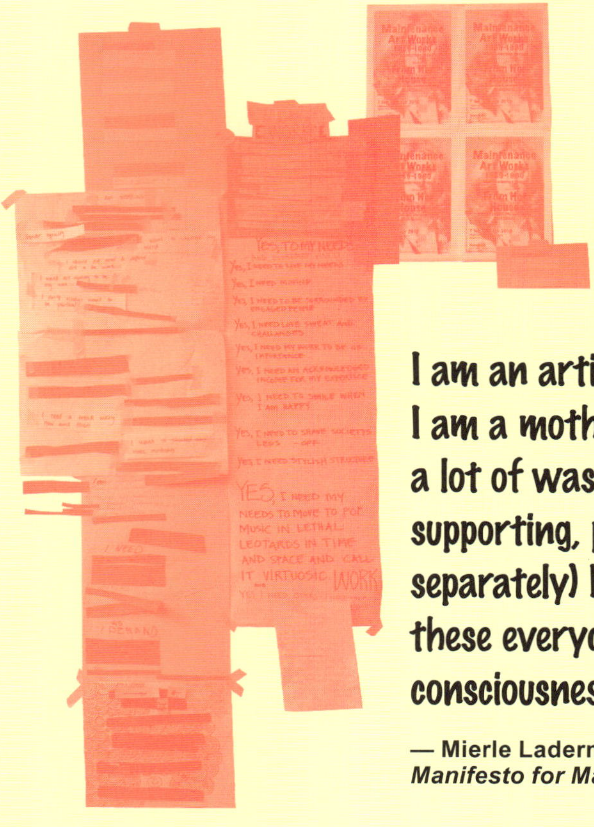

I am an artist. I am a woman. I am a wife. I am a mother. (Random order). I do a hell of a lot of washing, cleaning, cooking, renewing, supporting, preserving, etc. Also (up to now separately) I 'do' Art. Now I will simply do these everyday things, and flush them up to consciousness, exhibit them, as Art.

— Mierle Laderman Ukeles,
Manifesto for Maintenance Art, 1969!

Following the birth of her first child, Mierle Laderman Ukeles wrote a manifesto as a challenge to the oppositions between art and life, public and private. The manifesto is divided into two parts and lays out a distinction between what she refers to as two basic systems: 'Development' and 'Maintenance'. Development is associated with the male avant-garde and is focused on the new, change, progress, pure individual creation. Whereas maintenance, at least when performed at home, is generally associated with domestic work and the devalued labour of women. It focuses on preservation, renewal, replenishment, repetition. Maintenance tasks take, as she notes, 'all the fucking time'. The manifesto uses a feminist Duchampian trick (she cites Marcel Duchamp as an influence) and turns the everyday intimate tasks of domestic labour and the maintenance work of the home, such as cleaning dirty diapers, into ready-made performances.

Manifesto for Maintenance Art, 1969! uses the format of the manifesto in order to conceptualise and demonstrate a revaluing of the labour of everyday life, as well as the role this plays in building a collective struggle that can empower people to work towards change within their communities.

Home Works opened with an exhibition of works by Mierle Laderman Ukeles. The exhibition was originally curated by Krist Gruijthuijsen for the Grazer Kunstverein in Austria and was split between the art spaces Konsthall C and Marabouparken. The public programme for the exhibition used her practice to create a recipe on how to think about a manifesto today. The recipe was transformed into a workshop, which was then shared with students and artists. The purpose was to allow the participants to consider the boundaries between paid and unpaid labour, how much time they spent on it and their enjoyment in doing the cleaning, cooking and caring. Following the recipe is

the unofficial manifesto of Home Works – "How to work together" – inspired by Mierle Laderman Ukeles, *Manifesto for Maintenance Art, 1969!*

Ingredients

- Pens
- Blank tablecloths (in our case a blank bedsheet)
- Paper
- Tracing paper

Method

Key for this recipe is an open mind and a willingness to see and examine the details of our lives.

- Tell each participant to bring an example of a manifesto that inspired them or interested them in some way, prior to meeting.

- Spread out a large tablecloth on a table and give each participant a pen. Discuss: What is a manifesto? What claims do we want to make? How does personal experience relate to wider political structures? How does a manifesto operate ideologically and practically? How can a manifesto be a useful tool for developing critical art practices? How do we create shared manifestos? Use the tablecloth for notes.

- Continue taking notes on the tablecloth. Each participant reads the manifesto they brought, while the others take notes and discuss the manifesto. Question the act of writing a manifesto and how this manifesto can be central for art practices to think, make and live by. Use your own experiences, practices and struggles. How is your manifesto a way to learn about existing systems of value and how can it privilege other discussions and values?

- Grab some paper and make a list of the actions you identify as work you do during a given week. This can be an estimate and mash-up of items rather than a precise account. Use the tracing paper to turn your different works into a chart where you specify on an emotional scale your relation to the actions and also the approximate amount of time you spend on the actions.

- Pair up or work in groups and present and discuss your chart with each other. Keep working in pairs. Turn your chart into ten statements concerned with how you want to relate to your work.

- Combine your statements with your friends so it becomes ten shared statements.

- Categorise the statements into themes. Contextualise each statement with other statements. Make them abstract, make them real. What do they mean in real life? How can we carry them out? Clarify the statement with your preferred desire for change.

- Combine the statements into a manifesto and present it to the rest of the group.

Following the presentations

Cook together and host a public dinner *(see* *Public kitchen ↝ p. 145)*. Each participant invites two guests to join the dinner. During the dinner the group shares their manifestos with visitors and participants.

Col-labor-ation: a look back at the beginning of Home Works — *Jenny Richards and Jens Strandberg*

This conversation was conducted in 2015 and made for Kunstkritikk, a Nordic journal for contemporary art.

Kunstkritikk (KK): I wonder a little bit about your backgrounds, education and past projects. And how much of your own practices will you bring with you to Konsthall C? What kind of differences and similarities do you find in your professional backgrounds, and how do these reflect upon your expectations for the new job?

Jenny Richards and Jens Strandberg (JR/JS): We both trained as artists in Scotland, and often work with long-term research processes. Our practices are informed through working in artist-led spaces, such as Mossutställningar and Collective Gallery; artist-run galleries including Transmission Gallery and Embassy Gallery; and cooperative organisations – Interim kultur and Cubitt. Like Konsthall C, all these organisations were initiated by artists and focused on collaboration and creating new ways for artistic production, often supporting marginalised practices of artists at early stages in their careers, with an emphasis on artistic research and reflecting on conditions for working. This experience is the basis for how we will approach our time at Konsthall C, in which collaboration is key to our ideas on how we believe visual art should be generated. Konsthall C also shares in our organisational experience through its model of a rolling directorship, which we think is great as it brings in new energy and focus to the organisation.

In our previous work we have developed a commitment to different organisational models that are founded upon an idea of collaboration and which seek to push the boundaries of how art is produced and distributed. Collaboration is a central concern in our practices. In our previous work we have discussed the term and played with the idea of splitting it up as *col-labor-ation*[1], which is a way of underlining the labour of working together. Collaboration has in recent times been highly co-opted by corporations and finance capitalism as a labour-saving device, while, in our experience, collaboration has some of the most intensive labour processes. Working on your own – particularly within the art world – is far easier, as the art scene is geared towards an individual ego. We hope that our time at Konsthall C will encourage collective working processes and question the individualisation of artistic practice promoted by the art market.

[1] Labor according to the American spelling.

These ideas are key to our proposal for directing Konsthall C, which instils a work ethic that revolves around the flattening of a leadership position. Not only is Konsthall C known as a space where artistic experimentation is encouraged – its rich exhibition history exemplifies the many connections that have been developed between practices across different disciplines, which we are keen to further within our programme. It is also a place that, from our perspective, practices a radical form of organisational structure through its flat salary structure and open exhibition formats such as Centrifug (the spin dryer): a free exhibition space open for anyone to book and host exhibitions in *(see Collaborators and other chefs ➺ p. 10)*.

The focus of our research has been investigating issues of contemporary labour, particularly addressing themes such as the organisation of work, body politics and collective modes of production. This has been done through a series of long-term research exercises including *Domestic Art Practice*, *Manual Labours*, *School Workings* and *Home Economics*. These themes are quite literally reflected on the site of Konsthall C, which is situated in a community laundry where ideas of work and the gendered division of labour are ingrained in the architecture.

Our shared experiences in education has also influenced these concerns. We got to know each other through communal friends when we studied in Scotland, at Edinburgh College of Art and Glasgow School of Art respectively. Years after we finished in Scotland, we bumped into each other on a street in New York, which was the beginning of a long friendship. Since then we have been finding excuses to collaborate with one another.

We think our shared and distinct working methods will bring an energetic mix of knowledge and networks to Konsthall C as well as stimulate collaborations both locally and abroad. While our work catalyses around dialogic and process-driven ways of working, we are devoted to exhibition-making that visualises labour processes, not as a way of documenting them, but rather trusting that these processes are interesting and will generate compelling material for audiences. We are therefore really looking forward to launching Home Works with a solo exhibition by Mierle Laderman Ukeles, as highlighting maintenance work and visualising invisible labour processes are central to her practice.

KK: Konsthall C is known for its engagement with the local community, is this a way of working that will also be significant for the upcoming exhibitions and projects at Konsthall C?

JR/JS: Yes, working with the locality of Konsthall C and the nearby community is crucial to the programme, which responds to the site of the art space as a part of the community laundry, and investigates questions around the politics of the home and domestic work. It was emblematic for us that upon entering the building one chooses between the door on the right, leading to the laundry and house work, or the door on the left, which leads into the art space and artwork.

There is also a wider context that we want to connect to through the programme. The year 2015 marks the 40th anniversary of the United Nations' Women's Year which aimed to place the struggle of women on the international agenda. While the U.N. highlighted women's liberation within a global forum, the International Wages for Housework Campaign, a grassroots political movement that addressed the struggle of women within the household, gained some of its most significant ground in Iceland when ninety percent of the female population took a day off work for the Women's Day Off. We are interested in asking what those politics mean now, in the everyday workings of home life.

Group work and discussions are central to the programme, and we hope those processes can create a hub for the local community to meet. For example, during our first exhibition with Mierle Laderman Ukeles we are hosting a series of house warming dinners in our kitchen, which is also our office. It is a great way for us to get to know the community and see how we can best provide support and work together *(see How to organise a housewarming dinner ↪ p. 157)*.

KK: Can you see any disadvantages in focusing so heavily on the local community, as has been the case? Is there a risk that focusing too narrowly on the immediate surroundings creates a lack of attention, and if so, how will you approach this?

JR/JS: For us Konsthall C's commitment to the local community is an important one. As public space across the city becomes more economically driven the art space becomes a protected zone where it is possible to make new connections, share different positions and collectively work to negotiate the new cultural terrain we find ourselves in. However, this focus should not be narrow and we believe that Konsthall C's multilayered way of working is key to maintaining the art space as a space for political discussion. Embedded in Konsthall C's structure is the rolling directorship, which offers space for new approaches to exhibition making, and we intend to expand upon that throughout the programme.

We believe that an art space is a space of negotiation where people of different positions, interests and educations can meet and find shared areas of concern and relevance. We also believe in artistic processes that can build multiple ways of accessing and engaging with particular concerns relevant to artists and the local community in the wider socio-political landscape, spaces that produce aesthetic experiences that are visual, physical and non-didactic. It is this movement from local concerns to wider global challenges that we see as outlined in the theme of Home Works. We hope we can build meaningful exhibitions and events for a wide variety of visitors who will feel welcomed and keen to participate and shape the trajectory of Konsthall C and the Home Works programme.

Our research approaches are highlighted in the practice and array of works of Mierle Laderman Ukeles that evolved from her own struggle within the home. Born from a frustration with the fact that her responsibilities as a mother were seen as a distraction to her artwork, she wanted to test the boundaries of art by seeing both these forms of work as the same. Ukeles brought attention to the value systems associated with domestic labour and the white cube gallery. In both of these spaces the labour of their maintenance, upkeep and care is made invisible; cleaned away to leave only the smiling housewife or a shining art-piece on a plinth. By challenging the socio-political landscape she herself was forced to negotiate, Ukeles found a way in which her personal struggle could find common ground with wider political battles. Her practice is in many ways specific to the context of New York in the 1970s, but the work is still urgent today and can be re-situated to Stockholm and connected to the context here.

Her work also raises questions on the home as a space of comfort and security. By highlighting the home as a worksite, Ukeles touches on the ability of the home to conceal its role in the construction of normative power structures and as a site for the promotion of gendered, racialised and class-based violence behind closed doors *(see Race-proofing at home ↪ p. 78)*.

KK: Concretely, what artists and projects do you plan to show in 2015?

JR/JS: Home Works is framed around two, two-year research commissions with the writer Gunilla Lundahl and the artist Joanna Lombard. By working with long-term research we hope to mobilise a collective exploration into the contemporary organisation of work and the gendered division of labour. In a way, the solo exhibition with Ukeles is an introduction to the themes in our research and a prelude to our upcoming exhibitions. Our collaboration with Lombard will start off with a new work in the Centrifug space of Konsthall C and Lundahl has put together a bookshelf of literature corresponding to her upcoming commission. Both Lombard and Lundahl will be part of a soapbox discussion at the art space Marabouparken on International Women's Day.

Lundahl has drawn out a series of key questions for Home Works *(see This is how it began ↪ p. 39)*. The questions have formed a backbone through which the exhibitions and the events will grow. One of the questions is: What constitutes a home? The responses will take shape as a group exhibition, examining how our intimate spaces are built, maintained and transformed, and it includes works by Hiwa K, Anna Ihle and a new work by Gunilla Lundahl. We are also really pleased to present an exhibition this autumn with the Scottish artist Ciara Phillips, whose work we have been following since our time in Scotland.

Finally, we are looking forward to our long-term collaboration with Film i samtidskonsten (Film in contemporary art), which will see the presentation of a number of artists' film screenings throughout the year.

KK: How do you feel about your new positions, the history of Konsthall C, its political role and its place among other Swedish art institutions?

JR/JS: We are thrilled to be working alongside Anna Ahlstrand and we are dedicated to building an exhibition programme that is meaningful to the locality, the artistic community and that connects to larger socio-political issues.

As a two-year research programme, Home Works explores different constellations of how we can work with artists. Both of the two-year commissions provide a distinct framework that generates possibilities for collaboration between other artists within the programme and for new networks of artistic production to emerge. Konsthall C is a space that allows for these types of redirections, so that it can shift focus according to the changing nature of artistic production, the local community and the impact of wider political transformations. The art space plays an important role within the Stockholm cultural landscape, providing a unique platform for the development and support of experimental artistic working methods and marginalised practices. Konsthall C is, in our opinion, a space that puts forward critical practices that dare to question normalised methods of producing and distributing art, a legacy we are keen to continue. And while we are pleased to be holding a specific position within the visual arts ecology it makes collaborations across institutions even more interesting as we hope to be able to build meaningful partnerships with other art organisations throughout the programme.

We should probably get going with our Home Works now...

Women's Day Off Material. Photo: Women's History Archives, Iceland, 2016.

Workers Variety Show Looks for Members! Konsthall C, 2016.

100 days of need and greed, and a potential recipe for change, with Kristina Schultz

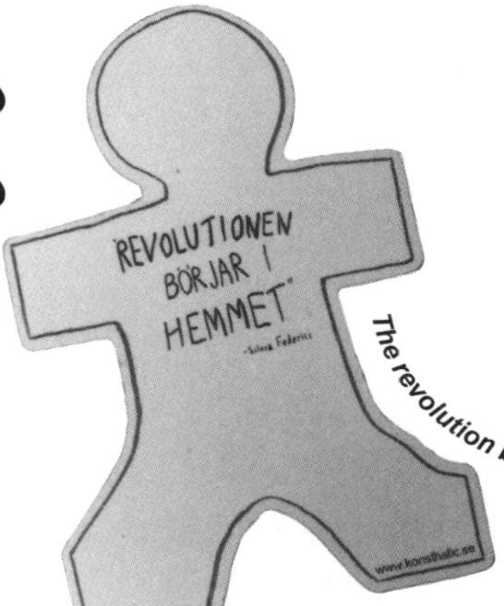

The revolution begins at home!

A work presented during Home Works, that deals with the economy of the home, is Kristina Schultz's research *100 Days of Need and Greed*, which challenges contemporary understandings of the home, consumerism and waste. In 2015, Kristina Schultz and her family stripped their apartment of all its possessions in order to rebuild it based on their needs and desires for living. The work aimed to construct a new home, influenced only by what was really necessary, both practically and emotionally. Life within the research became focused on the routine of eating together, and a series of spoons became the first tools that were required and produced. Yet, even this common instrument went through a process of rethinking how such a mass-produced object could be made anew. Was the outcome better, was it different to one you could buy from a store?

Other objects became crucial tools for the home, for instance, a pink fluffy pig that, although not requested, provided a companion that the artist's son, Liss, could play with. This gave Kristina Schultz and her partner, Johan Lindberg, some time to themselves. Thus, in this home, play came to be as necessary to their daily lives as eating. By emptying the house of all its material, the family was faced with their basic needs for survival. Their experiment intended to build a home from scratch and construct a life based on needs rather than greed.

The research shared a particular sentiment with activist and writer Silvia Federici's reflection:

> Through my experience at home ... I also discovered what I now call the 'double character' of reproductive work, as work that reproduces us and valorises us not only in view of our integration in the labour market but also against it.
>
> — Silvia Federici[1]

To many, addressing how one lives or changing one's relationships in order to practice a different kind of living might seem overwhelming.

Their home was a setting for exploring life in new ways and their experiment offered a glimpse into how it can be done. Johan Lindberg described that rather than *100 days of need and greed*, as a seemingly impossible exercise, what the experiment taught them was how easy it was to change, that what at first seemed impossible, a change at home, was in fact much easier than they had imagined. Demystifying this fear of change is the first step towards a whole home revolution.

What follows is a version of *100 days of need and greed*, here reworked into a recipe by Kristina Schultz. It focuses on how to change your entire life situation, where the space you define as home is used as a tool and an agent to kick-start the process. Of course, any room or collective space could be replaced as the main ingredient for this recipe.

1 Silvia Federici, *Revolution at Point Zero*, (Oakland, PM Press, 2012), p. 2.

Ingredients

- 100 days (or more)
- The place where you live
- A good portion of curiosity, tolerance and the ability to rethink

Collaborators

- An open-minded group of people (not necessary, but the more the merrier)

Temperature

A pleasant 21° Celsius (a high temperature can relieve the impression of the rather cold experience of an empty space).

Method

– Start getting rid of all the belongings in the apartment, they can be donated, sold or stored.

– Focus on believing in the new situation. Take a moment to step back and avoid rushing into the process.

– Try to actually enjoy the empty space.

BE AWARE,
HERE COMES THE TRICKY PART.

What are your basic needs for living in your apartment and how does this align with your true needs?

– Discuss these questions with the others involved and invite their opinion. Note down your basic needs and make a list. It is quite likely that you will end up with a long list, but do not worry, you have all the time you want to finish it. Start with the basics. Over time you will find out that your needs may change as your living habits are transformed.

– Gather the materials you need in order to build the objects, items and things on your list of needs. Try to use what you can find in your surroundings and let that lead your design process. Found materials will guide you as well as save time and money. This will enable you to engage in more complex needs that may require additional materials, parts or tools.

– Get down to it! Some knowledge of how to make things is helpful, but bear in mind that no one masters all materials and techniques. Do not let your shortcomings limit you. Focus instead on what you will learn. Also, do not let your designs limit you; be open-minded, to regard your designs as sketches can be helpful. Since you are the creator you can always rebuild or repair your items later on if something needs adjusting. Access to a workshop and to people with knowledge of specific techniques will help you on your way, but in the beginning there will probably be a lot that needs to be built in order to make your home liveable. Solve these functions first and foremost, rather than apply certain aesthetics or making objects in conventional materials and ways.

– Repeat the last three steps until you meet your basic living requirements.

– Still not satisfied? Try another recipe.

Enjoy!

Caring, cleaning and cooking: the double character of domestic work — *Silvia Federici*

> They say it is love. We say it is unwaged work.
> **— Silvia Federici**

With these words Silvia Federici begins her short essay "Wages Against Housework", written in 1975.[1] The text is central to the work of the International Wages for Housework Campaign that Federici co-founded in the 1970s, which sought to raise awareness of unpaid labour (such as housework) and its critical role in supporting

[1] Silvia Federici, "Wages Against Housework", in *Revolution at Point Zero: Housework, Reproduction, and Feminist Struggle*, (Oakland: PM Press, 1975), p. 15.

This conversation was originally published in Paletten Art Journal 3:2016 – #305: 37.

all other types of work. Over 40 years later the text is still a pivotal document in the analysis of domestic labour and the construction of female identity to better serve the reproduction of capital. For us, it is a text we often return to within our practices to deepen our understanding of the social and political structures at work in the categorisation of labour. Looking back on the text today can help us discuss the changes that have occurred on the home front, and the transformations and challenges waged against our gendered roles and expectations.

Federici is a teacher, writer and activist based in New York. She is the author of seminal works such as *Caliban and the Witch* and *Revolution at Point Zero*. The former builds on Federici's extensive research outlining the history of the body in relation to capitalism's expansion, arguing that the perceived division between body and mind are essential conditions for the development of labour power and the gendered categorisation of work. *Revolution at Point Zero* brings together a series of essays from 1975 to the present day, which reflect on the development of the 1970s feminist movement and arguments on reproductive labour and the political struggles Federici has engaged in.

In June 2016, Federici was invited to the symposium *The Home Within Homecraft*,[2] in order to reflect further on what she discusses in *Revolution at Point Zero* as the 'double character'[3] of reproductive work, which forms the basis for the following conversation. The text concludes with a reflection from Federici on her few days with us in Stockholm, discussing her involvement in the International Wages for Housework Campaign, home, care work, her family life and how she cared for her mother.

<u>Jenny Richards and Jens Strandberg (JR/JS):</u> Through our collaboration with Stockholm based writer and feminist Gunilla Lundahl, we have touched upon different aspects of reproductive labour including collectivity, constellations of home life and perspectives on child rearing. These different concerns are issues Lundahl has worked on over the last fifty years and which raise questions we can explore and interrogate through our current work together. If we use these questions as a framework for our discussion

2 Federici's theorising of the transformation of capital in the construction of the family, the housewife and the gendered division of domestic work has been critical in the development of the Home Works programme at Konsthall C, which the symposium *The Home Within Homecraft* was part of.

3 'Through my experience at home – through my relations to my parents – I also discovered what I now call the 'double character' of reproductive work as work that reproduces us and 'valorises' us not only in view of our integration in the labour market but also against it.' Silvia Federici, *Revolution at Point Zero: Housework, Reproduction, and Feminist Struggle*, (Oakland: PM Press, 2012), p. 2.

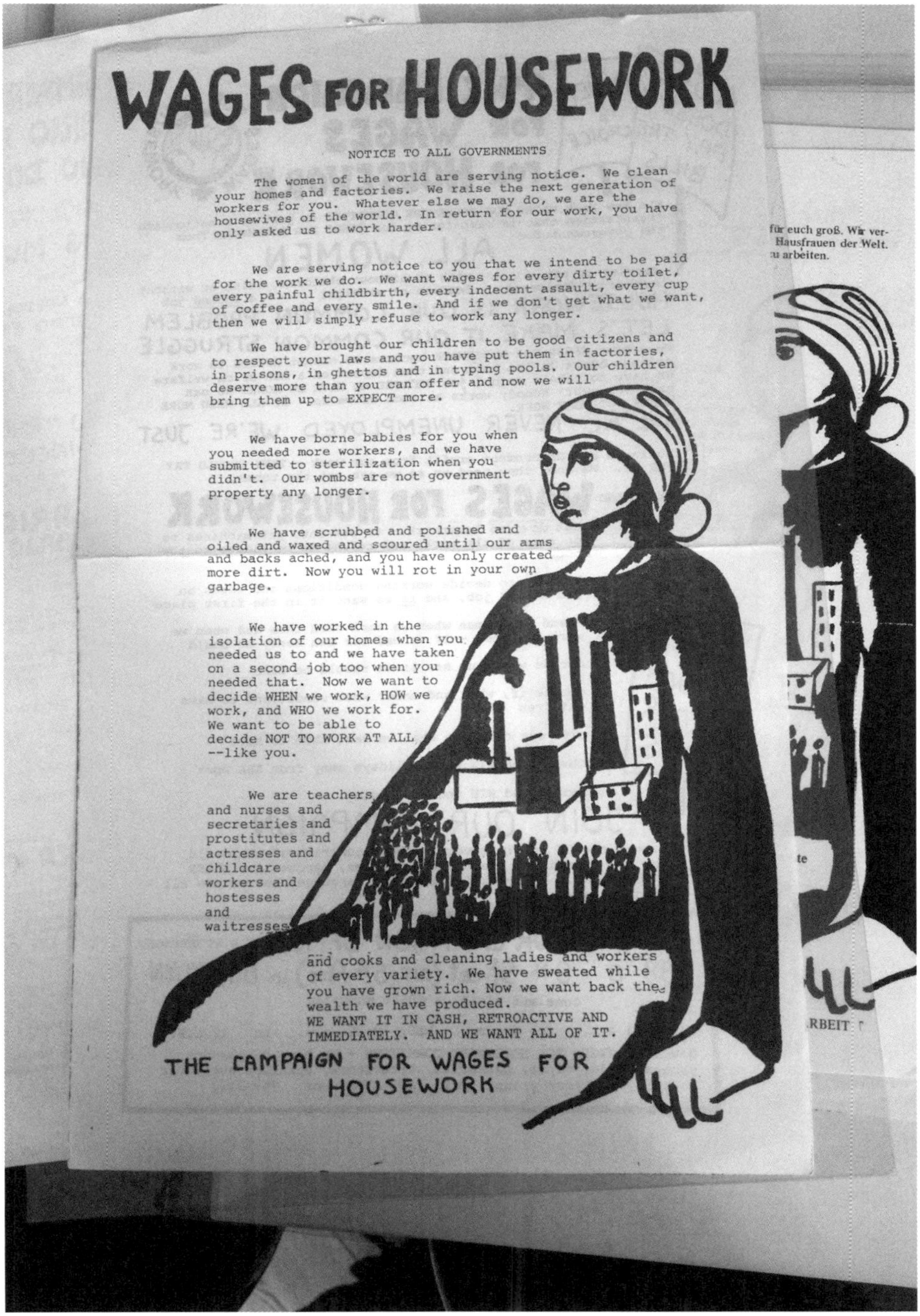

WAGES FOR HOUSEWORK

NOTICE TO ALL GOVERNMENTS

The women of the world are serving notice. We clean your homes and factories. We raise the next generation of workers for you. Whatever else we may do, we are the housewives of the world. In return for our work, you have only asked us to work harder.

We are serving notice to you that we intend to be paid for the work we do. We want wages for every dirty toilet, every painful childbirth, every indecent assault, every cup of coffee and every smile. And if we don't get what we want, then we will simply refuse to work any longer.

We have brought our children to be good citizens and to respect your laws and you have put them in factories, in prisons, in ghettos and in typing pools. Our children deserve more than you can offer and now we will bring them up to EXPECT more.

We have borne babies for you when you needed more workers, and we have submitted to sterilization when you didn't. Our wombs are not government property any longer.

We have scrubbed and polished and oiled and waxed and scoured until our arms and backs ached, and you have only created more dirt. Now you will rot in your own garbage.

We have worked in the isolation of our homes when you needed us to and we have taken on a second job too when you needed that. Now we want to decide WHEN we work, HOW we work, and WHO we work for. We want to be able to decide NOT TO WORK AT ALL --like you.

We are teachers and nurses and secretaries and prostitutes and actresses and childcare workers and hostesses and waitresses and cooks and cleaning ladies and workers of every variety. We have sweated while you have grown rich. Now we want back the wealth we have produced.
WE WANT IT IN CASH, RETROACTIVE AND IMMEDIATELY. AND WE WANT ALL OF IT.

THE CAMPAIGN FOR WAGES FOR HOUSEWORK

Wages for Housework material, MayDay Rooms archive, London, 2015.

with you, can you join us in speculating on the question we have asked ourselves: what is the home today and what has it become?

Silvia Federici (SF): Historically, the home has been a place where life is reproduced and where the people involved in the reproduction of life are connected through intimate relationships, by kinship, trust, affection; it is a place of social encounters. What we argued in the International Wages for Housework Campaign is that in the history of capitalism, the home has been subjected to all kinds of state interventions and legislations that have turned it into a centre for the production of labour-power. The Campaign read the home as a workplace, a workplace for women, the designated subject of reproductive work.[4] This means that the home, like reproductive work itself, has had two contradictory components that have produced a constant tension. On the one side the home and reproductive work have had to produce exploitable workers for the labour market, and on the other hand they have (re)produced our lives, and our struggles. Thus, the home has been both a place of subjugation and a place of resistance.

However, women's revolt against housework and economic dependence on men – starting in the post-World War II period – coupled with the restructuring of the global economy, has brought about a major restructuring of the home.

There is no doubt that the main objective of this restructuring has been to recuperate from that revolt, but it has also opened new terrains of struggle. The crisis of the male wage and the precarisation of labour, together with women's struggle for autonomy from men, have transformed the home in many ways. More and more people today, especially among the younger generations, form homes on the basis not only of marriage but also of friendship, political affinity, and of course, economic necessity, since the cost of housing has increased immensely.

Older people too are now getting together to form new homes, not

4 'The difference with housework lies with the fact that not only has it been imposed on women, but it has been transformed into a natural attribute of our female physique and personality, an internal need, an aspiration, supposedly coming from the depth of our female character. Housework was transformed into a natural attribute, rather than being recognised as work, because it was destined to be unwaged.' Silvia Federici, "Wages Against Housework", *Revolution at Point Zero: Housework, Reproduction, and Feminist Struggle*, (Oakland: PM Press, 2012), p. 16.

to be alone and because of their diminishing resources. As everybody is now realising, the concepts of family and home have been and are changing. For example, the home has become a place where people come together because they want to have a more collective experience and/or share expenses, without necessarily knowing each other before.

JR/JS: The changes within the home and the constellation of family roles also have an impact upon its younger subjects. What is your position on child rearing and how does it relate to your critique of reproductive labour?

SF: Parenting is a struggle;[5] I often quote a mother in Latin America who said, 'to be a good mother today is to be in a struggle for 24 hours a day'. Child-raising exemplifies the contradictions I mentioned before: you want to raise your children for their happiness, but at the same time you want to make sure they will be able to integrate into the labour market.

This implies imposing a discipline on them that is in contrast with their well-being. This is where the capitalist constraints operate. The happiness of your children is the goal, but this is juxtaposed with the pressure of having to discipline them to prepare them for employment. In other words, you have to prepare them both for the labour market and for the struggle against it.

JR/JS: How is it possible to be aware of your own role in perpetuating this constraint? Is it possible to deviate from this path?

SF: We have to be respectful of children, we must stop looking at them as human beings in training. This is how capitalists see them: they are not completely productive, therefore they are not completely human. We need to struggle against the violence against children. We need to change our concept

[5] 'That reproductive work is a labour-intensive process is most evident in the care of children and elderly people that, even in its most physical components, involves providing a sense of security, consoling, anticipating fears and desires. None of these activities are purely 'material' or 'immaterial' nor can be broken down in ways making it possible for it to be mechanised or replaced by the virtual flow of online communication.' Silvia Federici, "The Reproduction of Labour Power in the Global Economy", *Revolution at Point Zero: Housework, Reproduction, and Feminist Struggle*, (Oakland: PM Press, 2012), p. 107.

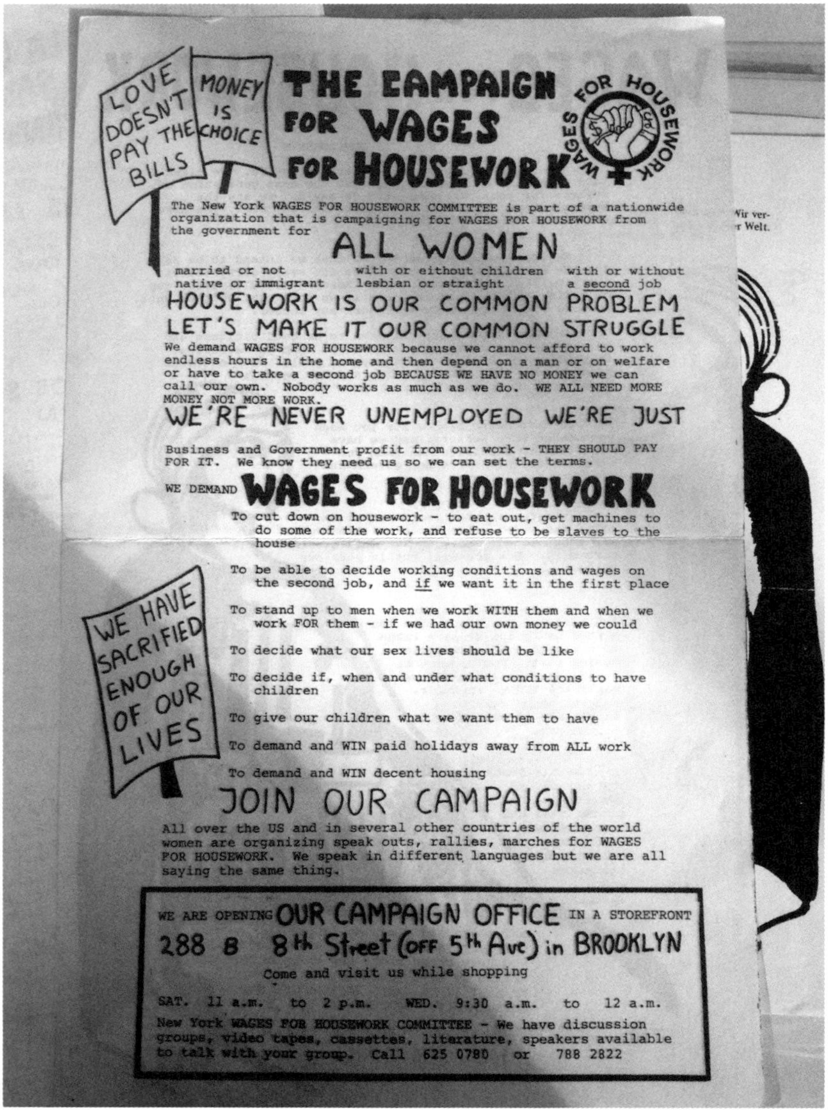

Wages for Housework material, MayDay Rooms archive, London, 2015.

of childhood and challenge the belief that it is a parental prerogative to beat children, because presumably they are too small to understand. At the same time, we have to make sure that we do not give the state more reasons to take children away from poor, proletarian families – migrant families or families of colour – which is happening all too often today.

The International Wages for Housework Campaign saw the women's liberation struggle also as a struggle for our children. We realised that in liberating ourselves from the drudgery of reproductive labour, we were also liberating our children. Women were always made to feel guilty for this struggle; for fighting against housework for fighting for time for themselves, away from their children.

The ideal mother has been the sacrificial mother; a woman who sacrifices her life, puts her needs last, in favour of the wellbeing of her family. We refused this model.[6] We realised it is a destructive model, for everybody. We realised that the moment you sacrifice yourself as a mother you also sacrifice the lives of your children. The sacrificial mother is always the mother who wants her children to give back to her the life she never had.

JR/JS: How would you describe the implications of the feminist movement's rejection of this role, the home and domestic labour?

SF: The rejection of the home, and of family life, was a strong tendency in the first phase of the women's movement. It was a refusal of a certain image of femininity, which we saw as extremely devaluing and a limit to our lives.[7] It was a rejection not so much of the home but of a life, a destiny that we knew

6 'The literature of the women's movement has shown the devastating effects that this love, care and service have had on women. These are the chains that have tied us to a condition of near slavery. We refuse then to retain with us and elevate to a utopia the misery of our mothers and grandmothers and our own misery as children! When capital or the state does not pay a wage, it is those who are loved, cared for, also wageless and ever more powerless, who must pay with their lives.' Nicole Cox and Silvia Federici, "Counterplanning from the Kitchen", *Revolution at Point Zero: Housework, Reproduction, and Feminist Struggle*, (Oakland: PM Press, 2012), pp. 34–35.

7 '... measuring work by the wages also hides the extent to which our family and social relations have been subordinated to the relations of production – they have become relations of production – so that every moment of our lives functions for the accumulation of capital.' Nicole Cox, and Silvia Federici, "Counterplanning from the Kitchen", *Revolution at Point Zero: Housework, Reproduction, and Feminist Struggle*, (Oakland: PM Press, 2012), p. 35.

would limit our possibilities.[8] That said, I have later learnt that many black women did not share the white feminist rejection of homelife. In a powerful essay called "Homeplace a Place of Resistance"[9] bell hooks points out that while white feminists were anxious to leave the home, black feminist saw the home as a place of resistance, and, above all, a place in which black people could feel valued, secure, and recognised in their humanity, whereas the world outside the home was a place of danger, and devalorisation. The rejection of home by white feminists in the United States and Europe, at first, was not critical enough, it did not distinguish the aspects of homelife that we should refuse and those we needed to preserve.

JR/JS: How does this relate to your own personal journey which starts from a rejection of housework within the International Wages for Housework Campaign to your presentation at the symposium here in Stockholm, which highlights the radical creativity and importance of the home?

SF: It was only when I joined the feminist movement and began to articulate a critique of the nuclear family as a construct of capitalist society that I began to realise that the drudgery and the sense of suffocation I associated with the family were consequences of the capitalist intervention in the construction of domesticity.

The nuclear family and the home, as we have known them, have been organised to guarantee the reproduction of the workforce and increase the productivity of labour. This is the reason not only for women's unpaid work, but for the individualised, atomised way in which home life is being organised. By identifying the function of reproductive work and the history

8 'Wages for housework, then, is a revolutionary demand not because by itself it destroys capital, but because it forces capital to restructure social relations in terms more favourable to us and consequently more favourable to the unity of class. In fact, to demand wages for housework does not mean to say that if we are paid we will continue to do this work. It means precisely the opposite. To say that we want wages for housework is precisely the first step towards refusing to do it, because the demand for a wage makes our work visible, which is the most indispensable condition to begin to struggle against it, both in its immediate aspect as housework and its more insidious character as femininity.' Silvia Federici, "Wages Against Housework", *Revolution at Point Zero: Housework, Reproduction, and Feminist Struggle*, (Oakland: PM Press, 2012), p. 16.

9 bell hooks, "Homeplace: A Site of Resistance", *Yearning: Race, Gender, and Cultural Politics*, (London: Turnaround, 1991).

of the capitalist takeover of family life, I was able to see the other side of that work and began to see the struggle that women, that our own mothers, that my mother had made against it.

JR/JS: How would you say these political revelations affected your relationship to your role within your own family and to your mother?

SF: For me, the women's movement was extremely important, not only politically but also personally (and of course we learnt that the separation between personal and political is a fictional divide). The women's movement enabled me to reconnect with my mother. Within the relationship between my mother and I, there had always been the historic battle around housework and around discipline. My mother would want me to behave in a certain way, the way women were expected to behave, which consequently meant that I saw my mother as the embodiment of that gendered discipline. I was also conscious that I did not want to repeat the life of my mother. I did not want to become a housewife, as she had been, because I saw her work was not socially valued, and she had to depend economically upon my father. But through the women's movement, through my new understanding of housework, I was able to see my mother in a different way, to see the work that she was doing in a different light. I became aware of the love that she put into her work, and as a result my relationship with her changed. I started to help her a lot more when I went home, sharing the housework, talking about housework, which was a big surprise to her. I also began to see her struggle and she started to reveal to me the ways she was struggling to not depend entirely upon my father. She told me how humiliating it was, when my father, who was the classical good man and gave her the greater part of his wage, oversaw her spending of it and wanted her to account for every expense. I never realised this and she had never said anything about it to me before. She told me how she was putting money aside so she could buy a pair of socks without having to account for them. That way she was also able to give me a little money too, because she knew that I was always penniless, and she was proud of these subversions.

In these apparently small things there is a whole world of struggle and that is part of what gave me the impetus to join the International Wages for Housework Campaign.

JR/JS: The feeling of not being entitled illustrates the embodied ideology that domestic work is not valued alongside other forms of work even by those performing it.

SF: The fact is that, when you depend on someone else's wages for your survival, you do not feel really entitled to that money, because you have not earned it yourself. So, even when one works full-time in the home, many women – like my mother – do not feel really entitled to the money their husbands or partners give them.

It was not only the broad theoretical understanding of how capitalism has used women's unpaid labour to expand the accumulation of capital that motivated my participation in the campaign, but also to see what economic dependence and a lack of money specifically have meant in the lives of women.

JR/JS: How did these personal experiences change your view of the home and reproductive work?

SF: Through the International Wages for Housework Campaign's analysis of how housework has functioned, I began to realise that this work can be very creative. There is not a more creative activity than reproducing life, producing the next generation. I am not referring only to procreation, but to all the activities, inventions and experimentations that are necessary for the task of creating new life. The task of deciding how to raise the children we bring into this world involves the process of deciding what the new society will be like, and what values we want to affirm.

There is a parallel here, in a way, with the work of cultivating new plants which also has a hugely creative component to it. Think of the generations of women who across South America select seeds to plant in order to grow better vegetables, better flowers, better food. It is a job that requires a lot of skill and sensitivity. That is how they have been able to produce 200 types of potatoes or 200 types of tomatoes. You need to know how to take advantage of the differences in the environment, of the patches of shade, of the wind, of particular types of soil.

So, by meeting women and hearing of their work I began to discover the cultural and aesthetic dimension of reproductive work, and the creative work that women have done around reproduction. Other examples can be found in the way many women have organised their house, grown plants, done beautiful sewing or how they have worked on the presentation of food; there is an enormous amount of art and creativity usually not recognised. Often people dismiss these creations, 'Oh it is the frustrated housewife that has no better avenues to channel her creativity,' but all of these things that men have often devalued – the curtains, the flowers, the knitted sweaters, the quilts – all of this is creative work. Women can be said to have been artists at every moment in history.

When you discover this other side of reproductive work, you realise that attached to it are some of the most powerful social relations on earth, the ones that shape our life and give us a taste of what life can or cannot be.

JR/JS: And in parallel then, how do you see the implications of your struggle on reproductive work? Can one say that this struggle was not only to liberate women from reproductive labour but to liberate reproductive labour itself?

SF: Reflecting on the different dimensions of reproductive work has convinced me that this work is central to the transformation of life, the transformation of the social system and the transformation of political work.

JR/JS: The International Wages for Housework Campaign was a key collective context for you to personally transform your concept of the home – can you expand further on the role of reproductive work in relation to the transformation of political struggle.

SF: I think often political work has failed because it has been separated from the reproduction of daily life. One of the greatest contributions of the feminist movement was to introduce a new type of politics, in which you do not separate the political from the personal – you do not separate politics from the reproduction of daily life.[10] This is why, from the beginning, the movement

[10] 'A lot of us have broken that barrier ... and discovered that the overalls did not give us any more power than the apron – quite often even less, because now we had to wear them both and had even less time and energy to struggle against them. The things we have to prove are our capacity to expose what we are already doing as work, what capital is doing to us, and our power to struggle against it.' Silvia Federici "Wages Against Housework", *Revolution at Point Zero: Housework, Reproduction, and Feminist Struggle*, (Oakland: PM Press, 2012), p. 22.

brought about a major transformation in the lives of women who were involved. As soon as you became a feminist, as soon as your consciousness was raised, being with other women gave you the sense that you could change your life; you began to question all your relations, beginning with your relations with men, but also your relations with your parents, with your children, with your friends. So very soon you were in an embattled situation, and this brings me to an important point, that this form of politics was at times painful and conflictual, but also immensely joyful. It was a politics that was lived and tested out everyday. It made you grow, in order to break many chains, and it came with a sense of discovery and joy.

JR/JS: In drawing this discussion to a close this seems like a great point to finish on. The emphasis on the joy of political work feels particularly poignant today, and it is something we try to remember and build on through our practices. Just as a final point then, is there anything from your conversations and time here with us in Stockholm that you would like to offer as a final comment? Or maybe something that touches upon this point – in how we might work for a joyful political struggle in our efforts to liberate the home and reproductive work?

SF: Rethinking the significance of reproductive work has made me realise how much artistic creativity women have expressed through this work, which has largely gone unrecognised, and how limited the concept of art is that we have all come to accept. Initiatives like Home Works do justice to this creativity by discussing how women have struggled to valorise their families, the people they love, and how their work has never only been shaped by the expectation they would produce disciplined workers for the labour market. We need spaces that affirm this creativity, places where people can meet, where people can circulate experiences, so that together we can confront the growing inequalities and racism.

During my time here in Stockholm I was inspired by Hildur Hakonardottir's tapestries[11] that seem to weave together the politics of their production – right out of an intimate kitchen – and the highly political struggles they are connected to. This was particularly highlighted in the

[11] As seen within the exhibition, *Expansions of Homecraft*, Konsthall C, 2016.

role the tapestries played in the struggle of the Women's Day Off strike in Iceland in 1975. The strike was hugely inspiring for the International Wages for Housework Campaign, as it demonstrated that when women stop, everything stops.

The need to reflect on the history of sexism and racism built into the many objects we use everyday within the home was something that Temi Odumosu taught us in her presentation during the symposium, which further highlighted the strategic role home life has played in shaping of our ideas, our imagination and our relation to the world. Like reproductive work, homecraft is a window that frames the contradictions women experience in our society and the importance of reproduction as a terrain of feminist struggle.

Hildur Hákonardóttir, Silvia Federici, Temi Odumosu, *The Home in Homecraft*, symposium, Konsthall C, 2016.

Race-proofing at home — *Temi Odumosu*

> To move beyond race I ground myself in my homeplace. In this house where I live, race has no place. As soon as I walk out the door, race is waiting, like a watchful stalker ready to grab me and keep me in place, ready to remind me that slavery is not just in the past but here right now ready to entrap, to hold and bind. No wonder then that I want to spend most of my life inside, in the sanctuary of home where there are no shackles, no constant reminders that there is no place free of race.
>
> **— bell hooks[1]**

In a conversation held at the New School in New York in 2015, bell hooks and Kevin Powell talked about black masculinity in the United States. After relaying an anecdote about getting racially harrassed at the gym, Kevin Powell goes on to explain the

1 bell hooks, *Writing Beyond Race: Living Theory and Practice* (New York: Routledge, 2013), p. 185.

dangers posed to black men's lives in public spaces, where one does not know whether they will get killed, marginalised or scapegoated. bell hooks replies: 'why do you not stay home more?'

> We have to see our homes as places of resistance. We have to look at our [African American] history and how much was started in the home … like Mary McLeod Bethune, starting the Bethune-Cookman College in her living room.
>
> **— bell hooks[2]**

Watching this conversation from my rented apartment in Copenhagen – as an Afro-British migrant in a city where I do not speak the language – I thought critically about what it takes to call a country and/or place home; somewhere for authentic being (at peace), for dwelling, for connection, for planting one's roots, for feeling free and comfortable. In bell hook's summation, the home is to be posited as a safe place for people of colour to avoid societal discomforts and be able to restore themselves as well as nourish the community. But home-steading in this way when you are mobile (nomadic, in motion, cannot stay put) is hard, and can be fraught with the presence of implicit bias. What happens when you are not the property-owner, and are 'borrowing' a space from strangers? How can we healthily navigate our time and/or inclusion in living spaces that are limited by rules, regulations, or other conditions such as the surveillance of neighbours? And, when does rest come for those placed in housing without freedom of choice? How do they experience the dwelling process?

Floating heads

bell hooks insists that protecting the sanctity of our home spaces from the 'watchful stalker' of race requires diligence, for it is not just a matter of the physical environment but also what/who enters there, especially by way of representations and media. She argues that a 'turning away from images' produced by the dominant culture has become a critical strategy for those seeking to transform the way they relate to others.[3] But, avoiding the discomforting realities of the world, specifically ghosts from a long

2 bell hooks, published online at: https://www.youtube.com/watch?v=FoXNzyK70Bk (Accessed October 2019).

3 bell hooks, *Writing Beyond Race: Living Theory and Practice* (New York: Routledge, 2013), p. 185.

history of colonialism and racialised slavery, is not easy. Haunting is complex and also embodied, and reckoning with its effects (that 'something happened' feeling) requires attentiveness to where the ghost appears, the reasons why it is there, and importantly what it is asking for. As Avery Gordon so eloquently writes, haunting describes:

> those singular and yet repetitive instances when home becomes unfamiliar, when your bearings on the world lose direction, when the over-and-done-with comes alive, when what's been in your blind spot comes into view.
>
> **— Avery Gordon[4]**

Such hauntings can come in many disguises, and take on different qualities depending on where you are in the world. I want to begin by reflecting on a particular domestic haunting in Denmark; the Cirkel Kaffe girl (*Cirkelpigen*), brand image of the Cooperative supermarkets' coffee. It is one example of a range of Danish food products that still use 'foreigners' on packaging and advertising, such as Törsleffs use of a middle-eastern man for vanilla, and the stereotyped Chinese 'yellow' head on Atamon syrup. Cirkel Kaffe's logo represents the head in profile and neck of a Black woman with cornrow-braided hair and a white headband. It was designed by Sikker Hansen in 1955 as part of a series of figurative 'types' for Fællesforeningen for Denmark's Brugsforeninger (FDB, later Coop). The image has become a signature for vernacular design, and even won an award in 2006 for bringing art into Danish everyday life.[5] You can see this Black woman's head everywhere in Denmark: not only on the coffee packet, but also on paper cups, serviettes, clocks, shopping bags, postcards, and posters on people's walls. She is even on the side of Coop's headquarters in Albertslund. Her image is so embedded in the overall Coop brand that in 2016, the company commissioned graduate students from the Spier arts academy in South Africa to produce a mosaic monument of the logo. This was also installed at the headquarters for their 150-year anniversary.

Sikker Hansen's rendering of a coffee-brown woman to represent an imported

4 Avery Gordon, *Ghostly Matters: Haunting and the Sociological Imagination* (Minneapolis: University of Minnesota Press, 2008), p. xvi.

5 See Lars Dybdahl, *Den danske plakat* (Copenhagen: Borgen, 1994), p. 81.; and a commemorative article produced for the Cooperative magazine in Liv Mygind, "Kvinden i cirklen: kendt fra kaffen", *Samvirke*, March (2016) 46-54. Published online at: https://s3.eu-central-1.amazonaws.com/samvirke/pdf/Samvirke_marts_2016.pdf

colonial product is very much of its time (a mix of romantic ethnography and exoticism with a dash of savvy design). It draws meaning and recognition from a long history of European trading with racialised imagery, using heads and bodies to do the metaphorical work of bringing Africa or India or Brazil into the living room.[6] Due to Cirkel Kaffe's successes as a logo, and because of brand longevity, it has been very difficult to analyse or critique an image that is essentially a Danish national trademark. Those that have already done so are labelled 'morality police' or 'po-cos' (postcolonial theorists or politically correct) who are failing to see the beauty and aesthetic qualities of the image.[7] Researching various examples of these *kolonialvarer* (colonial commodities), Mathias Danbolt describes the way such images satisfy a nostalgic view of the past in the present, for which it is very difficult to hold people accountable. When offence or disturbance is expressed, particularly by people of colour, their feelings are often met with denial or accusations that they are being too sensitive. Danbolt writes that 'the critique of racism appears as always already anachronistic: too late to rupture the historical precedent that has established the object's innocence in the past and too late

Cirkel Kaffe girl logo on serviettes.
Photo: Temi Odumosu.

[6] For research, see Elizabeth Kim, "Race Sells: Racialized Trade Cards in 18th-Century Britain", *Journal of Material Culture 7.2* (2002) 137–65; Raymond Bachollet et al., *Négripub: l'image des noirs dans la publicité*, (Paris: Somogy, 1994); David Ciarlo, *Advertising Empire: Race and Visual Culture in Imperial Germany*, (Cambridge: Harvard University Press, 2011); Malte Hinrichsen, *Racist Trademarks: Slavery, Orient, Colonialism and Commodity Culture*, (Zürich: Lit, 2012); and Dana S. Hale, "French Images of Race on Product Trademarks during the Third Republic," in *The Color of Liberty: Histories of Race in France*, eds. Sue Peabody and Tyler Stovall (Durham: Duke University Press, 2003, pp. 138–139.

[7] See Mathias Danbolt, "Retro Racism: Colonial Ignorance and Racialized Affective Consumption in Danish Public Culture", *Nordic Journal of Migration Research 7.2*, (2017): 105–113; Mathias Danbolt, "Mediestorm om kolonihistoriens aftryk i dansk visual kultur", in *Kampen om de Danske slaver: aktuelle perspektiver pa kolonihistorien*, eds. Jakob Ladegaard and Frits Andersen (Aarhus: Aarhus university press, 2017) pp. 148–166; Leena-Maija Rossi, "Licorice Boys and Female Coffee Beans: Representations of Colonial Complicity in Finnish Visual Culture," in *Complying with Colonialism Gender, Race and Ethnicity in the Nordic Region*, eds. Suvi Keskinen, et al. (United Kingdom: Burlington, 2009), pp. 189–204; and my own essay Temi Odumosu, "Open Images or Open Wounds: Colonial Past and Present in the City of Copenhagen", in *Openness: Politics, Practices, Poetics*, ed. Suzan Kozel, (Malmö: A Living Archives Publication, 2016), published online at: https://livingarchives.mah.se/files/2015/01/openness_final.pdf

to question the potential racist effects now'.[8] And, since the issue is always discussed in terms of competing perspectives (rather than historical entanglements), the dominant point of view usually ends the debate. Nobody wants to face the glaring phenomenon of Black-body commodification, likened to slavery as part of 'afterlife of property', and happening both on a commercial scale and intimately (insidiously) in our private worlds.[9] Danbolt describes the persistence of these colonial-imaged goods and associated objects as 'retro racism'; Leena-Maija Rossi in a Finnish context as 'colonial complicity'; Tavia Nyong'o as 'racial kitsch' (and an 'embarrassment').[10] What they all articulate, but which evades popular acceptance, are the ways in which these hauntings pierce the veil of (Nordic) innocence; that the very insistence of such images in monocultural (white) home settings, signals the presence of a ghost's 'lingering trouble'.[11]

The trouble that racialised objects and images can cause in public and private spaces is really the point of this small essay, which is an attempt to think alongside bell hooks about home as a 'safe space'. I want to suggest that our inner and outer realities are in constant dialogue, and therefore living with colonial imaginings exposes us, and our homes, to pollution – a continuous, low-level toxicity that we could call *slow violence* (to quote Robert Nixon).[12] This pollution does damage to minds, hearts, spirits, psyches, and it forces the body to do unnecessary extra work. What kind of work depends on whose body it is. And every moment of forgetfulness (historical denial) that normalises the presence of these disruptive things allows for the inherited rot to sink in further.

Figurative slavery

In her book *Plantation Memories: Episodes of Everyday Racism* (2008), Grada Kilomba uses the experiences and voices of Afro-German women as the theoretical

8 See Mathias Danbolt, "Retro Racism: Colonial Ignorance and Racialized Affective Consumption in Danish Public Culture", *Nordic Journal of Migration Research 7.2,* (2017): 105–113.

9 Saidiya V. Hartman, "Venus in Two Acts", *Small Axe: A Journal of Criticism 26* (2008): 13.

10 Tavia Nyong'o, "Racial Kitsch and Black Performance," *The Yale Journal of Criticism 15.2* (2002): 371–391. For Danbolt and Rossi, see footnotes above.

11 Avery Gordon, *Ghostly Matters: Haunting and the Sociological Imagination*, (Minneapolis: University of Minnesota press, 2008), p. xix.

12 See Rob Nixon, *Slow Violence and the Environmentalism of the Poor*, (Cambridge, Harvard university press, 2011). Nixon describes slow violence as: 'a violence that occurs gradually and out of sight, a violence of delayed destruction that is dispersed across time and space, an attritional violence that is typically not viewed as violence at all ... a violence that is neither spectacular nor instantaneous, but rather incremental and accretive', p. 2.

foundation for explaining how colonialism is activated in daily life. Using Philomena Essed's concept of 'everyday racism' as a guide for more subtle forms of violence, Kilomba narrates a definition of this term as: 'a "constellation of life experiences," a "constant exposure to danger," a "continuing pattern of abuse" that repeats itself incessantly throughout one's biography – in the bus, at the supermarket, at a party, at a dinner, in the family.'[13] One of the women interviewed by Kilomba (called Kathleen) retells her experience of constantly seeing an old-fashioned figurine of a Black boy on her white neighbour's balcony. This was a daily sight, which provoked discomfort and eventually rage. When Kathleen decided to approach her neighbour about her reasons for displaying this image of Black servitude, the woman said, 'she thought it was cute'.[14] Kilomba asserts that Kathleen had to endure the workload of being affected by racism, while also trying to divest its presence from the environment in which she lived. The German woman expressed her innocence when challenged, and then cited a Cuban 'friend' who also liked the figurine as a supporting defence. Such stories are instructive in pinpointing the ways coloniality disrupts processes of authentic human connection. The synthetic Black boy and its exhibition in public/private space was a fabrication, a performed substitute for something old – namely the master/slave relationship. But the figurine was also a sign of carelessness, an unwillingness by someone with inherited privileges to reflect on their actions, and therefore to equitably share space and time.

Historically, the home has been a space of racial and class performativity in Europe, especially in the lives of the privileged. For example, the inclusion of African, Chinese, and Indian children as exotic colonial servants at royal and wealthy estates, as early as the 16th century.[15] European art history is littered with family portraits representing Black children, who were symbolically laboured as a sign of imperial devotion, while simultaneously foregrounding the whiteness, agency, beauty, virtue, or youthfulness of the main sitters. The artistic term *chiaroscuro*, meaning the use of contrast between light and dark to create form, adequately conceptualises the function of these figures as props for showcasing the powerful. In real life, such children were usually enslaved and often referred to as a 'body servant', which means that (unlike

[13] Grada Kilomba, *Plantation Memories: Episodes of Everyday Racism*, (2nd ed. Münster: Unrast verlag, 2010), p. 45.

[14] Ibid, p. 122.

[15] For the sixteenth century origins of the painted page see Paul H. D. Kaplan, "Titian's 'Laura Dianti' and the origins of the motif of the black page in portraiture (1, 2)", *Antichità viva 21.4*, (1982): 10–18.

Arthur Devis. *John Orde, His Wife, Anne, His Eldest Son, William, and a Servant* (1754–1756). Oil on canvas. 94 x 96.2 cm. Yale Center for British Art, Paul Mellon Collection.

other domestic servants like cooks or drivers) they were always physically in attendance, fulfilling the direct needs of their masters and mistresses while keeping out of the way. At the same time, these children had an ornamental function, and were often considered 'playthings' who could be seen serving tea or hot chocolate, or appear in the company of other pets such as lap dogs, monkeys and parrots. The fact that these were children and not adults, maintained an illusion of safety and perpetuated the idea of unquestioned loyalty and obedience. Often when they became teenagers their roles would change to more distanced activities, such as horse grooming in stables.

A British painting from the 1750s by Arthur Devis exemplifies these dynamics. It belongs to a group portrait tradition called the 'conversation piece', which was a way to display practices of refinement in a domestic setting, especially for the landed gentry and aspiring mercantile class.[16] The painting is set in a reception room, decorated with portraits of ancestors and imported Chinese porcelain on the mantelpiece. It features a northern English landowner called John Orde reading the newspaper with his wife Anne. She turns towards Orde's eldest son, who has just arrived to offer her a pheasant he has shot. Next to him a young Black servant enters with a letter addressed to the head of the house.[17] These kinds of images were highly choreographed and incorporated advice from published manuals on proper living such as *The Rules of*

[16] To learn more, see Kate Retford, "From the Interior to Interiority: The Conversation Piece in Georgian England", *Journal of Design History 20.4* (2007): 291–307; and Matthew Craske, "Conversations and Chimneypieces: The Imagery of the Hearth in Eighteenth-century English Family Portraiture," *British Art Studies Issue 2* (2016). Published online at: https://doi.org/10.17658/issn.2058-5462/issue-02/mcraske

[17] This painting was one of several in an exhibition at the Yale Center for British Art, which critically engaged with the presence of these servants. See Esther Chadwick, Meredith Gamer and Cyra Levenson, *Figures of Empire: Slavery and Portraiture in Eighteenth-century Atlantic Britain*, (New Haven: Yale Center for British Art, 2014)

Civility (1703), which advised that it was 'very uncivil in company to 'speak to a servant in a language that the rest do not understand'.[18] Devis represented the family's Black servant according to the fashion at the time: dark ebony skin, expensive livery (his costume), a silk turban with gold braiding evoking the Orient and eastern harems, and with a silver chattel collar around his neck, marking his enslaved status. The inclusion of this boy must have been important as an expression of the family's status, because we know that Devis charged his patrons by each figure represented on the canvas.[19] Such imagery was, however, already normalised within the visual language of the empire, with examples from Russia and the United States to Sweden and colonial Mexico.[20] These figures were not only relegated to private paintings, but found their way onto all sorts of homewares, like sugar bowls, snuff boxes, fans, plates, and candlesticks, which became part of the domestic space – the domestic vocabulary.

We like to think of ourselves as having evolved from the behaviours of earlier times, and reading this text you might feel an unbridgeable distance from the idiosyncrasies of 18th century Europe. But what the so-called 'enlightenment' world teaches us concretely is that enslavement (like racism) was an exhaustive practice, which migrated from plantations to cities by changing its mode of expression.
In Europe, one form of bondage included the aesthetic whereby African bodies were visually coded into predominantly negative types and tropes. The ideas that strengthened the meaning-making process encapsulated theories of racial hierarchy by anatomists like Petrus Camper and Carl Linnaeus, spectacular stories of savagery and hyper-sexualisation in travel narratives, and biblical theories of an inherited curse. Not to mention all the treatises that have been written about the origins of skin colour and questions of beauty. 'The colours of beautiful bodies must not be dusky

[18] Antoine de Courtin, *The Rules of Civility; Or, the Maxims of Genteel Behaviour, As They are Practis'd and Observ'd by Persons of Quality, Upon Several Occasions*, (London: Printed for Robert Clavell and Jonathan Robinson, 1703), p. 21.

[19] Esther Chadwick, Meredith Gamer, and Cyra Levenson, *Figures of Empire: Slavery and Portraiture in Eighteenth-century Atlantic Britain*, (New Haven: Yale Center for British Art, 2014).

[20] The literature on this tradition is now extensive. I give an exhaustive summary in the footnotes of Chapter 1 in my book: Temi Odumosu, *Africans in English Caricature 1769–1819: Black Jokes, White Humour*, (London: Harvey Miller publishers, 2017), pp. 48–97. For African servants in Russia see Allison Blakely, *Russia and the Negro: Blacks in Russian History and Thought*, (Washington: Howard University Press, 1986), pp. 13–25. Fascinating Swedish examples can be found in Eva-Lena Karlsson and Hans Öjmyr, *Främlingen: dröm eller hot*, (Stockholm: Nationalmuseum, 1996), pp. 133–38; and they are discussed in a wider cultural and political context in Cecilia S. Henriksson and Patrick Gibson, *Svart i Sverige*, (Stockholm: Bladh by Bladh, 2012), pp. 58–63.

or muddy, but clean and fair', wrote Edmund Burke in 1753.[21] All of these cultural and aesthetic values were immediately fashioned into objects (a pipe in the shape of an African's head, for example). As Aimé Cesaire succinctly stated: 'Colonisation = thingification'.[22] This is the long history that haunts; haunts the Black and Brown body image at each and every turn.

Back at home

At its best, home can be a space of good feelings, a place we retreat to for restoration and sustenance before returning to our work in the world. One of the main reasons it has been difficult to shift thinking about vernacular images like the Cirkel Kaffe girl, or the figurine in Kilomba's German case study, is precisely because good feelings of life at home have attached themselves to those racialised images – good feelings of positive relations and having mastery over a domain. These were, after all, the intentions of those who designed racist Jim-Crow segregation imagery in the United States – cultivating an ambient racism for white Americans that felt good because it was being taught humorously by the mammy cookie jar, the grinning money bank, Aunt Jemima's maple syrup, and Uncle Ben's rice.[23] People have formed repeated intimacies around such objects, objects which also mark the familiarity of homespace. As Sara Ahmed reminds us, happiness is about the things we turn towards (it is an orientation), and the 'objects that give us pleasure take up residence within our bodily horizon'.[24] Without using too many words, the whole situation is deeply psychological.

bell hooks vision (for Black folks especially) of our homes as spaces of equity, healing, and care indicates that the phrase 'maximise your wellbeing' should be taken seriously.[25] Her rallying call asks us to reconsider the publicness and privateness of our activism, and she centres the home as the holding space for deep cultural memory; the ancestral echoes of grandmother's and great-grandfather's voices; the belly laughter and tears shared between long-time friends; the humming

[21] Edmund Burke, *A Philosophical Enquiry into the Origin of our Ideas of the Sublime and Beautiful* (London: Printed for R. and J. Dodsley, 1757), p. 102.

[22] Aimé Cesaire, "Discourse on Colonialism", trans. Joan Pinkham, New York, *Monthly Review Press* (2000): 42.

[23] See the pioneering exhibition catalogue: Berkeley art center, *Ethnic Notions: Black Images in the White Mind: An Exhibition of Racist Stereotype and Caricature from the Collection of Janette Faulkner: September 10-November 12, 2000* (Berkeley: Berkeley Art Center, 2000).

[24] Sara Ahmed, *The Promise of Happiness*, (Durham: Duke University Press, 2010), p. 24.

[25] bell hooks, *Writing Beyond Race: Living Theory and Practice*. (New York: Routledge, 2013), p. 189.

of the blues; the moon, the music, the art, the magic, the births, the deaths, the spirits, and the medicine.

My last assertion here is that it is time for some spring cleaning. Time to begin the delicate process of race-proofing our homes, which is to say clearing out outdated and redundant colonial junk, and then paying attention to, making safe and soft and welcoming our sanctuary spaces, for love and authentic connection to thrive.

Part 2. Cooking

(Collective processes)

> **The familiar world begins with the writing table, which is in 'the room'. We can name this room as [Edmund] Husserl's study, as the room in which he writes. It is from here that the world unfolds. He begins with the writing table, and then turns to other parts of this room, those which are, as it were, behind him. We are reminded that what he can see in the first place depends on which way he is facing.**
>
> — **Sara Ahmed**[1]

Sarah Ahmed examines how we orientate ourselves and our thinking in relation to the familiar by paying attention to the things we face rather than the processes behind them. She asks how would the philosopher Edmund Husserl's world have unfolded if he had paid attention to the processes behind his writing desk? Her text inspired us to relate her thinking to how labour is organised, acknowledged and valued. What labour is infront of us and seen in society and what labour is made invisible?

Part 2. zooms in on some of the behind-the-scenes elements and *hidden* work that was carried out during the making of Home Works, which did not have a public face.

1 Sara Ahmed, "The Phenomenology of Whiteness", *Feminist Theory 8* (2007): 149.

The work, processes and activities behind that which was seen by visitors when entering the art space; the ongoing collective work that often began around the kitchen table orientated by the domestic objects in the kitchen. Much of this activity took the form of workshops that set up co-learning situations where artists, activists and the local community could come together, discuss politics and experiment with making, performance and writing. To come together and meet people you have not met before meant that processes evolved from a place of not knowing. While collective, this did not mean the methods of working and spending time together were structured around consensus. Rather, the intimacy of this 'hidden' work encouraged vulnerability and the sharing of knowledge from personal experience, creating a space where anger, contestation and desire could be expressed.

Most of the workshops and experiments that are explained in these recipes were carried out in Home Works' kitchen/office. In some cases they directly informed the work displayed in the exhibition. In other instances they remained hidden, as tasty breadcrumbs, objects to orientate ourselves from our kitchen table.

How to make political theatre? with Stephan Dillemuth

In January 2016, the artist Stephan Dillemuth converted the Home Works building into a temporary sculpture workshop and rehearsal space for those who joined the *Workers' Variety Show Looks for Members!* Over ten days, members worked together, sharing their working conditions, and translating their work experiences into improvised performances while the limbs they used during their working days were cast into plaster sculptures. Members signed up to the workshops through an open call, and during their intimate time together they learnt about the history of the workers' theatre movement, particularly how it began in Germany around 1880s within *Arbeiterklubs* (workers' clubs).

These workers' clubs existed throughout Germany; the aim was for workers to entertain and to educate one another. It has been discussed as a form of grass-roots culture, in contrast to the bourgeois culture of the state theatres. Each member of the theatre was a producer who contributed to the development of a show according to their own skills. Known in Germany as *Bunter Abend* (colourful evening or variety show), these shows included everything from sketches, magic tricks, gymnastics, poetry, singing and dancing. Through these variety shows workers informally exchanged stories of their work experiences and encouraged each other to challenge their exploitative working conditions.

In a similar way, the *Workers' Variety Show Looks for Members!* brought together a group of people with different occupations, which allowed them to share their work experiences. It was a way of casting light on the challenges they were facing and collectively understanding different working conditions. The theatre offered a discussion forum, improvised performance exercises and body casting techniques, which culminated in a variety show and a party, only for those involved in the workshop.

The exercises on the following pages were carried out during Stephan Dillemuth's workshops and can be seen as short recipes for how to examine your working conditions in order to find collective ways to change them.

Members:
Aina Backman, Kristin Broberg, Stephan Dillemuth, Sophie Erlandsson, Merituuli Holm, Rebecca Hubbinette, Hashem Nazari, Jimmy Offesson, Siri Osterman, Fatemeh Rafiei, Jenny Richards, Konstanze Schmitt, Jens Strandberg, Malin Ståhl, Jo Tengblad Söder, Marika Troili, Anita Wernström, Nathalie Wuerth

ARBETAR
REVY
SÖKER
MEDLEMMAR
Var:
Konsthall C
16 Cigarrvägen
T-bana (Hökarängen)
SE Konsthallc.se
FÖR MER INFO.
Maila: osa@konsthallc.se för att anmäla er.
I samarbete med: The Nordic art association (NKF) & Konstfack
Programmen genomförs i samarbete med ABF Stockholm.
Med stöd av: Goethe Institut Stockholm, Stockholms Stad, Kulturrådet & Stockholmshem

How to make political theatre?

I think there is a basic difference between cooking and art making.

(Stephan Dillemuth)

I am not a cook that uses people as ingredients.

I am not a kitchen that people use to cook their food in - I am not a toolbox. There is no recipe we can follow to do the right thing.

Workers' Variety Show Looks for Members! was not an attempt to make a tasty workshop. And anyway, what does 'tasty' mean? One of us had an advantage of knowledge and institutional relations. Other people had the advantage of experience and expertise in their respective professional and extra-professional fields that we might call 'life'.

The idea of the workshops was to bring together these fields of knowledge, experience, expertise and institutional support in order to create new knowledge and shared experiences; to talk about our work and work experience. One of us was speaking about the history of the workers' theatre. Another was speaking about efforts to entertain, to agitate, to educate, to propagate.

We tried to activate these narratives using historical methods that you can find below, recipes perhaps?

Cantastoria

Cantastoria comes from the Italian for story-singer. It is a theatrical form where a travelling narrator sings stories depicting old prints and paintings with scenes of marketplaces. There is a scene in the Georg Wilhelm Pabst and Bertolt Brecht film *The Threepenny Opera* (1931) where Ernst Busch uses this technique. Watch it for inspiration.

METHOD
- Draw a story about an experience at work.
- Explain the experience, pointing to each drawing in turn.
- Make up a song.
- Sing what you have just explained, pointing to each drawing in turn. You could use a part of the audience as a chorus or a human beatbox.

Choral speaking

A sung monologue or report on your work introducing others in the group to facts, statistics, numbers, arguments.

METHOD
- Practice singing your information or argument.
- Ask others to sing in response to your monologue in solidarity with or protesting against your position.
- Mix short sounds with lengthy noises
- Moderate your voice and amplify it with enhancing and desirable effects. For example, try using a mechanical voice.

Invisible theatre

METHOD
- Get on a bus.
- Pretend to be making a phone call.
- Talk loudly about your problems at work.
- Turn to the person next to you, discuss what you just spoke about on the phone.
- Raise your voice, let other people know.

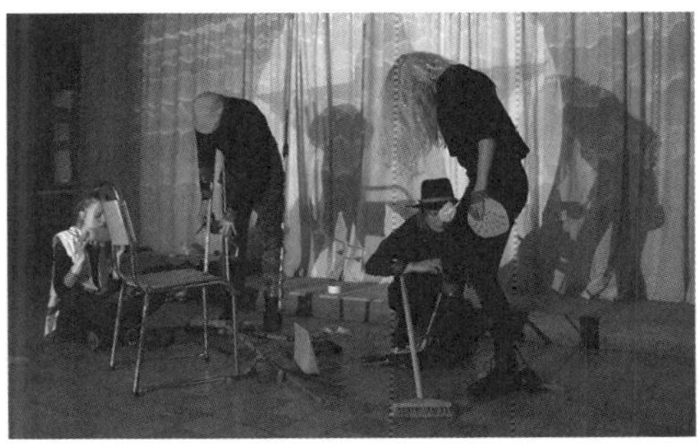

Machine exercise

METHOD
- Try to emulate a machine. Your body moves like the mechanism of a machine.
- Synchronise your movements with a partner.
- Imitate the noise of a machine together.
- Make the machine more complex by adding more people from the group to the machine.
- Create a collective machine. For example, during the workshop we created a collective dishwasher after eating together by forming a human chain where we passed dishes to be washed, dried and put away.

Tableau vivant

Tableau vivant, translates from French as 'living picture'. It is a static scene containing one or more actors or models, often dressed up in costume, carefully posed, with props and/or scenery. *Tableaux vivants* can be seen today in the form of living statues; street performers who pose in costume.

METHOD
- Envisage your worst work experience.
- Ask some friends/workshoppers to recreate the scene as if it was a photo.
- Take a photo and give it a title.
- This could be extended to a sequence of images that make up a story. Create a scene – the actors carefully pose – then lights off/curtain closes – the actors change into a new pose – lights on and again curtain opens.
- You can expand this with costumes.

Here's an example of a Choral speaking exercise, written by Jimmy Offesson during workshops that were a part of the *Workers' Variety Show Looks for Members!*

1

Once upon a time there was a worker and he had a family of co-workers.

This particular worker was working very hard for his family of co-workers.

He had several jobs throughout the day.

He started ~~on~~ the morning on his first job.

(Now I need your help and imagination... what was his first job for the day?)

After lunch he started on his second job.

(Again...) ~~The~~ And what was his 3rd job?

2

Now you understand that he was very hard working.

Now you also understand that the day had turned to night.

It was time for the worker to go home to his family of co-workers.

It was a long walk through the dark streets of the city.

(I need: one worker
a city of sounds / houses.
three people making a mysterious mood tune)

3

When the worker walked through the city he heard:

- Hey, worker

He looked around but couldn't at first see anyone.

- Hey, worker

He turned around and saw ~~the~~ a man. Little did he know that this was the capitalist.

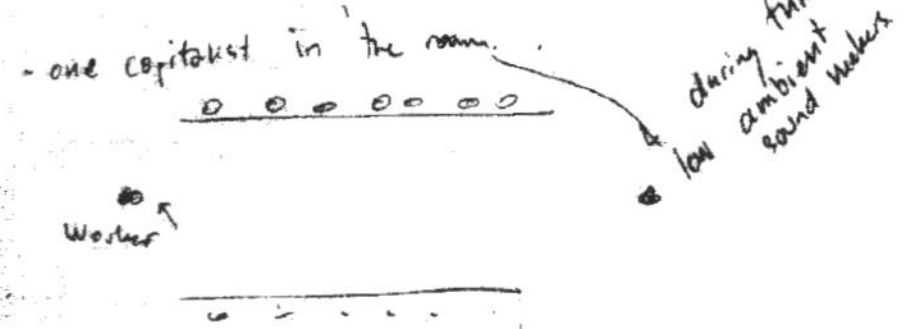

WORKER 4B

capitalist: Where are you going worker

you: Home, to my family

where do you family live?

At the end of this long street

I see, I have never been there

Ah, it is a happy home. My family is a spirited people.

I see, do you mind working for me?

Now? No I have done so much work today.

I pay you.

(you hesitate...)

I pay you very much. ... YES.

5.

And the worker said yes.
(ambience sound stop).

And the capitalist went to the worker's family of coworkers. At the end of this very long street.

And worker did another job.

\- - - - - -

It was breakfast time when the worker came back home to his family of coworkers. To his luck: it was his day off so he looked forward to a long rest from his long work.

But first he wanted some food.

6.

The worker sat down.

(sitt vid gaveln alla ska stå upp och stirra på honom när han äter)

Then he ~~broke~~ noticed that something had changed. At first he thought he was tired. But something had changed.

7A

He said:

What big
eyes you have?

He said:

What big
ears you have?

He said:

What big
mouths you have?

They said

OUR BIG EARS
ARE FOR LISTENING
TO THE CRITIQUE
OF OUR WORK
SO, THAT WE CAN
IMPROVE IT

They said

OUR BIG MOUTHS
ARE THERE
TO BE FED
SO WE ARE
STRONG FOR WORK.

8

The worker listened
and accepted this
new truth that his
family of coworkers had
adopted.
Time went on
(capitalist sound) money...
... and time went on.
The esteem and spirit
of the family diminished.
They soon got depressed.

...
One day an enlightened
worker from another city
paid them a visit.
(now he stands / they sit...)

9A

He said -

What big eyes you've
got?

- they answered

- NO, Your big eyes are
to spot and see the
injustice ~~that~~ in how you
and your fellow coworker
~~is treated~~ is paid differenty
is treated differently.

7B
9B

They said

OUR BIG EYES
ARE FOR LOOKING
AT OUR WORK
AND THE WORK OF
OTHERS
IN ORDER TO
EVALUATE THE WORK
AND PAY IT
ACCORDING TO
THE RULES OF EFFICIENCY

He said.

What big ears you've
got?

they answer

NO, your big ears
are for listening to
your own desires and
for listening to the needs
of your fellow co-worker

He said

What big mouths
you've got?

they answer

No, your big mouths
are for speaking of
the injustice you have
seen and heard.

Now, my fellow co workers
I believe there is someone
here not belonging to your
family.

10

With new energy
and revitilised perception
the family could clearly
see that they had
an un-invited guest.
(ambiance AND capitalist sound)

In the corner (drag one person to the corner (march on)

sat the
capitalist,
~~who~~ with piles of money (spread money)
around him. Money that
the workers had earned.

What were they going to do with
him?
~~think~~ of a sentence... I film it.
→ that is the solution / next step story ending

Who is the third pedagogue? with Joanna Lombard and Gunilla Lundahl

Developing exhibitions and conducting artistic research in close relationship with the area and the local community were central to Home Works' activities. It was an attempt to embed the research in the community in order to find out whether art could be a pedagogical tool for coming together and collectively learning from each other.

Martinskolan, a local Rudolf Steiner school, is one of Konsthall C's neighbours. The pupils and staff were actively involved with Home Works, by participating in workshops and performing in the art space. School, like the home, can be seen as one of the central institutions for a child's development and learning. Play can be a way of learning, but learning can also be a form of play. In many of Home Works' collaborations there was an examination into how artistic methods connected to histories of different forms of pedagogy. The programme wanted to find ways to support forms and processes of learning that are often excluded from education curricula, and that seek to develop other ways of understanding the world. Martinskolan, with its implementation of Rudolf Steiner education methods, was an important discussion partner for this investigation.

The Room is the Third Pedagogue by Joanna Lombard was developed for Home Works in 2016. It began with Joanna Lombard spending time in the area, exploring activities in the neighbourhood that connected with her practice. After joining a meeting at Hökarängens stadsdelsråd, *(see Collaborators and other chefs ↷ p. 10)*, she noticed an advertisement for a children's choir at Martinskolan. Joanna Lombard was part of a choir during her time in the Steiner education system, and thoughts of her own children's enrolment in a similar school in Stockholm sparked curiosity, which led to a year spent with the choir and the production of a new film. Joanna Lombard's experience of attending a Steiner school, however, lacked the inclusive, collective experience the education aimed to create. From her time there and as a member of the choir, she recalled a sense of not belonging or fitting in. Unlike the children in this choir, her participation in the school choir had been mandatory.

Joanna Lombard's time with the choir included joining rehearsals, repetitive exercises, restaging common songs from Steiner pedagogics, and playing around with musical instruments. She found points of contact that were later developed into short film sequences in collaboration with the artist Eva Rocco Kenell. The film was a way of trying to understand the ambivalent position she holds towards the Steiner pedagogy.

What is the relationship between how one is shaped by institutions and how one is shaped by our own desires? And how is one influenced and formed by the many different individuals that constitute an institutional community?

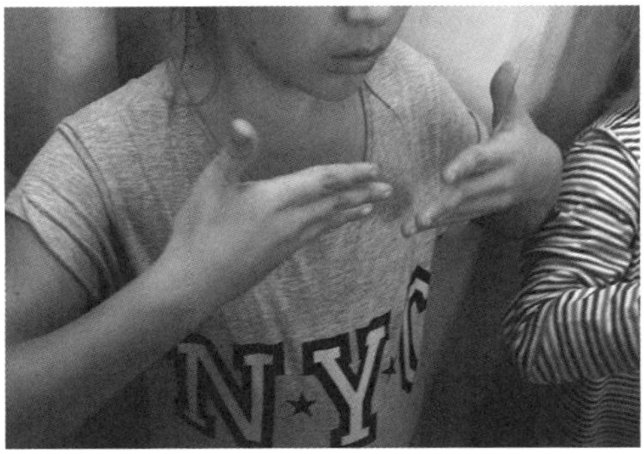

Below is a number of pedagogical methods to experiment with, written by Gunilla Lundahl for Joanna Lombard's exhibition.

Rudolf Steiner

Rudolf Steiner started a school for the children of workers at the Waldorf-Astoria Cigarette Factory. There he first tried out the pedagogical ideas that are applied in Steiner schools worldwide today. In Sweden there are about forty schools, the first of which was started in 1931. Rudolf Steiner drew on his experiences from his time as a tutor in a family where the youngest child was perceived to be uneducatable. With patience, empathy and attention he managed to awaken the child's capacity for learning, and the boy successfully found a way to study and learn.

METHOD
Teach someone else something they do not know.

Friedrich Schiller

Friedrich Schiller, poet, playwright and philosopher, was appointed honorary citizen of Paris at the beginning of the French Revolution. When he saw violence taking over, he began to write *On the Aesthetic Education of Man* (1795). It deals with the two contradicting forces that rule life. On the one hand, the propensity towards form that ends in total petrification, on the other, the propensity towards materiality, which, in the end, leads to chaos and complete dissolution. Two contradictory poles, also expressed as intellect versus sensuality, reason against feeling. He suggested that the way out of the struggle between these forces was play. Only in play can a person really become human. Play makes us free from the instincts that rule us. Play makes us free from intent.

METHOD
Invite someone to play a game with you that they have not played before.

Johann Heinrich Pestalozzi

Johann Heinrich Pestalozzi worked with orphan children around the turn of the 18th century. He wanted to know how personal responsibility, or a willingness to act, emerges in a person. He also pointed out that all meaningful education directs itself simultaneously to the head, the heart and the hand. These principles have been relevant for many centuries.

METHOD
Share a story of when you learnt something that affected your head, hand and heart.

Friedrich Fröbel

Friedrich Fröbel, inspired by Johann Pestalozzi, wanted to support the unique capacities and needs of children through the development of educational materials that would gradually lead to new insights. He believed in the creative instincts of children and looked at play as a child's way of recasting experiences: singing, dancing and culture would promote the development of children. This pedagogy had some impact in Germany, but was eventually banned as it was perceived as being a source of social dissonance.

METHOD
Make a comic describing what a future school might look like.

Maria Montessori

Maria Montessori was an Italian physician who was interested in the conditions of deprived children in Milan in the late 20th century. Because the children were impoverished, they were considered uneducatable. Maria Montessori wanted to demonstrate that such an assumption was incorrect, and she prepared materials that would support children in their own journey of discovery and learning. Her experience as a woman also widened the pedagogical debate, a debate that was frequently dominated by men. She is also considered an important feminist.

METHOD
Do the washing-up with someone you do not know.

John Dewey

John Dewey was an academic and philosopher from the United States. He has produced a prolific body of writing on educational matters and he developed the concept 'learning by doing'. His pragmatic commitment was to create conditions for a democratic society. He created an experimental school that offered insights into the way the shape of a room can determine the type of dialogue and conversations that occur within it. John Dewey was also interested in Lev Vygotsky, a teacher in the Soviet Union in the 1930s. The Stalin regime erased his learning methods, but his writings make him relevant today, especially his interest in language as the basis for all communication, and the learning that comes through language. He said that the teacher should be the train track upon which the students (coaches) move freely and independently.

METHOD
Decide on a topic of conversation, then try this in a number of different rooms. Note how the conversation changes.

Celestine Freinet

Celestine Freinet gave rise to his own movement during the 1920s and 1930s. His school was started in the French countryside with the aim of supporting the children of peasants and developing their role in society. He bought a printing press for the school, which was an important tool in their education. The children created their own teaching materials, starting with issues that were relevant to them. They exchanged material with other schools, and over time they created their own library.

METHOD
Buy a printer and set up a children's newspaper in which the children are the editors and producers of the content. Share this with your local schools.

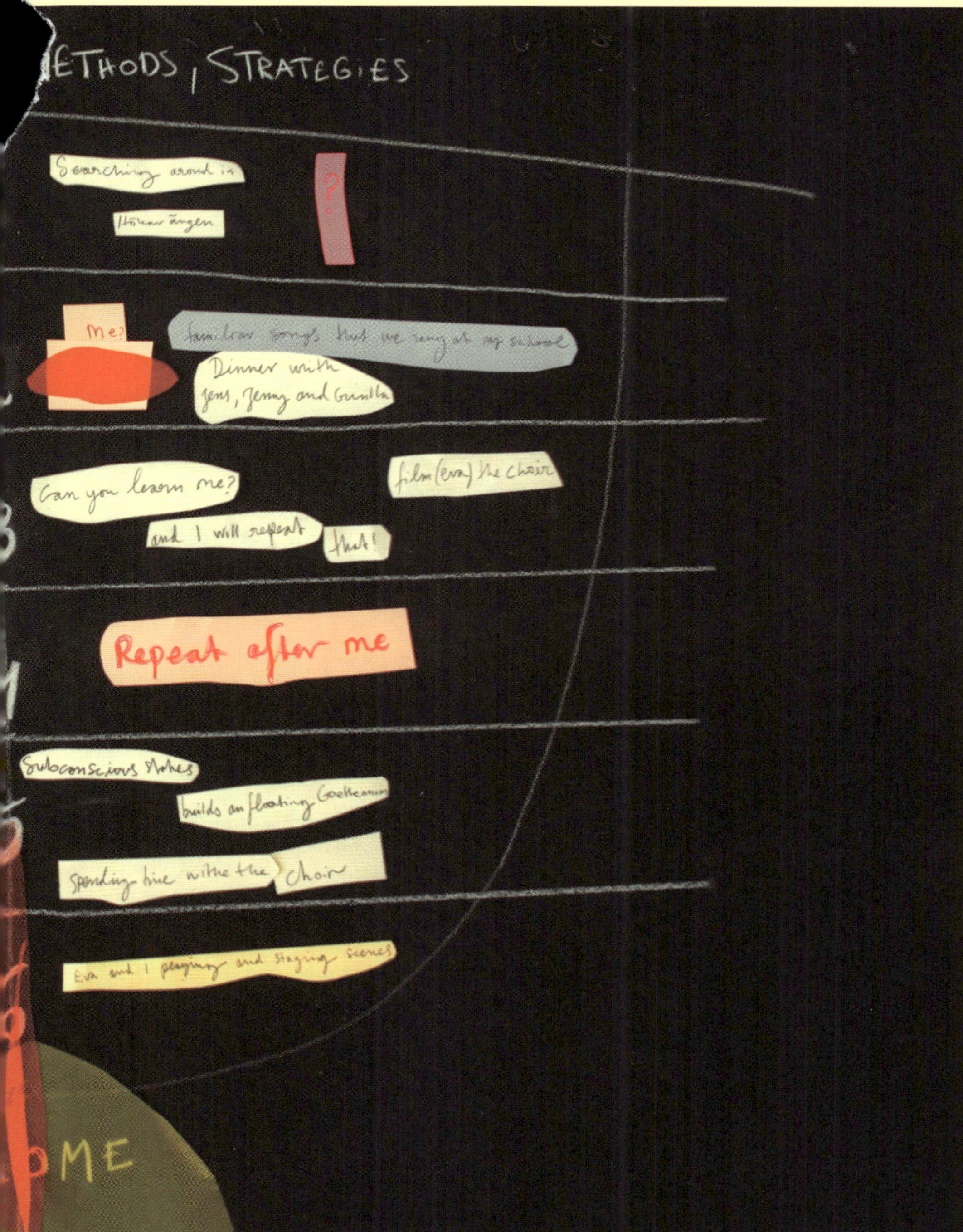
ETHODS, STRATEGIES
Searching around in
Hökarängen
?
me?
familiar songs that we sang at my school
Dinner with
Jens, Jenny and Gunilla
film (eva) the choir
Can you learn me?
and I will repeat
that!
Repeat after me
builds an floating Goetheanum
spending time with the
choir
Eva and I playing and staging scenes
ME

Loris Malaguzzi

Loris Malaguzzi, active in the anti-fascist struggle in Italy, opened a day care centre and a school in the Emilia region at the request of women working in the rice fields. His education put emphasis on children's free creativity, a creativity that by its beauty and wealth of imagination aroused amazement and interest within art institutions. He emphasised that his methods were not meant to make artists of all children, but to give each child a foundation for becoming a free thinker. In the pedagogy of what came to be known as the Reggio Emilia approach, teachers talk about 'the third pedagogue', which is to say the environment, since it was felt that the room and the tools in it were complementary to the two teachers in charge of a group of children.

METHOD
Go camping in the forest. Pay attention to the environment and how it complements your thinking.

Paulo Freire

Brazilian educator Paulo Freire wrote a book entitled, *Pedagogy of the Oppressed* in which he called for critical reflection and action in pedagogy. He attacked the 'culture of silence' in which people are excluded from knowledge about the reality that governs them. He participated in a literacy campaign, and was jailed before fleeing the country in 1964. Some years later he went to Harvard University and worked for the United Nations before returning to Brazil in the 1980s. 'Freedom is not something you get, it must be conquered', according to Paulo Freire, whose books are now read again after years of oblivion.

METHOD
Paulo Freire used the concept of decodification as a way to situate yourself in your lived reality. It was a concept that reflected on the different components that made up a situation, a way to understand the place you find yourself in, whether at work, in school or at home. He likened it to the way a photographer brings a motif into focus.

In a group, decodify the situation you are in. Think about the information you have about the situation, who and what is in this situation with you? In what way do the people you are with understand the situation differently? Allow each person in the situation to talk about how they understand their respective position and why. This is a way of gathering information in order to build up a picture around real situations and real people, and the way privilege and power is executed in different ways.

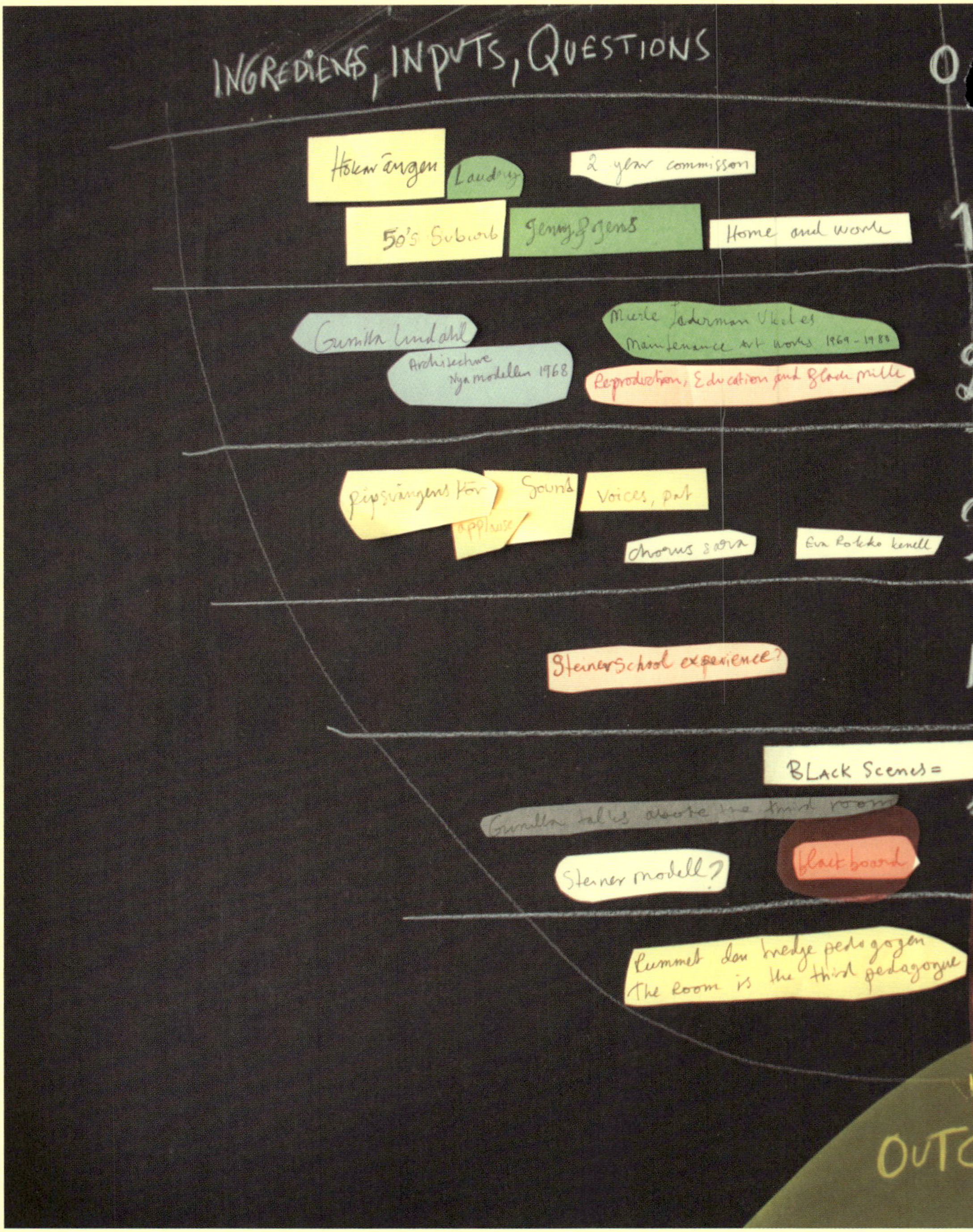

***Parabola formula*, by Joanna Lombard.**

How to make a balloon bass, with Toncirkeln

Toncirkeln[1] is a collaborative work by Shida Shahabi and Anna Sóley Tryggvadóttir. During Home Works, Toncirckeln converted the kitchen/office into a temporary music studio and instrument-building workshop. In the workshop the artists invited a group of 12-year-olds from Martinskolan, located near the art space, to collectively create musical

1 Swedish for tone circle.

instruments using kitchen appliances and other materials they found at the art space.

The workshop took the format of a study circle to learn about how to understand one's surroundings through sound. In the book *Spaces Speak, Are you Listening?* Barry Blesser and Linda-Ruth Salter discuss the aural architecture of different spaces and their social components.[2] The book draws attention to the intangible, experiential boundaries of a space rather than its built margins, accentuating the often overlooked knowledge that the soundscape of an environment offers.

For Home Works, the group explored the soundscape of the domestic environment of Konsthall C's kitchen/office. Not only were cups, glasses, plates, bottles, shredders and strainers rebuilt into musical instruments, their activation in the kitchen drew attention to the aural architecture of the art space and the narratives the sink, dishwasher and cooker exude.

The work amplified the seemingly hidden sounds of domestic labour and raised questions about the categorisation of music and what materials can be used for making music. What are accepted as soothing and difficult sounds, and why? How do different sounds effect us? These and other questions tie into the historical lineages of improvised music production within the domestic environment as well as into larger political narratives.

For example, you might think of the construction of instruments in the 1700s, such as the now well-known banjo, created by enslaved African workers and brought to the Americas during the transatlantic slave trade. These non-linguistic forms of communication for political ends have displayed their potency. Instruments were banned on many plantations in the United States, as landlords understood their communicative potential.

For Home Works, school children from Martinskolan reworked the sounds of the building into an aural soundscape of the kitchen. This was performed during a live concert for the rest of their class, who listened to the repurposed and amplified sounds while laying across Stephan Dillemuth's exhibition installation.

This recipe shows how you can build a bass using a plank, a balloon and an elastic band.

2 Barry Blesser and Linda-Ruth Salter, *Spaces Speak, Are You Listening? Experiencing Aural Architecture*, (Massachusetts: MIT Press Cambridge, 2007), p. 21.

Ingredients

- 2 elastic bands no shorter than 1.5 metres (you can find them at a haberdashery or you can remove them from a pair of old jogging pants)
- A wooden plank no shorter than 1 metre.
- 1 balloon (the bigger the balloon the more sound, but standard size works as well)
- 2 chopsticks

Method

- Tie the elastic band around your wooden plank and blow up your balloon.

- Stretch the elastic band and put the balloon between the band and the wooden plank.

- Add two chopsticks on either side, or both sides of the balloon.

- Try playing your balloon bass.

- You can also use the chopsticks as drumsticks on the balloon.

The elastic band can be of various sizes and thickness. This will give you different sounds. You can also experiment by attaching many elastic bands at the same time.

You can build and use a contact microphone and a small amplifier if you want your bass to be louder.

A real sourdough: an art space and a bunch of children, with Marie Ehrenbåge

What is the role of children in society today? How does a child articulate their thoughts or position when their writing and speech are still developing? Can we imagine any political possibilities beyond those of speech and the limits of language? How can art be a tool for articulating other political imaginaries?

These were some of the starting points for *Back to the Future*. The exhibition built on a collaboration established since 2011, between Konsthall C, the local council (Farsta stadsdelsförvaltning), local preschools and their teachers. The collaboration led to a series of annual exhibitions showcasing the

work of four and five year-old children.

Back to the Future parts I and II were the Home Works programme's contribution, based on a collective investigation into the impact the home has in forming our views of the world, whether that concerns a consciousness of our gender, or our position within the family.

Artists were invited to deliver workshops to ninety-three preschool teachers. Together, they shared pedagogical methods including narration and collective collaging, which culminated in a toolbox that the teachers could use when back at their preschools. During sessions at the preschools, questions around the home were discussed, as well as questions concerning homelessness and how this connects to societal inequalities. Following this, the pedagogues used the toolboxes to create artworks with the children, which were later displayed in the exhibitions.

During *Back to the Future part II*, by Jenny Berntsson and Seçil Yaylali, 500 preschool children were invited to not only exhibit but activate their artworks at the art space. Children carried their artworks like placards, as though marching at a demonstration, and collectively shouted their demands.

The children from the year below joined the demonstration, and were introduced to the idea of what an art space can be, the work that goes on there, and how artworks can be tools for 'demonstrating' opinions.

Collaborators

- 300 preschool teachers
- 500 5-year-old artists
- 500 4-year-old exhibition visitors

Ingredients

- 1 local council administration
- 1 art space
- 1–2 artists (or more)
- 3–5 preschool teachers specialising in art
- 1 technician
- 3–5 exhibition hosts

Method

- First month, pour the local council administration and the art space into a jar, close the lid tightly.

- Second and third months, shake the jar every now and then. Establish the themes of the exhibition with the council. Email the preschool art teachers and bounce different ideas around with them. Do not be afraid to try things out and see what works.

- Write a contract for the council administration, the art space and the involved artists which clearly states what is expected from each party.

- Fourth month, add the artists to the jar and stir gently. Leave the lid off to allow the mixture to respond to unknown active ingredients.

- Fifth month, pour everything out onto a large table. Present the thematic of the year, make sure that everyone understands the ideas and that they are excited about the thematic. The point is to allow the participants to add their own flavour to the mix, as things always taste better when discussed communally.

- Sixth month, the preparations are finished!

The point of this recipe is to involve children in the activities of an art space at a young age so they feel that the art space is a place they can go to and become a part of. Central to this recipe is that there can never be too many cooks in the kitchen. Do not see the vast number of collaborators as a problem that could turn the dough sour; rather, see the multiple cooks and collaborators as a way of developing the sourdough starter.

Solidarity versus individualism hither and thither — *Khasrow Hamid Othman*

'I have always been amazed by solidarity!' is the first line of Sara Pilotes article "Solidarity vs. Individualism: The Power of Mutirão". It continues:

> ... to me, seeing people getting together to help each other, fight as a group instead of alone and be there for each other is the hope that the world can become a better place. For me, solidarity presents itself as a hope that in the future things will improve, even in the presence of pain, disasters and wars. If there is solidarity something good will come of it all.
>
> **— Sara Pilotes[1]**

[1] Sara Pilotes, "Solidarity vs. Individualism: The Power of Mutirão", (2011), published online at: https://www.rioonwatch.org/?p=1762 (Accessed 20 March 2020).

It was these ideas of solidarity that came to mind in 2015 when my son Hemin unexpectedly connected me with a German artist and an art space in Stockholm.

The situation was as follows: an art space in Stockholm – Konsthall C – had invited the artist Hiwa K to an exhibition called *Open House*. For the exhibition, they asked Hiwa K to address the architecture of the home through his minimal sculpture *One Room Apartment*. The sculpture depicted a house built in the minefields of Iraqi Kurdistan, which Hiwa K saw when driving there in 2007. The view of the isolated home in the deserted landscape shocked him, and he went on to develop *One Room Apartment* in order to highlight the new forms of living that were emerging in Iraqi Kurdistan after the destructive Gulf Wars. A way of living that centred around individualised homes that differed dramatically from the communal dwellings that had previously been the norm. While the official objective of the war in 2003 was to remove Saddam Hussein from power, for Hiwa K it also seemed to be a cultural war in which United States imperialism violently reshaped Iraqi living practices. Transforming communal dwellings into individualised homes.

The house Hiwa K had seen on his journey in 2007 was originally located in Iraqi Kurdistan, but it also spoke to the situation in Stockholm, as one of the capitals with the most individualised households in the world.[2]

Reconstructing *One Room Apartment* was not easy, it was a large sculpture and the building process was complex, particularly for a small art space like Konsthall C. The piece follows the same scale as the original house, but stripped of three of its walls, leaving just one wall, a staircase and part of the roof hanging freely from the remaining wall. *One Room Apartment* can be described as a sculpture that appears large and heavy, yet at the same time fragile and vulnerable.

During the production of this work, Hiwa K was stuck abroad and was not able to finish the sculpture. Through a Facebook message he reached out to his friends for help with the construction, and it did not take long before his Canadian friend, my son, responded to his message, saying that his dad was an engineer based in Stockholm, Sweden. On Wednesday 16 May 2015, I received a video call from Hiwa K. I remember the conversation also because a few days earlier I had undergone surgery on my left eye, and I was still waiting for an operation date to correct my right eye. Hiwa K explained the situation, and in order to avoid the embarrassment of not

[2] According to European statistics published online at: https://ec.europa.eu/eurostat/statistics-explained/index.php?title=People_in_the_EU_-_statistics_on_household_and_family_structures#Single-person_households. (Accessed 20 December 2019).

finishing the sculpture in time, he asked if I could assist with the rendering of the sculpture.

A momentary network of solidarity emerged. Within a few hours I had connected with my son Hemin in Vancouver, an Iraqi-born artist based in Germany, an art space in Stockholm and a team of stressed workers. The next day I received the following message on Facebook:

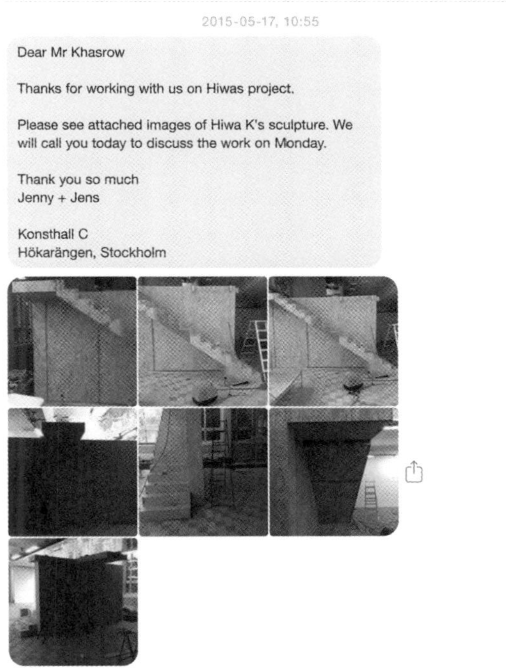

My initial concern was that the structure had been made from cheap OSB boards, instead of stone and concrete, which are the building materials that are commonly used in Iraq. Hiwa K had explained that his concern had nothing to do with aesthetics, nor the colour of the sculpture. He wanted the sculpture to give the right visual impression of the house he had seen in Iraq. To solve this, he wanted to render the sculpture entirely with a mixture of sand and cement, which can be difficult when you use OSB boards. This is due to the fact that the surface of the boards is glued and slippery, which complicates the way the cement adheres to the board. With only a few days left until the opening of the exhibition, Hiwa K asked if I could provide some building expertise for how to render the sculpture. So, I joined the install-team at Konsthall C to see how we could accomplish Hiwa K's goal.

Due to my eye operation, my role was to guide the workers at the art space. Solidarity played its role, and we managed to collectivise and learn from each other while at the same time fulfilling Hiwa K's requirements for the sculpture. *One Room Apartment* embodies the expansion of the phenomenon of individual homes across Iraq after the occupation. However, here in Stockholm, the process of building the sculpture also built a sense of collectivity, a network of solidarity, or as Pilotes ends her article: '[Solidarity is] about the sense of pride one experiences as an individual and also as a community, to see things improve through collective effort.'

Hiwa K, *One Room Apartment*. Part of *Open House*. Konsthall C, 2015.

How to render a house? with Khasrow Hamid Othman

In what follows is a recipe for the render that was learnt during the installation of Hiwa K's sculpture. There are many possible finishes, please select your own as you see fit.

Ingredients

- Sand
- Water
- Cement
- Wire mesh
- OSB boards
- Gravel
- Steel float

Method

- Prepare the surface before starting. Make sure that the surface you are rendering is free from dirt, dust, oil, grease, paint, silicone or any loose material. At Konsthall C, *One Room Apartment* by Hiwa K was built using OSB boards. This is a cheap material, but it is also slippery which makes it more difficult for the cement to adhere to the surface. In order to make the cement stick, we covered the house in wire mesh.

- If you are building a house indoors, as we did at Home Works, make sure that the floor you are working on is strong enough to carry the load, as the construction will be very heavy.

- Use safety equipment. Cement creates dust and debris that can be dangerous without the right safety equipment. Wear a dust mask, as well as safety goggles and a thick pair of gloves when mixing cement.

- Now, mix the right amounts of cement, sand, gravel and water. The precise ratios will vary depending on the type of cement, so make sure to check your bag or the instructions that come with the cement you use. However, as a general rule of thumb, you will need one part cement, two parts sand, and four parts gravel. It is easier to mix the cement if you rent a cement mixer, but if you do not have access to this, you will need a bunch of friends to keep turning the cement so that it does not set.

- Apply to the wall. Use a steel float and apply the first layer of render to the wall. The mixture needs to be fairly thick, if it is too loose it will fall off, and if it is too thick it will be hard to apply. Keep applying the render until you have reached the desired thickness. Once the thickness has been reached, use a straight edge such as a metal leveller and scrape off the render using a sawing motion. After this, gently use the steel float to smooth the surface. There are a few different ways of rendering a wall. For example:

    - Bagged/patterned finish is achieved by rubbing a ball of damp hessian into the surface, which produces a pattern depending on the style of rubbing.

    - Sponge finish is when you mop or dab the hardened surface with a damp sponge, which can create a sponge-textured finish.

    - Roughcast finish is achieved by throwing and flicking the final coat onto the surface to achieve a roughcast finish, no retouching is carried out, the way it lands will be the way it looks.

    - Textured finish can be achieved by the addition of a coarser aggregate, that is to say larger gravel components are added to the mix for the final coat.

- Cleaning is important! Rinse and clean all the equipment. Make sure that they are free from dirt, as it will be difficult to use them in the future otherwise.

- Enjoy your new house!

Not knowing your home — *Jonna Bornemark*

Jonna Bornemark is a philosopher whose thinking is informed by real life situations and their connection to contemporary politics, ideas that are explored at the Centre for Studies in Practical Knowledge at Södertörn University where she is Professor of Philosophy. Her latest book uses the philosophy of Nicholas of Cusa to unpack the politics of measuring and monitoring and the effects of new public management and neoliberal ideologies in contemporary care systems.[1]

We met Bornemark for tea on a rainy day in October 2019. She was rushing between interviews and talks, teaching and picking up her children from school.

1 Jonna Bornemark, *Det omätbaras renässans: en uppgörelse med pedanternas världsherravälde*, (The Renaissance of the Unmeasurable: Arrangements of the Pedantic World Domination), (Sweden: Volante, 2018).

Jenny Richards and Jens Strandberg (JR/JS): We thought we would start off this conversation with a simple yet complex question. Do you work at home?

Jonna Bornemark (JB): Yes, always. Initially, when I hear that question, I think of the paid work that you do and that you can do at home, and I like to write and read at home. However, when you slow down your question, it forces me to ask what is 'home' which I spontaneously associate with the personal, a family place. I also think of the Centre for Studies in Practical Knowledge at Södertörn University. That space is not just my professional base, but also a space where I feel at home. Both spaces are nurturing and secure places, a kind of home.

Then I also think of 'work', and one thing that is much needed in my personal home is a proper clean-up, as I am very bad at prioritising cleaning. From that perspective, I do not work at home. But the term 'work' is an interesting one. It tends to be associated with the labour you do in order to earn money, which of course is one part of it. The other part is the necessary tasks we need to do, and these two parts are not always connected. Much of paid work is fairly meaningless, and a lot of unpaid work is meaningful and very important. I think one of the problems is how we use the term 'work' indifferently and a lot of paradoxes arise from that. It would be interesting to see if a clear distinction between these two meanings will be made in the future.

We often skim the surface of words and their meaning. When we slow down and look closer at the words in a simple question like the one you just posed, it can go off in all kinds of directions. This is something artists should do, as it shows how a new world order can grow from small sentences.

JR/JS: One aim of this Cooking Book is to zoom in on the *hidden* side of the Home Works programme as a way to draw out the hidden work that went into its making. To better understand and discuss the concepts 'home' and 'work', we transformed the art space into what we have called a 'public home' *(see How to create a public home → p. 239)*. We wanted to connect the resources we had access to at Konsthall C with the Stockholm housing crisis and use the space as a way to experiment and speculate about other ways of living. What do you understand by the term 'public home?'

JB: This is an important question. One of my first jobs was working for the *Folkets hus* (People's House) organisation,[1] whose idea is to create what they call a 'communal living room'. For me, there is a risk of romanticising such an idea about living in harmony, but it has been a strong ideal in the Swedish context. Now, in a time of neoliberal ideology, fuelled by an individualised system, we seem to want to get rid of collective spaces, this ideal does not fit, which is probably why it has come to play a less important role.

One of the problems with the idea of a communal living room, is the way it seeks to create uniformity and harmony. The political theorist Chantal Mouffe would question the necessity of people being alike in order for such commonality to take place. If we follow her thinking, she argues that the idea of a communal living room is predicated on consensus.[2] I think one thing that happened with the People's House movement was that there was an underlying aim of making people alike and suppress differences.

For example, my job was to visit the People's House organisations around Sweden in order to hear about how they worked with youth, and how they dealt with integration. Some of them functioned well, but I remember one place in particular that did not have any youth-related or integration activities at all. When I asked why, I was told: 'we tried that ten years ago, but they would not take their shoes off, so we had to cancel the programme.' The example is funny, but it shows a pitfall with regard to consensus when certain people feel like a place belongs to them, while others need to play by their rules in order to gain access.

My position is more complex. I think we need spaces with communal living rooms at cultural centres or 'public homes', as you put it. In this case, we can say there needs to be a 'we' in order for these spaces to exist, but at the same time the definition of 'we' constantly risks becoming too narrow, and there is a risk it becomes: 'we are the ones'. To me, this is a movement between *intellectus* and *ratio*,[3] between not knowing who 'we' are and organising stuff, and the needing to know who 'we' are and what group we

1 The People's House movement is a movement and organisation that organises cultural activities. The national organisation was officially formed in 1905. Today, it consists of 500 membership organisations.

2 Chantal Mouffe, *On the Political*, (London: Routledge, 2005).

3 Jonna Bornemark is referring to the specific concepts developed by the philosopher Nicholas of Cusa as explored within her book, *Det omätbaras renässans: en uppgörelse med pedanternas världsherravälde*, (Sweden: Volante, 2018).

want to work with in order to organise stuff. I think we always need to think of the many aspects of these concepts and rethink what we can do with them.

JR/JS: Maybe this is a good point to backtrack. You write about Nicholas of Cusa in your recent book, and you started to talk about some of those ideas in your response just now, but can you give a short definition of the terms *intellectus* and *ratio*?

JB: The idea is basically that human experience is always taking place on the horizon of 'not knowing', we can always know more. Central to the idea is that the horizon is not a wall. It is not that the things we can know are on one side of the wall and everything we cannot know is on the other side. That is a bad invention of Modernity as it splits up the world. Instead, the horizon of 'not knowing' is exactly that we can go to the horizon and find knowledge about, say, the islands there, but that the horizon has moved. In one way, we can never know everything, knowledge is infinite, but we can always know more. It is important to keep these aspects together, as we cannot choose one of them.

Intellectus, simply put, is the human capacity to stand in relation to horizons of 'not knowing' and explore *what* is important and *how*. When we have verbalised what is most important, and we vaguely know how to do it, then we use *ratio*, which is organising and measuring used in order to structure and order the world. *Ratio* can be described as a worldview or a verbalised map of our existence.

There should always be movement between *intellectus* and *ratio*. For example, we know that democracy is important on our map, but do we know what democracy is? Maybe we need to not know what democracy is in order to find out what is important in democracy. This is a movement from *ratio* to *intellectus*. Once we have asked ourselves what democracy is, we can reinsert our findings back into *ratio*, which then needs to be reformulated, developed and changed. We get into trouble if we cut off the connection between *intellectus* and *ratio*, as we would think that the world is complete and fully defined.

JR/JS: How would you think about these concepts in relation to the work we do at home? With that we mean the work that is often unrecognised but central to all other kinds of production. How do Nicholas of Cusa's concepts relate to notions of 'work' and 'home'?

JB: Let me start with someone else's terminology. Simone de Beauvoir speaks about 'immanence' and 'transcendence'. She would say that the unpaid work at home is pure immanence. Transcendence is the creation of projects, which, in line with Jean-Paul Sartre, is the essence of humanity. From this perspective, the *only* purpose of housework is to uphold life. I think this is problematic in de Beauvoir's writings, and to me this is a major problem with her texts.

If we include relational work, like caring for children, sick or elderly people in the concept of home working, both Sartre and de Beauvoir would most likely say that it might develop you as a person, but it is not transcendence. From this perspective, labour at home is neither *ratio* or *intellectus*, it is just pure 'nature' and goes around in circles. However, we know that we need to follow time in order to do this type of work. This is interesting, because time is in itself a kind of circle. Housework requires you to listen to the specificity of time and lived experience. In this way it is closer to time, since it is closer to life. I think this is perhaps why it often slips into this notion of being 'natural'. It becomes too close to life, and life has not been valued. Value, in today's society, has become more about getting away from lived reality in order to create culture and human reason.

When things become *ratio*-fied they tend to slip away from time. Rather to say that this situation is new, specific and unique, it builds a logic based on generalisations and abstractions. This tendency to leave life is one of the problems with the civilisation we are part of, which I think should listen more to time and life.

Both immanence and transcendence are part of an *intellectus* and *ratio* structure, as both are about creating projects and reshaping the world, and hence creating yourself. For example, emotional work is dependent upon horizons of 'not knowing' – *intellectus* – as to see someone living is always to enter into a relationship, which you do not fully know. This is what it means to be a human being. I cannot know what you are thinking, but you can give me horizons. Cleaning is of course a way of organising and building worlds. A world where we can be at home, where everything is in its proper place. This is a good example of what *ratio* can do and what solutions it can find.

For example, my desk needs a box for my pens, a second box for my rubber bands and a third for rubbers. I also need to get rid of the pens that do not work. This is *ratio* at work.

Value is totally central here. If we work with the four concepts *ratio*, *intellectus*, immanence and transcendence, it becomes clear that today in Sweden, society mainly values *ratio* and transcendence, when in fact they all need each other. Value is always there. If we listen closely, it is easy to hear how we use our words, as some concepts can appear banal or clichéd, and it is precisely the banal and clichéd that tells us what we are taking for granted. If we go back to this idea of value, it is clear that work at home is part of a process that involves both *intellectus* and immanence. Taking care of children, for example, requires that you listen to the uniqueness of each child at every moment, which demands *intellectus* skills. But it is centred around taking care of the child, feeding them, putting them to bed, and keeping them reasonably clean. These could be called activities of immanence. However, at the same time, an *intellectus* process would also be about stopping and asking yourself what exactly working at home involves. Why is it thought of as going around in circles? And why is it bad to go in circles?

Only by listening closely and taking another look can we change what we value most and how we value it. Today, it is necessary to revalue these things, as we are realising that we cannot go on living in the same way. Therefore, we need to reconsider and change our values.

JR/JS: You have written extensively and critically about manuals and instructions. When we were working on this book, we were thinking about how we could create recipes developed from the practices we worked with at Konsthall C. We realised that we might be doing the exact thing that you have been criticising, and we felt it would be interesting to also be critical of this format and discuss how the recipe might connect to efficiency and measurable politics. Are we simplifying complex, artistic procedures into bullet points and manuals? And what does that do to the complexity of Home Works, its specificity and context, now, a few years after it was made?

JB: The short answer would be: we simplify things all the time and we should not be afraid of it. What is important, however, is how do we use recipes or manuals. By whom and to what ends were these instructions made? And how do they relate to the economy? Manuals and recipes are one way to gather and save experiences. Without having seen yours, I am guessing that they are artistic and open-ended. Recipes that in themselves can be brought into new *intellectus* reflection and new specific contexts and situations. In this way, recipes are tools, which outline important insights that we want to share. This is how I think recipes and manuals should be used.

That said, an important philosophical question lies behind the production of recipes and manuals, which has to do with the relationship between generalisation and specificity. Humans often move between these poles, and it is in this movement that problems arise, since we tend to forget the point of what we are doing. In other words, we need to gather together and build a common world, which in a way we can call a home. We need to have a home, but a home is there to take on new situations.

JR/JS: It is interesting how this links to knowledge of cooking, and how cooking is passed on to new generations as practical knowledge, which seems to hold an embodied specificity.

JB: Yes, and we all know that following a recipe is one thing, but having the skills that lead to success is another thing. I often follow recipes in detail, but my cinnamon buns do not look anything like the ones in the pictures. Hence, there is a practical knowledge attached to cooking that is not found in the recipe, but that can be learnt by doing.

Aristotle talks about *techne* (craft or art) and *phronesis* (practical wisdom), which are the two aspects of practical knowledge. *Techne* is two-sided and can be formulated both as, for instance, a manual as well as embodied knowledge, for example, riding a bike or tying your shoelaces. *Phronesis*, on the other hand, is being able to judge a situation and act in a 'good' way, that is to say responding in a way that is as productive as possible for those involved.

These two parts of practical knowledge are also in play in an *intellectus* and *ratio* relationship, but to Nicholas of Cusa, maybe practical knowledge is about moving between *techne* and *phronesis*, to make use of automatised embodied knowledge based on experience and to summarise it in manuals, but also to relate to the specificity of the situation.

However, there is also theoretical knowledge, Aristotle calls this *episteme*. *Episteme* is true at all times and in all places. Such truths are reached through generalisation and abstraction. Generalisation occurs when we see a common trait among many situations, and this is how we formulate concepts. The experience of, for example, blue can often be summarised in the concept 'blue'. Abstractions on the other hand, build theories and develop new layers or concepts. For example, when you write down a recipe you might write: add flour, water and butter. However, if you start in an abstract way, you might build layers of what we understand a recipe to be, that is the metalevel.

Unlike Aristotle, Nicholas of Cusa's concept of knowledge does not take its starting point in the difference between practical and theoretical knowledge. *Intellectus* as the capacity to stand in relation to 'not knowing' is practical as well as theoretical. We do this in relation to specific situations, it is fundamental to our ability to act, to see *what* is important to do in a given situation. This is practical knowledge, but we also stand in relation to horizons of 'not knowing' in more abstract or theoretical ways, connected to knowledge acquisition. For example, this can relate to which 'whatnesses' are relevant in life at large? Like, what is life? What is a good life?

Ratio combines practical and theoretical, 'whatnesses', in a system, a process that *techne* is part of. But this system is never completed, it constantly goes back to being an *intellectus* investigation.

In the case of this Cooking Book, the movement between *intellectus* and *ratio* might be achieved through the making of recipes that allow us to build on earlier experiences and practical knowledge that we can use in new situations where we need to use our own capacity for *intellectus* and *phronesis*.

JR/JS: *Ask Again!* was a research project that we began in 2016.[4] It was an attempt to mobilise domestic workers and art workers in Stockholm and raise awareness of working conditions for domestic workers. The work developed as a collaboration with Kommunal, the union for domestic workers in Sweden, to work within the existing support system. We managed to set up one meeting after we had tried to push the work

4 *Ask Again!* was based on Ask! (Actie Schone Kunsten) that took place at Casco in Utrecht (2011). For more info about ASK! see Binna Choi and Maiko Tanaka, eds. *Grand Domestic Revolution Handbook*, (Utrecht: Casco and Valiz, 2014).

for six months. Unfortunately, the meeting did not get us very far. The management of Kommunal was very interested in the collaboration, but we found that they could not see the point of working closely with workers.

Looking back, it was quite a naive attempt in many ways, but what we are interested in discussing with you today is the wider philosophical question around Sweden's relationship to institutions and political organising, and the potentials and pitfalls of this system, specifically in relation to Nicholas of Cusa's notion of 'not knowing'. Could you explain how you look at the relationship between this concept and political organising, as well as the possibilities for organising outside the walls of the art space? How can we, in institutions, think about creating spaces of 'not knowing' within other institutions, such as Kommunal, which, from our perspective, are fundamentally opposed to the idea of 'not knowing'?

JB: I have been talking about resistance and micro resistance, and, if I understand your research correctly, you were looking to build an alliance with the workers that you thought had a lot to resist. Your question was, how do we build alliances and how can we help them in their resistance? To me the question is about where resistance comes from?

The neoliberal system in the form of new public management does not only mean a lot more paperwork, as workers are monitored and manualised through regulatory documents, it is also a rationalisation of our understanding of work. The system of monitoring workers is very old and has grown this century in the lowest paid sectors. For me, the neoliberal system is anorectic, based on calculations. For example, in home care for people who are older you might have fifteen minutes for showering, five minutes for dressing, ten minutes for washing up. What is forgotten is the space for making the process possible. In the manuals and on paper it looks possible, but everyone who works with home care knows that it is not how reality works. This probably will not change until it reaches the middle class, as the lowest paid workers can always be exchanged and do not have space to resist or even perform micro resistances. In a way, they do not have power.

As I understand *Ask Again!*, wanted to contribute to the union's way of organising workers in Sweden and show how the workers do have power. This will probably take time, as the unions abandoned the workers a while ago, and bought into the neoliberal, new-public-management way of organising. From my perspective, the unions missed these questions, as they only see salaries and ways to raise those salaries. This is of course an important question, but there has been a fixation on this issue, which has meant that they miss so many other questions that are also important. Collective Agreements and juridical economic perspectives seem to be the only perspective the unions have and there is little resistance in this.

We should also keep Gayatri Spivak's ideas of representation in mind and ask ourselves how can we talk for someone else's experience? How do we build alliances? One way to do that would be to get into their experience and let them talk. Create a space where they get to explain their practical knowledge in relation to everyday concrete experiences. I think one of the questions is, how do you express resistance when there are no words to describe it?

To create a space is one thing, to have the words to verbalise is another. In your project you maybe thought that there were words already in place. Words that you would have in common and could use. But, for example, I was only able to write my recent book because I worked for ten years with these concrete experiences of people working in care situations. I also think it would have been impossible to write that book if I had worked as a nurse for ten years because of lacking the language to describe certain experiences. As a researcher you need to be able to listen, and not only to the stories, but also to the work in order to dig into the stories.

I believe in alliances and I believe in the way you thought about the work, even though you maybe did not find the right words this time. To give birth to new ways of verbalising resistance is one of the challenges for the workers' movement. Researchers tend to speak for people, but I prefer it if research participants write and reflect in their own words. We need new ways of listening in order to build these alliances, but not that alone, we also need to show the possibilities of verbalising and how verbalisation demands alliances.

I am not sure if the problem with your research was that you went through the management of Kommunal but maybe there was not enough time to build up a language that allowed a resistance to be verbalised.

JR/JS: This idea of an active listening is interesting, as it is not just listening but also a way of digging in and carving out problems and questions. One of the exhibitions during Home Works looked into home craft as a tool for creating new ways of living. This was an investigation into the radical forms of creativity generated in the home that challenge hegemonic values of patriarchy and production to expand the notion of what homecraft can be.

You have been teaching practical knowledge at Södertörn University. What politics do you see in homecraft and how do you see that in relationship to taking power over one's living conditions?

> JB: I would start by talking about matter. I had this discussion once with a person that was a wood whittler. He said that he had an intimate relationship to the wood he worked on. I would say his whittling practice listened to the wood, to understand how the knot and branches could be used to his advantage. To have this careful relationship to matter is, for me, political. I think in today's culture of consumer and mass production, we do not have a clear relationship to matter. Instead we tend to focus on the matter we do not have. As soon as we own it, it melts away. But how can we listen to the matter around us and build relations to it? If we have these intimate relations to matter it becomes a relationship rather than a thing.
>
> Matter has become something that is dead, something impersonal. The philosopher Giordano Bruno had this idea of self-forming matter, where matter is an integral part of living structures. In his words, the world is something that is constantly taking shape, which is such a different relationship to matter.
>
> For example, the mother of my former partner lived in the same house for about sixty years, until she, late in her life, moved into a care home. When they moved her from her house, it was clear that she would not have much longer to live. It was like her house was an outer skin that had been removed. The matter of her house and her body had melted together. I think this is quite common. Your house has traces and holds different possibilities, you work out paths and patterns for how to do things. Your house becomes a part of your automated system that your body navigates in without reflection. Taking a person out of this environment can probably be quite abusive.
>
> I think we underestimate the matter part of a home. That is perhaps why cleaning, for example, has a political radicality in taking care of the matter and can create a different attitude towards what matter is. Being a

materialist is perhaps not the problem. Maybe we are not materialistic enough. Instead we should aim to be better materialists and pay closer attention to the details and matters that are around us. It is when we start paying attention to the specificity of matters that new worlds open up.

A home is thus a *ratio*: a structured and ordered verbalised world we can live in, a place where our rationality stands at the centre. But we are not at home in such a home if it is allowed to become a pure rationalisation, and thus abstraction – away from life – as it takes place in time at specific and unique moments. Instead we are more at home when we can leave home and stand in relation to everything that is not familiar to us, the world that overflows us. And do this both in relation to matter – where a piece of wood can surprise us and open up a new direction – and in relation to other living creatures where, for example, love for a child means creating a world that is a home that should be changed; and that in relation to new thoughts which can change how we understand ourselves. Home is maybe where we can both be ourselves and change ourselves.

Who needs an umbrella when you cannot leave your home? with Bolaget and Gunilla Lundahl

This is what happened when
Lilian Lindblad Domec received care at home
with art and life, with playfulness
and seriousness; with imaginative solutions.
It is about the Umbrella System and the
working conditions within the social care sector.
I met with people in their homes in Hökarängen,
the so-called 'customers'
the generation that once settled in *Folkhemmet*
(The People's Home).
Mutual starting points for conversations
about different aspects of the same topic
– work and life
care in the confines of the home.

— Gunilla Lundahl, *The Need for Umbrellas*, (2017).

For the exhibition *Open House* (2015), Gunilla Lundahl created a collaborative work that looked into how the home changes when you grow older, how it becomes a workplace for other workers, and how it changes your perspective of home life.

This work began during a conversation at one of the house-warming dinners. Gunilla Lundahl wanted to share the friendship that had formed between her friend the artist Lilian Lindblad Domec and her care worker, Thomas Gilek. In light of Lilian Lindblad Domec's dependency on Thomas Gilek and his professional role in the personal space of her home, Gunilla Lundahl sought to create a different relationship that would confront the reorganisation of life through the care system.

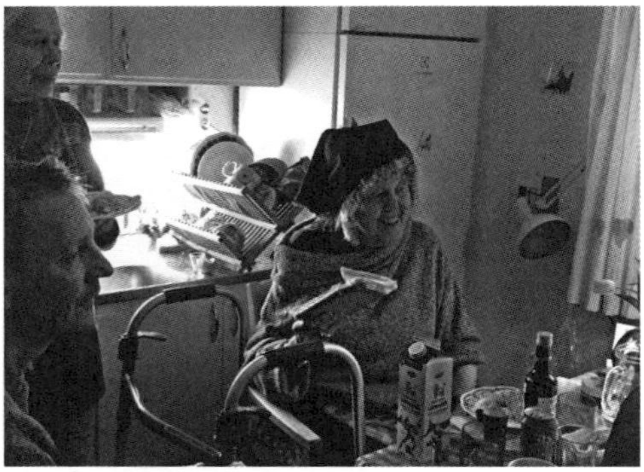

Lilian Lindblad Domec, born in 1922, was one of the pioneers of early animation in Sweden. She invited Thomas Gilek to work with some of the drawings from her last animation. Thomas Gilek produced postcards with collages depicting the absurdity of contemporary life and the history of art, which were distributed across Stockholm. As they travelled across the city via the postal service, they became a kind of expanded animation, as the collages were collectively animated by the people that handled and received them.

Playing on the professionalisation that intruded on their friendship, they formalised their collective artistic work by setting up a fake company, Bolaget, which means The Company or The Company for Living, and alludes to Systembolaget, the government-owned chain of alcohol stores in Sweden which is often simply referred to as Bolaget.

The reason this section is entitled *Who needs an umbrella when you cannot leave your home?* refers to both Lilian Lindblad Domec's position at home but also to *ParaSol*, the overarching or umbrella managerial system for home care in Stockholm at the time. This system tracks movements, and monitors the time care workers spend in people's homes via a mobile application. The work of Bolaget and Gunilla Lundahl's research developed a critique of this umbrella system.

Clara Lindblom – a local politician responsible for social care in Stockholm at the time – joined a discussion at Konsthall C along with activist groups such as Hemtjänstupproret (The Home Care Insurrection). Pressure was put on the City Council to ban this disciplinary technology; a technology embedded in a long history of attempts to make social work and care work more efficient.

Gunilla Lundahl widened her research by working with Hökarängens hemtjänst, a cooperatively run home care organisation. She interviewed fifteen local residents who relied on home assistance in order to be able to live within their own homes. Through these conversations, Gunilla Lundahl listened to the different meanings 'the home' had for people. To some, home was the objects that evoke memories, to others it was a safe place for meeting family and friends. Others discussed the home as a place for creating sustainability, built on knowledge that many brought with them from growing up in the countryside. Some discussed the home as a place that was built for and connected to women's work and different roles.

Throughout the conversation and through the stories that people shared with Gunilla Lundahl there emerged homes based on care, collaboration and friendship, similar to the relationships that had been forged between Lilian Lindblad Domec and Thomas Gilek.

Sadly, some time after this research and exhibition both Thomas Gilek and Lilian Lindblad Domec passed away. However, their work lives on, sparking inspirational ways of working and living, and building new conceptions of what home and work can mean when shared with others.

What follows is a recipe for community organising over the dinner table.

Ingredients

- A desire to work with others
- A good ear to listen with
- An openness to finding curiosity in the everyday
- The energy to make contact and meet people in their own contexts
- A sound recorder
- Agreement contracts
- Time (which is not monitored or measured)

Method

- Think about who lives in your local area.

- How is it possible to meet your neighbours?

- Could you invite your neighbours to your home for a coffee or dinner? Can this start a conversation around how other people understand what home is?

- By knocking on the doors of your neighbours, do you find out a little about who you live with and what kind of services they need to rely on at home or in the community?

- What services are available in your locality?

- How is it possible to meet people who are working in these services?

- Do you book a meeting with an organisation that manages home care to find out how they work? Or hang out at the local supermarket and see who is shopping for someone else?

- Finding out about people's experience of the home and what kind of support they need there can be very personal, so building friendships and trust is the first step in learning about what the home can mean to different people of all ages.

- Whose home is a workplace?

- Have your neighbours become your collaborators?
- What issues do you find among your neighbours and the services they use? How do their issues connect with yours?
- After some time you may want to record an interview with some of your collaborators, for this you should always get permission and be clear about what the interview is for. Do you want to write an article on the issues you have discovered?
- Think about how to author the information you are gathering, how do you pay your respects to all the collaborators in this research endeavour?
- With whom do you and your collaborators want to share these findings? Would sending a letter to a politician focused on these issues be productive? Or do you want to first share it in the local newspaper and ask whether anyone else wants to discuss these problems with you?
- Can postcards like those by Lilian Lindblad Domec and Thomas Gilek be a good vehicle for sharing information between collaborators and the people you want to speak with?
- What kind of change can be seen through your activities? Is it possible to measure this type of community organising?

Leftovers

Situating yourself in a community. Learning about the history of the community and about who lives in the area. Learning different perspectives on what a home is and how different homes are constructed. Building a community where there may not have been one before. Making new friends, neighbours and collaborators. Learning new methods for working in groups. Breaking the isolation of the home.

Lilian Lindblad Domec and the hippos

Where did the hippos come from?
I was drawing animations at Filmverkstan.[1]
A wonderful place
created in 1973 to be a space for experimental film.
Material equipment and tutoring was provided for.
I had an idea about two hippos
then digitalisation arrived.
Filmverkstan closed down.
My hippos ended up hidden within my couch.

The time passed and I grew old.
Received home care, an escort to the outside world
Thomas.
With *The Svea Life Guards* musical parade on his mobile phone
it became easier to get down the stairs.

One day we found the hippos within the couch
completed and already cut out.
I asked Thomas to take one of the drawings.
The hippos had empty speech bubbles
What should we fill the bubbles with?

New powerful expressions are needed
said Eva Marklund while visiting.
Like those of Captain Haddock.

[1] Filmverkstan was an organisation that ran workshops and shared resources to support people to experiment with film. It was run by the Swedish Film Institute and Swedish Television between 1973–2001.

Thomas likes
Cabaret Voltaire in Zurich
so now Dada became useful.

Suddenly, a postcard lay on the doormat
from Thomas
with two hippos.
The idea was born.
The hippos could start travelling the world
with the help of the post office.

The first postcard went to Karin van Dijk.
What a surprise – a reply came.
An analysis, a thesis, an essay, a review
In short, a poetic rant.

Now we were four
we founded Bolaget.

Thomas where do you get everything from?

REVOLUTIONARY CONSCIOUSNESS
BOLAGET MEDIA
ARS GRATIA ARTIS
MARK
Ecce Homo
Ecce Homo
rekommenderas av Bolaget.
FANTASINS LÖSNINGAR
It's All in Your Mind
Vi tillåter oss
dessa historiska och
magiska motto för
att framhålla detta
faktum! - Flodhästen
simmar igen
Bolaget
Gunilla
11258

Who needs an umbrella when you cannot leave your home?

The umbrella system - Gunilla Lundahl

The home care system was created to offer nursing and care to those who need it.
Meetings take place when getting care, around work in the home.
A meeting between people from different worlds.
It concerns life.
Doors open for the new extended family
'to care for people as they grow older is the best and most rewarding work one can do, if it were not for...'

With LOV (a law concerning the freedom of choice of welfare and care providers)
the amount of social care companies quadrupled.
Home care was transformed into a market.
In Hökarängen, you are offered a choice of around 120 different companies,
difficult to keep track of, a lot went wrong.
Where did the money and the time go?
Scandals.

In order to grasp all this, Stockholm City Council purchased
ParaSol – a system that was made for the industry.
It became an umbrella system for Swedish health care
effective from 1 July 2014 for everyone in the home care sector.
ParaGå became the management system for those working with care in the home.
A GPS and an app that tracks your movements
what you do and when. ParaGå documents what you have done.
Do not forget the codes.
Work is carried out according to the schedule in the app
deviations must be reported and repriced.
Now the freedom of choice is over for the 'customer' and staff
needs and desires are instead identified by a care administrator
who places an order to a company
making sure that the money from the council is sufficient.
The managers of the company create a schedule.
That covers the tasks that fit within this umbrella system.

The Home Care Insurrection had already been formed.
Strikes were held at the company Aleris in the southern part of Stockholm.
It was followed by a 'lockout'
attendance and demonstrations
an unworthy system. A motion of no confidence.
The joy in the work disappeared.
Stress and the feeling of insufficiency. No flexibility.
The home care system should be organised by those who work in it.
Out with ParaGå
instead, work in small groups that can provide
continuity and security based on the knowledge at hand and on need.
The network Common Welfare agrees.

It requires a lot of experience, habits, and imagination
familiarity within a sector to master the system.
Give workers a decent salary and schedules that give space
for lunch and travel. The cooperative Hökarängens hemtjänst manages
'we become friends with those we meet.'
But 60 percent of all the companies are not offering collective agreements.
Breaks and time for walking vanish.
Many employees are paid an hourly rate with precarious conditions.
'A clear connection between the system and the organisation is missing,'
a district committee points out.
Those managing the system need educating in order to understand.
The integrity of the 'customers' is at risk.

More people are living longer. The politicians want to streamline and save money.
New public management rules.
Work in the homes should be free.
Proposals to raise costs for the 'customers' are presented
to many poor older people, who built the welfare state,
the *Folkhemmet*, (People's Home).

In a world full of incomprehensibilities,
Bolaget
Lilian Lindblad Domec and Thomas Gilek
call for imaginative solutions.
Thus care in the home became an elixir of life.

With the help of the home care staff of Hökarängens hemtjänst
could Bolaget's hippos find their homes with
14 senior residents of Hökarängen.
With the help of the postal service they came back
With the message of what a home is.

Stockholm on 18/5

To Councillor Clara Lindblom
City Hall

This is my situation. I am 93 years old and I have received care at home for 8 years. It has worked just fine. I have received the help I need and have had the joy of meeting people from all over the world. At the same time, I have been privileged enough to have some of those people return and, because of that, they have become important to me. I have also experienced the effect of the so-called smart phones, which I see as a tool for monitoring staff, based on a form of managerial distrust. There is much to be said about the ideology behind this form of new public management. A lot has been written about it. What scares me is that the relationship between staff members and the receivers of care should be kept within 'professional' boundaries, that is to say, if one happens to have common interests, or if friendship arises, or simply the feeling of safety that can arise from long-term cooperation. Apparently, there have been dubious situations in connection with personal assistants. But, to let these isolated incidents of workers abusing the situation become the guiding principle for an entire sector is, as far as I understand, illegal. One is innocent until proven guilty according to the law.

But please, authorities that control these issues, is it not rather encouraging that people can create meaningful encounters in this rather harsh Stockholm environment where there is so much loneliness?

Lilian Lindblad Domec

PS.
At Konsthall C, an art space in Hökarängen, there is an exhibition based on interviews with older residents from the area. It draws connections to the home care service and I think a lot of it could be interesting for you.

You are most welcome.

Recipes from the public kitchen

There can be a lot of cooking involved in running an art space. Prior to the Home Works programme, the artist group, akcg, had raised money to install a kitchen in the office, which made it possible to cook and offer food and refreshments to visitors. During the Home Works programme, the kitchen was used constantly and a dishwasher was added; possibly the best two thousand Swedish krona spent during the programme. The money was raised by renting out the art space for a photography shoot to a large department store in Sweden. The dishwasher was kindly installed by Mats Strandberg, Jens Strandberg's dad.

Chilli sin Ukeles

The following chilli recipe was served at the opening of an exhibition with Mierle Laderman Ukeles during the first Home Works' exhibition. In preparation, there was a lot of cooking, exhibition organising and public programme planning. We were nervous, our hands were sweating and small wet rings had formed in the armpits of our shirts. The bulk of the chilli had been prepared the night before the opening, so we only needed to put it in a pot and cook the rice at the event. That same night, at 3.30 am, one of us woke up, ran to the toilet and threw up. Shaken and scared by the incident they managed to fall asleep again. The next day we were afraid we had caught a stomach bug. We were not sure if the pot of chilli at the art space had been affected by the potential virus, the last thing we wanted was to give a hundred people a stomach bug. After taking it slow in the morning, it was decided that the sudden sickness was due to nervousness. To ensure there was no possibility of bacteria, we boiled the chilli thoroughly for more than two hours. Hence this dish should always be prepared with a pinch of nervousness, as it gives it a distinct flavour of openness, excitement and a small risk of failure. This recipe feeds up to 50 people.

INGREDIENTS

6	packs sweetcorn (frozen)
20	onions chopped
10–15	carrots chopped
15	peppers
15	garlic cloves
20	cans of black beans (rinsed and drained)
10–15	cans of diced tomatoes
10 red	chillies deseeded and chopped
10 tsp	chilli powder (add more for more spice)
15 tsp	ground cumin (add more for more spice)
15 tsp	paprika powder (add more for more spice)
	oil
	salt and pepper (you can also add cocoa powder if you have some)
2kg	rice
30	pinches of salt
2.5 litres	of water

METHOD

- Cut the carrots into strips. Dress in oil and cook them in the oven on a tray.
- Deseed the peppers and cut into strips. Dress in oil and cook in the oven on a tray.
- Heat the oil in a big pot, sauté onions and garlic.
- Add fresh chilli, cook for 5 minutes.
- Add beans and sweetcorn to the pot.
- Add spices and let it all cook together for a few minutes, so the flavour develops.
- Add tomatoes and reduce the heat, cover and simmer.
- Prepare the rice while the chilli is cooking.
- Drain and wash the rice.
- Add salt and water and cook on low heat until the water is gone.

Serve with care, love and excitement.

Collective lentil soup with orange juice

This soup was served during a workshop with a group of students from Konstfack, an art school in Stockholm. The aim of the workshop was to write manifestos *(see What recipe is needed for a Home Works manifesto?* *p. 46)*. The manifestos were written collectively and in pairs. For the presentations the group was in charge of the cooking. Each participant invited two extra guests and presented their manifesto for the group. This recipe feeds up to 25 people.

INGREDIENTS

	oil
20	carrots
8	potatoes
1 to 2	cartons of orange juice
15	onions
2	packets red lentils (1.6kg)
1	bag of ground cumin
	coriander leaves
	lots of vegetable stock (check during cooking so that it gets the right thickness)

METHOD

- Chop the onions, carrots and potatoes.
- Use a large saucepan and gently heat the oil.
- Fry the onions, add the potatoes and carrots afterwards.
- Stir it in the oil.
- Cook it with a lid on for 3-5 minutes so that the onion and carrots get a bit softer. Be careful not to burn.
- Add cumin and coriander.
- Add the red lentils.
- Add orange juice and some vegetable stock.
- Allow it to simmer for at least 30 minutes or until the lentils have softened.
- Use a hand-blender and blend it together to a soup consistency.

Serve with fresh chopped coriander.

Large communal macaroni pie, by Jennifer Bailey and James N. Hutchinson

Eating and cooking together was not only the backbone of the Home Works public programme, it was also central when hosting workshops with artists, students and groups who were interested in delving into questions of domestic labour and the home, building conditions for our own sustenance into the process of working together.

In 2015, the format of the dinner and communal cooking was used to frame a workshop with ten artists from Scotland. It was part of a collaboration with Collective's Satellites programme, which supports artists at an early stage of their career. The collaboration began with discussions on the topic of domestic labour and culminated with a communal dinner. Guests who could share information about the Stockholm art scene and its collaborative and self-organised activities were invited to join. The dinner took place in November, a time when Stockholm can be dark and cold. This heavy carbohydrate dinner recipe is not only filling, but warming and cheap to make for a large crowd. The pie was the main dish for the occasion and served around 20 people.

Macaroni pie is usually found in Scottish bakeries. While traditional versions tend to be individually sized, this recipe employs some unusual methods to create a striking centrepiece. Ideal for moments when you have guests on their way, no internet connection, a poorly stocked local shop, and limited kitchen utensils.

UTENSILS

- 1 wire coat hanger
- 2 pieces of string
- A bottle of wine
- A large pie or flan dish
- A mixing bowl

INGREDIENTS

1 pat	butter
1 bag	plain flour
1 block	generic Swedish cheese, grated
	Parmesan, either a wedge or a tub of sprinkles
	mustard
	salt
	pepper
1 bag	macaroni (or other tubular pasta)
1	tomato (optional), to make the dish healthy

METHOD

- Cut a lump of butter from your pat and attach it to one corner of the coat hanger using the string, so it hangs freely. Hold the hanger by the hook at the top. This is your scale! Attach the packet of flour to the other corner of the hanger and gradually remove flour from the bag to balance the scale. Put the flour into a bowl and repeat the process, you need double the weight of flour to butter for your pastry.

- Add a pinch of salt to the flour. Rub together the butter and flour mixture using your fingers until it resembles fine breadcrumbs. Bring together the mixture with a small quantity of cold water. Knead the mixture lightly into a smooth ball. Wrap it in clingfilm (if you have any) and – if your guests are not due imminently – place it in the fridge to rest for about 20 minutes.

- While the pastry dough is resting, prepare the béchamel. Cut an identically sized lump of butter to your previous one, and melt it in a saucepan. Add two heaped dessert spoons of flour per approximately 50g of butter (this should be easy to work out) and mix until smooth. Add the milk in small quantities until a smooth sauce is created, then add two or three teaspoons of mustard. Add the generic Swedish cheese in handfuls, ensuring that each has melted into the sauce before adding the next. At this point you might be getting quite stressed, especially if people are arriving, but try to avoid overheating either yourself or the sauce. Start adding the parmesan and taste as you go. Continue until you think you have achieved the maximal level of cheesiness and clagginess your guests can tolerate. Season and add more mustard if the sauce does not taste of much.

- Boil some water in a saucepan and cook the macaroni until al dente. Drain the macaroni and combine with the béchamel.

- Grease the pie or tart dish with some of the remaining butter. Roll out all but a small handful of the pastry using a wine bottle, place on the tart dish and lightly form the pastry to the shape of the dish. Place in the oven and blind bake for at least 5 minutes, 15 ideally. If your oven has a temperature gauge, set it at about 180°C.

- Roll out the small piece of pastry, and, using a small knife, cut out the letters M A C A R O N I P I and E. Remove the blind baked pastry from the oven and pour in the macaroni mixture. If you have decided to make the healthy version, slice the tomato, and place slivers in the centre of the pie. Top with any remaining cheese and place the pastry letters thoughtfully on top, spelling out whatever words you can make with the letters available. Place back in the oven until the cheese has browned and the pastry letters are cooked.

- Place the dish at the centre of the table and serve.

Hökarängen's vegetarian climate smart cooking group

During one housewarming dinner, a couple of neighbours who were keen to cook joined. They were part of a self-organised cooking group and called themselves Hökarängen's Vegetarian Climate Smart Cooking Group. The group cooked vegetarian food as a way to discuss how climate change and climate change activism can be tied to our eating habits. Often, they met at their respective homes to cook together and learn recipes from one another. Learning collectively, without a leader, draws on a long tradition of higher education in Sweden where people meet in study circles. The tradition of making study circles and collectively learning from one another is central to working class struggle in Sweden. Hökarängen's Vegetarian Climate Smart Cooking Group feeds into this history and is a study circle that practically learnt together and shared recipes.

The group cooked as a way of learning by doing. There might be a recipe to follow, but when making collectively there is space for discussion, which encourages experiments and deviations. Add more of one thing, take away something else, eat with a different vegetable. These collective cooking sessions were an excuse to develop a sense of creativity and collaboration, like any artform there is an element of the unknown in the process of making. Their principles included, do not fear the result, enjoy the process and share it with others.

If you want to cook together with others, it might mean you need a space to do it, so as many people as possible can join the collective cooking. The lack of space was one of the problems Hökarängen's Vegetarian Climate Smart Cooking Group faced. During Home Works, the art space's kitchen/office at Konsthall C was offered as a site for the group's meetings and cooking sessions. Smells of fresh ginger, onion or the sweet aroma of chocolate would fill the art space, wrapping the exhibitions in another layer of sensory experience. Alma Forssblad and Iréne Grollman are two active chefs in the group. They became good friends and expanded their cooking in collaboration with Home Works, so that large numbers of visitors could experience their tasty, healthy smoothies, dips or salads.

Sometimes visitors were greeted with a request to help with the preparations. 'Can you deseed this pomegranate?' 'Please can you wash the lettuce?' Cooking together blurred the roles of who was a visitor and who was staff, whoever was keen to get involved was drawn into the cooking cacophony! The result, a feast to share and talk over! When there is food to eat together, there is always something to discuss!

The group have kindly shared a delicious recipe for Tomato and Saffron Stew with Aioli and Foccacia, that feeds up to 30 people and was served during The Women's Day Off symposium in 2015. The recipe is in Swedish so may need translating first. The recipe is a guideline not to be stuck to, but to be played with! Best carried out with others!

1. Sätt ugnen på 200 grader. Blanda alla torra ingredienser. Rör ner filmjölk och sirap. Blanda väl.
2. Häll upp i en smord brödform och grädda i nedre delen av ugnen drygt 60 min. Låt gärna brödet vila några timmar efter att det är klart innan det skärs upp, men det går även att äta det tidigare.

Tomat- & saffransgryta med aioli och foccacia

Allt gånger 5

Gryta

√1 dl gröna linser 5dl
√40 g färsk ingefära (hellre något mer än mindre) 200g
√1 stor gul lök 5 lök
2 påsar saffran 10 påsar
√2 burkar (800g) hela tomater/~~körsbärstomater~~ 10 burkar
~~3 dl vatten~~
√3 medelstora potatis 15 st
√200 g persiljerot eller palsternacka 1kg
√2 medelstora morötter 10

kaffe

2 tsk farinsocker
~~1 tsk spiskummin~~ finns
√2 tsk hela fänkålsfrö
√2 kanelstänger 10 kanelst
~~½ tsk kanel~~
√3 stjärnanis
√3 lagerblad
2 ½ tsk salt finns

1 dl russin
Ät med bröd eller matgryn och aiolin

1. Koka gröna linser ca 20-25 min i saltat vatten.
2. Finhacka ingefära. Grovhacka gul lök, skala och dela grönsakerna i bitar ca 1,5 cm stora.
3. Hetta upp ett par msk olja i en gryta/kastrull och bryn ingefära, gul lök och saffran ett par minuter.
4. Tillsätt tomat och vatten samt grönsakerna och alla kryddor (Vänta med russinen).
5. Koka upp och låt puttra under lock på låg-medelhög värme ca 15 min. Tillsätt russinen och låt grytan stå och puttra ytterligare ca 10 minuter tills grönsakerna är lagom mjuka. Tillsätt linserna och smaka av.
6. Servera grytan med bröd eller matgryn och aioli.

Aioli Vegansk alternativ havre creme fraish.

~~1 äggula~~ 5 ägg finns
√en skvätt citronsaft eller 2 citron
~~ca 2 dl olja, gärna rapsolja blandat med linfröolja~~ 1 flaska finns
~~1-2 pressade vitlöksklyftor~~ finns

1. Vispa äggula, citronsaft och salt i en stor bunke med en spiralvisp tills allt är ordentligt blandat.
2. Tillsätt olja, först några droppar i taget och sen i en tunn stråle, under kontinuerlig vispning så att du ser att emulsionen tjocknar. Här är det bra att vara två så att en "droppar" i olja medan den andra vispar.
3. Blanda ner vitlöken och smaka av med salt/citronsaft.

Recipes by Hökarängen's Vegetarian Climate Smart Cooking Group, 2015.

ARBETAR
REVY
SÖKER
MEDLEMMAR

Part 3. Eating

(Communal ways to experience art)

> **Home values are always in permanent mutation, and today, those which deal with the kitchen are precisely the most capable of radically changing preset gender roles and domestic labour structures.**
>
> — Anna Puigjaner[1]

Eating today, can often be an isolated act. Home Works aimed to support communal eating situations and develop what could be described as a semi-public kitchen. The kitchen/office at the art space was often transformed into a collective space for cooking and dining throughout the exhibition and events programme. It facilitated the support of artistic practices that encouraged social engagement, and offered a way for the questions and politics associated with the artworks on display – around hospitality, collective processes and communal experiences – to be enacted within the art space. Conversing with others over dinner can create a more intimate encounter with art, in contrast to wandering around an exhibition with little opportunity for discussion.

1 Anna Puigjaner, "Bringing the Kitchen Out of the House", *e-flux Architecture*, published online at: https://www.e-flux.com/architecture/overgrowth/221624/bringing-the-kitchen-out-of-the-house

Part 3. shares some of the ways in which Home Works developed different communal encounters with art through involvement in print workshops, choir rehearsals and a fashion show. The recipes reflect on the methods for working collectively and generating broader public engagement with artists and their work. Eating together was central to a lot of the activities discussed here. These texts reflect on the politics and potential that eating together offers for other ways of being and coming together in an art space. What does it mean for an art institution to take on the role of host? How can an art space become a site for building community? And how could this challenge social fragmentation today? Or, as Anna Puigjaner contends, in other words, how might eating together become an act of political resistance?

How to organise a housewarming dinner

When Home Works moved into the art space and its neighbourhood, the programme began with a number of housewarming dinners, a form of social gathering that was repeated throughout the programme *(see Recipes from the public kitchen → p. 145)*. The dinners were framed as a series of moving-in parties that were an attempt to get to know the area and its community. The sharing of food and conversations was a way to discover areas of mutual interest and find out how the programme could be relevant to concerns within the neighbourhood. It can be described as an attempt to open up the art space, to tell the local community that the space was theirs to be used, and that it was there to be shaped and be a part of. The housewarming dinners aimed to encourage private discussions, provide a place for friendships to develop, create a relaxed atmosphere, and set the scene for how artists, locals and visitors could meet and get to know one another. The dinners were part of an attempt to build a public home, but can also be seen as artforms in themselves by creating a platform and situation for community organising, creative conversations, happenstance and undetermined encounters *(see How to create a public home* *→ p. 239)*.

The dinners continued throughout Home Works and were a starting point for many of the commissions that were developed during the Home Works programme, as many productions were collectively made within the community. For example, one of these commissions was *Warm Friends, Cold Cash* by Ciara Phillips. Many dinners were held, and much food was shared together. Ciara Phillips turned the exhibition space into a temporary print studio, thereby subverting the art space as a site where visitors encounter the products of an artist's work. Instead of presenting a static and finalised exhibition, Ciara Phillips invited groups, activist organisations, and neighbours to produce new prints with her, which expressed subjects that aired the collaborators' concerns. Printed posters were then pasted up around the art space asking visitors to 'support your local *hemtjänst*' (home care),[1] or shouting 'artist-run, it's a fucking marathon'.[2] Amidst the physical and collective work of printmaking, collaborators often ate together, shared coffee and built informal connections with the artist and others they had never met before. These moments were both a mode of artistic and curatorial production and an informal way for the Home Works programme to learn from the community and get to know new collaborators. One memorable dinner was held at the end of Ciara Phillips' commission. The art space was at this point full of new prints, colourful messages, dirty tables and aprons. The dinner was a space where guests could make prints and work with Ciara Phillips, as well as discuss the ongoing research of the Home Works programme. People moved between stirring the soup in the kitchen/office and stirring printing ink in the art space, thereby blending and blurring the line between art and domestic work.

The following recipe is an example of how you can use an art space to organise a housewarming dinner, to get to know your neighbours, find out about local concerns and to see how your work can be embedded in the community.

Based on the first meal we made for Ciara Phillips during *Warm Friends, Cold Cash*, she has written *Macaroni with veggie sausages, peas and optional ketchup*, as a playful analogy for how to work with others.

Ingredients

- Dinner recipe *(see Recipes from the public kitchen* *→ p. 145)*
- Things to cook with
- Space (can be your kitchen, an art space or another space for organisations)
- An open door
- Communication
- Time
- A pinch of money
- Tablecloth
- Fabric pens

Method

- Set a date for your dinner.

- Send a dinner invitation to people you would like to start a conversation with and let them know that you would like to hear about their ideas and concerns. For example, during the *Open House* exhibition in 2015, Gunilla Lundahl made contact with The Home Care Insurrection, and this became a relationship that was cultivated

[1] Printed in collaboration with the activist group Hemtjänstupproret (The Home Care Insurrection).
[2] Print made in collaboration with the artist-run space Nýló (Living Art Museum).

Macaroni with veggie sausages, peas and optional ketchup *(or possible instructions for leading a collaborative workshop)*

Ingredients: *A group of 10-15 is ideal*

Quick cooking macaroni
Veggie sausages
Peas
Ketchup (optional)

Method:

You ~~will~~ *may or may not* know all of these ingredients separately, but the trick is to bring them successfully together. The macaroni cooks in three minutes, the sausages in sixteen, the peas in three and the ketchup, well, it's ready, but maybe you need to take it out of the fridge so that it doesn't cool everything off when applied.

context

Let's imagine you are cooking this meal away from home. *(eg. Konsthall C in Hökarängen)* The oven is unfamiliar to you and you're not sure how long it will take to warm up. You could ask your hosts but even they probably won't know how long it will take to reach 180 C. You just have to start. Turn the dial and watch the light come on. If you are lucky you will hear a fan whirring in the background, then you will know that things are really getting going.

With the stage set, you can lay out the sausages. *(a technique / a framework)* I like to keep this part simple - just line them up, nothing fancy - but you can set them up however you like. When the little red light on the

Think John Cage - begin anywhere

*

front of the oven goes off, open the door and carefully place them in. Bear in mind that you will need to rotate them, but you can come back to this later.

ask questions

In the meantime find two saucepans that you can fill with water and place them on the stove at high heat. Add salt if you want to reach the boiling point sooner. The macaroni is the foundation of your meal, a creamy coloured filler, and the peas are the brain food, little green orbs of input. Both are best served al dente, that is to say that each should have some tooth. Overcook either and you will be sorry.

people doing things

Soon the steam will be rising, the windows fogging and a quiet symphony of gurgling and sizzling filling the kitchen. Bask in the warmth of it all without forgetting why you are here. Timing is key and careful observation and testing will yield the best results. The macaroni is a good case in point - left for too long and it will turn to mush, but exercise caution when testing it too soon or boiling water nestled in its curve can easily burn your tongue and the discomfort will stay with you for days.

conversation

With all of the ingredients nearing completion and presentation close at hand, prepare to dish it up. Think of the ** plate as a platform for bringing together varied content, and an offer of something new. You may be hungry, but don't be lazy. Consider aesthetics, they are closely linked to taste. Perhaps now is the moment to add a splash of colour? The choice is yours.

* take action

** output

during *Warm Friends, Cold Cash*. You never know where conversation might lead!

- A good way to expand your community is to ask everyone who is attending the dinner to bring a friend or two. That way you can also reach out further with your housewarming dinner.

- What food will you prepare? You could cook on your own, but cooking with others can be more fun. New ideas, untold stories, and local histories all surface through conversations, and when cooking together you can talk and share the labour of preparing the food.

- Cook, host, serve and discuss.

- When discussing over dinner, use the tablecloth to make notes and map out interests and concerns the dinner guests raise. For example, during *Warm Friends, Cold Cash*, Ciara Phillips began by asking those who had joined what concerns mattered to them at that time. She made notes during the conversation in order to draw up connections and common ground as well as differentiate between people's ideas.

- Be open to the unexpected and nurture the relationships that are created. Relationships formed during *Warm Friends, Cold Cash* continued to develop and grow during the rest of the programme.

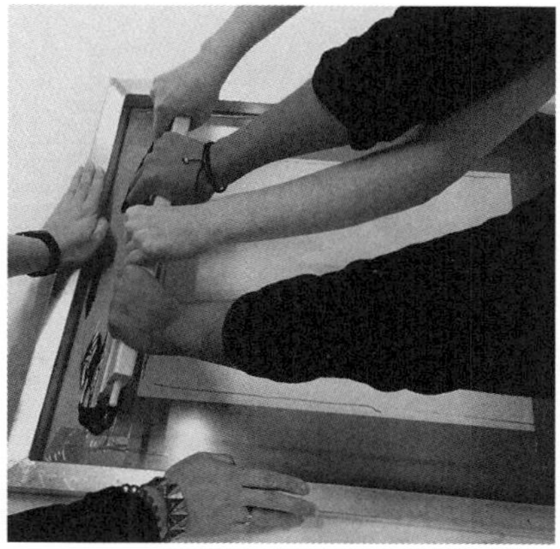

CASH
FRIENDS
WARM
FRIENDS
CASH

The politics of eating together, or eating together in politics — *Silvia Federici*

Our second conversation with Silvia Federici took place in 2020, four years after our first discussion. This time we held our conversation on a Friday evening over Skype, from a small apartment in a suburb of Stockholm to her home in New York.

Jenny Richards and Jens Strandberg (JR/JS): Hi again Silvia, it is great to be continuing some of our discussions around cooking and organising with you! In our previous conversation in 2016, you talked about the aesthetic dimension of housework *(see Caring, cleaning and cooking* *↪ p. 65)*. The creative act of organising one's home and the importance of the presentation of the food we eat.

As this book takes the format of a cooking book we wanted to pick up the conversation where we left it, and discuss further the politics of eating and eating in politics. Can you clarify some of your current perspectives on the politics of eating together, how food and activist work are linked, and how you are working around these questions?

> Silvia Federici (SF): I would say that food is everything in a way. Food and sex are among the main engines of our lives.
>
> I think we should discuss food and the politics of eating in two ways. First, we need to understand food in relation to our health. Food, which is the source of life, is now often a source of death, because of its contamination, as agriculture relies on chemical imputs to force exhausted soils to produce. Secondly, there is the question of food and power. Who owns food? Who controls the food supply? We can see, for example, the power of corporations like Monsanto, who have tried to appropriate and modify the seeds available to farmers. And we have seen how food crops have become objects of financial speculation, exacerbating the problem of hunger in the world, to the point that in Haiti, because so many people were starving, women were cooking mud pies to deal with the hunger. Controlling the food supply means controlling people's lives. Without food there is no possibility of resistance. Without food there is no life. Corporations understand that, which is why the struggle over food is becoming more and more intense.
>
> From this perspective, a key political question today is how to make a good, nutritious meal. Food gives us life, but it can also give us death, and it can also kill those who produce it, so lethal are the chemicals used within food production. Studies show that the number of deaths by cancer among farmers, among food producers has escalated worldwide, and also that women who eat contaminated food, through nursing, pass the poison it contains to their children. Still the main problem remains hunger, which affects more and more people.

There has been a lot of organising and networking around 'food politics' with organisations like Food not Bombs[1] that, in the 1990s, recovered unwanted food, created cookhouses and, 'regularly served free food in public spaces' to poor and working class communities.[2] But as soon as the police and local governments understood what they were doing, it was outlawed, using as a pretext the question of 'hygiene'. In San Francisco, in the United States people were arrested for giving food to homeless people. Clearly, the government forbade this food distribution because they saw what a power it has in bringing people together, and because food distribution exposed the fact that in the richest country in the world so many go hungry.

Another struggle is for agricultural practices that do not poison the earth or our bodies. I am currently working on a text for a handbook on feminism and ecology that draws on what is happening in Latin America, where rural/Indigenous women are leading the struggle against oil companies and other mining activities that are contaminating the soil, the waters, the air, and in their struggle the question of food production is central.

(JR/JS): It is coming into consciousness that it is important to organise with food and that eating together is an integral part of political gatherings. One thing we have discovered recently is that for many people it can feel overwhelming to know how to involve themselves in politics when there are so many disasters looming, from climate, to health and the economy. We believe just having a meal together can be a political act and can be a first step in getting involved in political work. What for you are the politics in eating together?

(SF): The politics of eating together has a long tradition. Think of the word 'companion'. It is made up of *com* and *panis*, which means 'with bread'. The idea of companionship comes from the practice of eating together, to 'break bread together with another person.' The expression has medieval roots,

1 Food Not Bombs was formed in Cambridge, Massachusetts in 1980 by anti-nuclear activists and is an all-volunteer organisation dedicated to nonviolent social change. Food Not Bombs has no formal leaders and strives to include everyone in its decision making process. Each group recovers food that would otherwise be thrown away and makes fresh hot vegan and vegetarian meals that are served outside in public spaces to anyone without restriction. www.foodnotbombs.net/new_site/ (Accessed March 2020).

2 Chris Crass, *Towards Collective Liberation. Anti-Racist Organizing, Feminist Praxis, and Movement Building Strategy*, (Oakland: PM Press, 2013), pp. 37–105.

referring to the time when you broke bread with others, as you ate from the same dish. Through sharing the bread solidarity was born between people.

This experience has grown over time in different contexts. In the United States, this practice was enlivened during the Occupy movement, when hundreds of young people came together in camps, not only talking together, but cooking together, deciding how to sustain themselves collectively. People got in touch directly with farmers, to avoid depending on the market and corporations. They wanted to break the control the market has on food production and distribution and circumvent agriculture's entwinement with the chemical industry, which is filling crops with all sorts of contaminants. CSA (Community Supported Agriculture) are also motivated by this need for more autonomy and more control over what we eat.

Another aspect of the politics of eating together is the sharing of information. Cooking is a profoundly cultural act. In the Occupy movement there were people from all kinds of places, so cooking together was a broad cultural exchange. This is all part of the experience and politics of eating together.

Sadly, eating has become a purely utilitarian act, it is like going to a gas pump and filling yourself up. We are now a 'fast food world' with consequences that go well beyond our own stomachs, though the ubiquitous rise in obesity should be sufficient to warn us of the danger fast food poses to our lives. Fast food also brings a 'de-materialisation' of the eating process.[3] While the nutritious content of food disappears and the taste of what we eat becomes more uniform, with local differences fast disappearing, the component made of pills and supplements increases. Ironically, some 19th century socialists dreamed of a future in which we would eat purely to satisfy our metabolism's needs. The German socialist August Bebel, for instance, was so enamored with the idea of a scientific management of food consumption that he dreamed of a day in which we would go around with a packet of powders that would give us everything, all the minerals and other substances our bodies need to survive.

[3] See Raj Patel, *Stuffed and Starved. From Farm to Fork: The Hidden Battle for the World Food System*, (Brooklyn: Melville House Publishing, 2007), and Eric Schlosser, Fast Food Nation. The Dark Side of the All-American Meal, (New York: HarpersCollins, 2002).

'The food problem (he wrote) is a purely chemical one. What until now vegetation has done industry will henceforth perform and more perfectly than nature itself…. The time will come when everyone will carry a little box of chemicals wherewith to provide his food supply of albumen, fat, hydrates, carbon, regardless of the hour of the day or the season of the year…'.[4] He looked forward to us eating the kind of food that astronauts eat in their voyages to space.

Eating together is one of the main social practices; it signifies sharing, trust, friendship. In some Indigenous traditions of South America there is a long preparation for food to be eaten at the annual *fiesta*, eating together resignifies their belonging to the community. Eating is not just feeding our bodies with nutrients, but it is a profoundly social act. Preparing food and eating together is a vital part of the material and cultural reproduction of people and communities.

The struggle over food, then, implies much more than the question of food itself. It also implies the continuity between us and the earth, the animals, the waters. Food connects us to a complexity of relations none of which can be ignored. For me, thinking of food in cultural and ecological terms is to go beyond the periphery of our skins. Our bodies are not self-enclosed; our skin does not set the frontiers of our relation with the surrounding world. Our bodies are porous. They extend and continue into the surrounding environment. They respond to and connect with other bodies. Food brings this reality to us in a very concrete way.

We are made of the food we eat, but the food comes from the earth, the trees, the air and the labour of other human beings. Out of food we can expand our perspective into interlocking universes continually merging into each other.

(JR/JS): We relate to the emphasis of collectivity within cooking and eating together. Many of the activities described in this Cooking Book also encourage this.

(SF): The question of eating collectively speaks to what we share in a process of struggle. Do we share only a vision of the world to come or also affective

[4] August Bebel, *Women and Socialism*, (Zurich: Socialist Literature. Co. 1879), p. 288.

experiences? The moment of eating together is where affective relations can be built.

Eating with others is different from eating alone. When you eat alone, you feed the 'body machine'.[5] When you have dinner with other people there is, potentially, a nourishment richer than food. The sense of collectivity is not an abstraction, it has a material basis; sharing experiences and joining our desire with that of other people. It creates a common interest and a common culture.

(JR/JS): To think of the question of taking control over food supply and production, for example by growing your own food and also having the possibility to eat with others, brings up a question of space. We need space for these activities but access to space is becoming increasingly difficult particularly in urban areas. Who has the possibility of access to space for growing food or a big enough home to eat with others?

(SF): Yes, eating collectively involves reclaiming space. It reminds me of the Movida Madrileña, the countercultural movement which saw people claiming their 'right to the streets' after Francisco Franco's death in 1975. *Movida* means to move and is in contrast to the idea of the restaurant, where you are sitting in a self-enclosed space.

Our struggle must include the reappropriation of space. Struggles need an infrastructure of space and resources. We need space in which to join, discuss and take decisions collectively, but space has become a luxury few can afford. In New York, most people now live in tiny apartments and everyday more people are being evicted and pushed to the streets. In addition, developers construct one-room apartments fitted with a microwave oven and a bed, where it is impossible to bring friends home. We are becoming birds in a cage.

5 The 'body-machine' is a recurring idea in Silvia Federici's book *Caliban and the Witch*, (New York: Autonomedia, 2004), rather than examining Karl Marx's concept of 'primitive accumulation' from 'the viewpoint of the waged male proletariat and the development of commodity production', she examines it 'from the viewpoint of the changes it introduced in the social position of women and the production of labor-power…, which includes a set of historical phenomena that are absent in Marx, and yet have been extremely important for capitalist accumulation.' One of these points is the 'mechanization of the proletarian body and its transformation, in the case of women, into a machine for the production of new workers'. (Ibid. p. 12) She writes; 'We can see, in other words, that the human body and not the steam engine, and not even the clock, was the first machine developed by capitalism'. (Ibid. p. 146.)

The fight against being closed in and to have space, so that we can host people, is fundamental. It is part of the process of building sociality. There is a material aspect in commoning that cannot be ignored. It is about reclaiming land, space and control over food production. It is about having time to meet, and to collectively decide what we need.

> Elements of a communally based society are still around us, though subject to a constant attack that has recently intensified. Capitalist development requires the enclosure of communal relations. Privatisation now extends to every aspect of our existence. Not only are lands, forests and fisheries privatised and turned to commercial use. Everything from the water we drink to our body's cells has a price tag or is patented, and government spare no effort to ensure that companies have the right to enclose all the wealth on earth and force us to pay to gain access to it.
>
> This is why the idea of the commons – of reappropriating our relations with other people, to overcoming the individualism that is inculcated in us from birth – exercises such an attraction on our collective imagination.
>
> **— George Caffentzis and Silvia Federici[6]**

On the other hand, we can see an increase in exclusionary communities, or what I call 'gated commons'. They appear as commons but they are built on an exclusionary principle.[7] They are Christian, or all white or admitting only people of a certain income or profession. Many times these communities have gates and are policed.[8] There are many gated communities in the United States, people realise that coming together has certain advantages. You are not completely alone, you have access to resources, you can strike a

6 George Caffentzis and Silvia Federici, "Commons Against and Beyond Capitalism", *Re-enchanting the World*, (New York: PM Press, 2019), pp. 86–88.

7 Ibid. pp. 86–88.

8 'It is hard to ignore the prodigal use of 'common' or 'commons' in the real estate discourse of university campuses, shopping malls, and gated communities. Elite Universities that cost students 50,000 dollars a year call their libraries 'information commons'. It is almost a law of contemporary society that the more commons are attacked, the more they are celebrated.' Ibid. p. 86.

better bargain in commercial negotiations if you act as a group. People are realising that there is a value and protection in coming together. However, they come together not on a basis of a set of values that enhance our sociality, as not everyone can become a member of these gated commons. Rather it is about wanting to be with those who are like yourself. I call these 'defensive commons' instituting new forms of apartheid.

(JR/JS): One of our goals for the Home Works programme was seeded in our idea of creating a 'public home'. We wanted to see if we could transform the art space, from a place where one can experience art to a space where one can come and be with others as a form of art. Our concept of the 'public home' is something we are trying to articulate within this book. What is the relation between *public* and *home* and when put together, what do you get?

(SF): Feminists have been rethinking these relations. *Public* and *home* have been written as opposing and antithetical to each other, meaning the home is seen as a place which has no public character. This is a mistake. There is nothing that is private in the home. In the International Wages for Housework Campaign we spoke about the home as a place of production, the production of the work-force, which is carried out daily and generationally. Our homes are isolated from each other but they form part of an assembly line catering to the production of labour-power and as such they are terrains traversed by strong power relations. This means that domestic, familial and sexual relations are relations of production, they are integral to the process of capitalist accumulation. As we often said, the state is in our bedrooms and the kitchens.[9]

On the other hand, you have the *public* which is very structured and has been based on exclusion. Who is part of the public and who is not? The public has been the place of the white male, of the man of property, or

[9] '…as housewives, women are not suffering from capital, but… precisely from the absence of it. Our problem, it seems, is that capital has failed to reach into and organise our kitchens and bedrooms, with the two-fold consequence that a) we presumably live at a feudal or at any rate precapitalist stage; b) whatever we do in these kitchens and bedrooms is at best irrelevant to any real social change. For obviously, if our kitchens are outside of capital, our struggle to destroy them will never succeed in causing capital to fall.' Silvia Federici and Nicole Cox, "Counterplanning from the Kitchen", *Revolution at Point Zero: Housework, Reproduction and Feminist Struggle*, (Oakland: PM Press, PM Press, 2012), p. 29.

of the white waged worker. It has certainly not been the place of women, migrants or other non hegemonic ethnic groups. For me the public is a place of exclusion and a place marked and structured by all kinds of boundaries. Here too a transformation has to happen and walls have to be torn down. (As we write, statues are coming down in public space. They are statues of slave owners and a variety of military men and legislators who supported slavery and other forms of institutional racism. This is a necessary step, but much more is necessary. The material conditions of life, with regard to health, employment, housing and education have to be changed for social inequality to be eradicated from the social body).

The feminist movement has exposed these false dichotomies like that between *the public* and *the private*, and called for a reorganising of our reproduction in a more cooperative way, breaking down the walls of our homes, putting an end to the isolation in which we cook, eat and resolve the many problems daily confronting us. We need to resignify our space and show how the division of labour is also a division of space. The public and the private reflect the division of labour and the hierarchies that are built upon it.

<u>(JR/JS):</u> Most art spaces construct and divide space based on a division of labour. When you enter a gallery or an art space, it is often cleared of any evidence of work. It is often in the back, or downstairs where the work happens. For us, the idea of a public home, attempted to break down that dichotomy through cooking and eating together in our kitchen/office space and in the art space *(see How to create a public home → p. 239)*. Looking back, it was an attempt to ‘mess up’ and rupture the white walls of the gallery and see what would happen if we avoided the compartmentalised and sterile process in much art production and presentation. It brought up questions like: what kind of commons and communities could this space support?

To support and organise the commons today feels ever more urgent, and to us the idea of eating together as a commoning activity is very poignant. Particularly now, when we can see an increase in racism and a mobilisation of the far-right, in Sweden and across the world, that has been able to mobilise collectivity around exclusions and populist rhetoric. Why do you think they have been so successful?

<u>(SF):</u> The collectivity you talk of is a collectivity fed by hatred. Racial hatred, the hatred that motivates white supremacists is a defence of privilege.

It comes either from the knowledge that the prosperity one has achieved is based on the appropriation of the wealth of others, for instance in the United States, the land of Indigenous people and the wealth produced by slavery. Or, in the case of white working class racial hatred, it is motivated by the belief in the hope of gaining some privilege purely on the basis of one's skin, obtaining privileges at the expense of the exclusion of others.

It is successful because it is sustained by an institutional system that benefits from it, that encourages it, in so many different ways, that at every turn (at least in the United States) discriminates, with regard to housing, employment, healthcare, that prevents Black people, Indigenous people, and those who have migrated from benefiting from the wealth they produce.

On the other hand one can think of racism and exclusionary policies as a form of self-induced impoverishment. There is a great loss, from the point of view of our humanity, in such hatred. Hating other people seems to be the only thing that makes racists feel good about themselves. If they were not so dangerous you would think of them as pitiful.

(JR/JS): This distinction between far-right collectivity based on hatred and the concept and practice of the commons that people can be part of, contribute to and share in, is important. For us, this also connects to a theme within the book around hospitality as a practice to build an infrastructure in which people, regardless of their background, position or situation can be a host or a guest.

(SF): It makes me think of the 1970s when I, and other people, when traveling to other countries, could stay with women I had never met before. My home was also one of those houses where people could stay. There was an international common space that was built with thousands of homes of people connected through being in the same social movements. Your house was always ready with a bed and food for guests. This is still happening but it is under threat. Now you have 'couch surfing' and Airbnb among others. Hosting people is being commercialised and some of the spontaneous comradeship and generosity that had emerged through the feminist movement and other movements has gone.

The so-called sharing economy is a misnomer. It is not sharing, it is renting. Today, even within the movement, to stay at other people's places is more difficult, first because the cost of rent has gone up and second because everybody's space has been reduced, and because the trend is to rent what space is available, even if it just a couch.

(JR/JS): How do you relate the notion of hospitality to your work in the International Wages for Housework Campaign? How did you organise around food then?

(SF): We always had food whenever we had our meetings. The memorable times would be when we had our international gatherings, once or twice a year, and when women from other countries would come. These were powerful moments, not only did we eat together but we sang, listened to music, talked, sometimes danced. They were those moments of affectivity building, community building. This was happening not only within our campaign but across the feminist movement. This is one of the great contributions of feminist movements. Women are determined to not reduce political activism to purely political discussion or protests, but to engage in politics as a form of community building.

A month ago, the women's group I work with had an event here in New York with Rafaela Pimentel, one of the spokeswomen from Territorio Doméstico, a domestic workers organisations in Spain.[10] She gave a powerful talk on the way they had begun to organise, and one of the things she insisted on was the importance of making time to eat food, sing songs and dance together. The importance to do something joyful, to creating bonds, the importance in bringing some pleasure into our lives. In every struggle it is important that you reproduce yourself and have activities that are not only oppositional, but activities that are constructive and build solidarity.

We need to come together not just to plan or demonstrate but to reproduce ourselves. We need some joy in our lives in order to keep on fighting. Often the struggle depletes us. Making food and dancing is part of the joyful militancy I have advocated for. There are just too many sad militants! If there were more joyful militancy, more people would be engaged in political work.[11]

[10] Territorio Doméstico is a space of struggle for the recognition of the rights of domestic workers. Their motto is "BECAUSE WITHOUT US THE WORLD DOES NOT MOVE".

[11] Silvia Federici, "Feeling Powers Growing: An Interview with Silvia Federici". In Carla Bergman and Nick Montgomery eds. *Building Thriving Resistance in Toxic Times*, (Baltimore: AK Press, 2017), pp. 243–258.

(JR/JS): And finally, we were wondering if you would like to contribute a recipe to the book. What would you cook for the struggle, if you would cook today?

> (SF): I would make a soup of garlic, onions, potatoes, spinaches, collard greens, and if available some good tomatoes, all seasoned with oil and spices. This is the kind of food that has fed proletarians throughout the ages and that does not destroy our environment or cause suffering to animals, though regrettably we do not have the viewpoint of the potatoes and the greens on this matter. It has become one of my favorite staple dishes.

What if the sea could talk? — *Dady de Maximo*

> Dady De Maximo's mixture of haute couture and political activism is not a cynical tactic, it is … another positive … artistic and political contribution. Much of the public can relate to a fashion show. A fashion show is a form that everyone understands. It was one of the most moving moments of my long career as a curator and art historian, to see a procession of people walk slowly down the catwalk wearing life vests and holding barbed wire while refugees, some of whom had made the voyage themselves, looked on. Another model wore clothing made of sacks used by the United Nation Refugee Agency (UNHCR). De Maximo's performance piece *If the Sea Could Talk* was by no means sensationalism; it had nuance.
>
> **— Tone Olaf Neilsen in Clemens Bomsdorf**[1]

[1] Tone Olaf Neilsen in Clemens Bomsdorf, "Without words, they communicate what people must endure …", *Contemporary And*, (2015), published online at: https://www.contemporaryand.com/magazines/without-words-they-communicate-what-people-must-endure/ (Accessed March 2020).

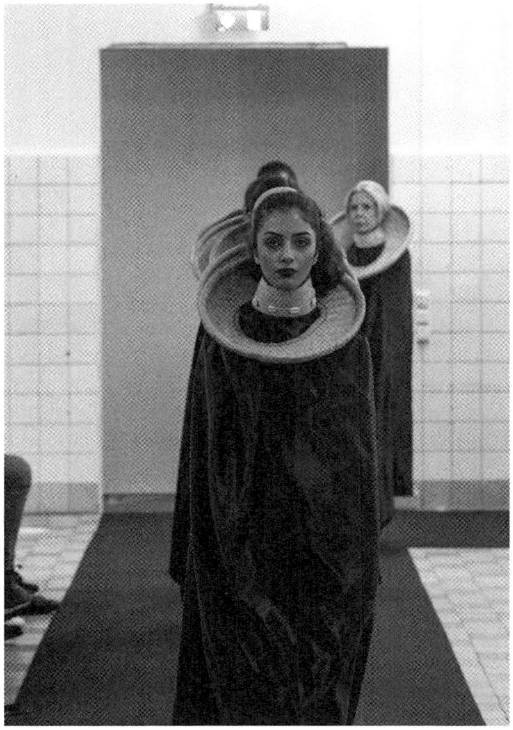

Dady de Maximo, *If the Sea Could Talk*, 2017.
Photo: Kristoffer Rozenthal.

In order to pay tribute to the disappeared refugees and those who have died in waters, oceans, seas, desserts, containers, and rivers I wrote the article "If the Sea Could Talk" in the Danish magazine visAvis.[2] It shared stories of my friends alongside statistics of people migrating to Europe and those missing in the Mediterranean between 2006 and 2011. The purpose was to pay respect to the people behind the dramatic headlines and the shocking images of human migration broadcast in the media; to the people whose bodies are filled with stories of individual courage, tragedy and compassion – stories that are rarely told from their point of view. It was an article for the thousands of people that have crossed walls covered with barbed wire, sailed across the sea in unseaworthy boats, travelled clandestinely or in containers without air. It was for migrants and refugees that have left their homes, risking their lives in a desperate quest to find safety and a better life.

"If the Sea Could Talk" was an important article for me to write, but it was not enough. I wanted to do something more for the struggle of migrants and not limit and label myself a journalist who observes or interprets, but to position myself as part of that same struggle. I am an artist, human rights activist, filmmaker, fashion designer, journalist and survivor of genocide in Rwanda, and the story of silenced migrant voices spoke to me. For it was also my story. I was sure that there had to be other ways than writing an article to break the silence of these voices and share the stories that preoccupied my thoughts.

My 'other way' came in the form of a fashion show, a platform interesting

[2] Dady de Maximo, "If the Sea Could Talk", *visAvis*, (2013), published online at: http://www.visavis.dk/2013/02/if-the-sea-could-talk/ (Accessed March 2020).

to me as it attracts a lot of media attention. Unlike the article it does not rely on the viewer's ability to understand a specific language. But how could a fashion show, part of an industry connected to consumerism and unethical working conditions, be a platform for political action? How could a fashion show speak to an audience that would never pick up visAvis magazine and engage in migration politics? How could a fashion show be a platform to amplify the silent voices of migrants and refugees?

While fashion and politics may not seem to go hand in hand, I believe fashion can be a platform that has the potential to influence and change social views. In some ways it is the fact that fashion presents itself as separate to politics that I found enticing. To pair fashion and migration politics is unexpected, and that is exactly what drew me further into working with this form. I wanted to see if it was possible to work with the form in order to question the distance of the fashion world to migration politics, a distance constructed to alleviate the connection and responsibility of the fashion industry to migration struggles. I wanted to demand the attention of the fashion world, and by doing so demand the attention of a much wider public. I wanted to ask them to really listen to how refugees and migrants are not only forced to abandon their professional life, families and homes, but also to understand the ways in which they are rejected by society when they arrive in Europe, where they are unable to work, build a home or access education. I want them to attend to these multiple stories of rejection, the things people are forced to abandon, as they hope to build careers, support their family and start a new life in Europe. It is important to remember that migrants are, in many European countries, not allowed to live freely, or rent apartments. Instead, like in my home of Denmark, they are forced to live in detention centres, prison camps where they are deprived of their fundamental rights. Their state of

Dady de Maximo, *If the Sea Could Talk*, 2017. Photo: Kristoffer Rozenthal.

precarity is deepened through their living situation in these camps, which can last for years without any idea of when it might change.

"If the Sea Could Talk" grew into a fashion collection and a show dedicated to and inspired by my friends from Somalia, Sudan, Libya, Tunisia, Eritrea, and others whom I have met in Europe.

Initially, I wanted the fashion collection to be colourful and light, a symbol of hope, something reviving, that could offer strength to those beginning new lives. However, my heart was filled with testimonies from migration journeys. I wanted to find a way to work with fashion in which these sides of the story could be acknowledged and shared. I began sculpting clothes using materials that connected to my own history of migration, as a way to build solidarity with many other people and their migration stories. This evolved as a methodology in the research for the fashion show which tried to listen and find ways of translating the complexity of migration through storytelling. I wanted the fashion show to explore the possibility of whether it could offer another way of listening to and working with these stories that so often go unheard. In order to experiment with this idea, it was crucial to also be aware of the ethics and respect that are necessary in order to share someone else's story. What methods and approaches are necessary when working with storytelling as a medium for political change?

The development of the fashion line began with workshops with different people such as professional models, local artists, refugees, migrants and volunteers, bringing together a diverse group to discuss questions of migration. The workshop allowed those who had experienced the migration journey a chance to tell their story and their experiences, while at the same time local artists could use their skills and professional experience to learn together and amplify some of these narrations.

When it came to making the actual clothing, I wanted the clothes in the fashion show to highlight the political issues through their design, but also through their production process. During the workshop, participants brought material connected to their stories which could be incorporated into the research and project. For example, in my case, if I were to think about a material from my story I would think of papyrus. In Rwanda during the genocide against the Tutsis in 1994, some Tutsis were able to survive by hiding in the marshes and within trees and bushes like the papyrus.

In another example, a person that had migrated to Sweden talked about the importance of water when you are fleeing. They reflected on the materials they had

Dady de Maximo, *If the Sea Could Talk*, 2017. Photo: Kristoffer Rozenthal.

with them on their migration journey to help them carry water. When one needs to flee from their home, they have to face the question of what to bring and what to leave behind. For one participant, their struggle to carry water was the key part of their migration journey. In response to these memories they produced a T-shirt with sewn water bottle holders. While far from a solution to their trauma or the global struggle of migrants, the workshops offered a way to respond to an experience and memory through collective making, and allowed a way of telling their story differently.

Another example saw the use of barbed wire, which was used to symbolise the suffering and control of refugees. The inclusion of this barbed wire in the fashion line meant that this material was then worn on bodies. Wearing barbed wire was, for me, a strong statement and signalled the rejection and isolation of migrants and refugees, as well as the materials used in migrant and refugee deportation and detention camps, where refugees are deprived of some of their fundamental rights. UNHCR – the United Nation Refugee Agency – tents were another material that was used and worn in the fashion line, and indicated the materials of a refugee's home and how refugees live together.

For the public presentation of the fashion show I invited different people with different experiences to wear the clothing. This meant that some people, with no experience of migration, would be clothed in other people's stories and material reality. I wanted the clothes to perform in this way on those invited to be part of the show, to share with them, and others with no experience of the struggle of migration, that when there is a disaster, the disaster does not choose its victims. We might call people migrants or refugees but behind these labels there is a story and a person who has lived through things that cannot be seen from the outside.

How I wish the sea could talk, but of course this is not possible. But let's take a leap, let us think that it can, what would we hear if we could listen to the voices in distress, the voices of refugees leaving their country and seeking a place to live away from wars, conflicts, disasters, injustice, hatred, genocide, discrimination, torture, rape, harassment, famine?

Listening to the sea, with Dady de Maximo

Prior to the development of Dady de Maximo's *If the Sea Could Talk* fashion show,[1] he held a number of workshops at Konsthall C exploring questions of the home and migration.

What can the silenced voices of the sea teach us about what a home is? Migrants are not only forced to leave their homes but are also prevented from making new homes when they arrive in Europe. In what ways is home a privileged space, that many people do not have access to? And in what ways are certain types of homes forced on migrants by their host countries? In Sweden, homes began to be standardised in the mid 20th century, thereby creating a specific physical and

[1] *If the Sea Could Talk* was originally commissioned by CAMP (Center for Art on Migration Politics) in Copenhagen. The work was reproduced, with some alterations for Home Works at Konsthall C in 2017. CAMP is a non-profit exhibition space for art discussing questions of displacement, migration, immigration, and asylum. http://campcph.org.

social architecture for people to fit into. In Sweden's case, as in many other countries, the home was designed around the idea of the heteronormative nuclear family with the kitchen specifically optimised for use by one woman. This standardisation offered a framework that supported certain types of home-making while excluding others. Sweden's attitude to migration can be drawn in parallel. People who are given the right to stay, are expected to fit into Swedish logic and standards and to maintain and perform the ideals of the dominant culture they have been pushed to call home. This recipe is a reworked version of a workshop Dady de Maximo presented at a symposium during Home Works. The workshop aimed to initiate a discussion between the home and forced migration.

Ingredients

- A number of tennis balls
- A timer

The tennis balls symbolise the sun and a boat you are using to make passage to Europe. Prior to GPS and digital devices, people used the sun to orientate themselves and navigate the sea. Today, boats are used in emergencies or conflict situations in which people are prepared to leave their homes and everything they know behind. Precarious boats are navigating across the Mediterranean Sea to unknown contexts, countries and cities. Those within the boats may know little about where they are travelling. The host country may not know (or want to know) much about the migrating persons, their stories, where they come from and what their experiences are.

Method

- Choose one person to lead the workshop.

- The workshop leader reads the instructions from now on. The element of the unknown is an important part of the exercise.

- Split the group into smaller groups. Each smaller group should be around 3–4 people. This is your 'family'.

- Give each family 1–2 tennis balls.

- Put the tennis balls on the floor in front of them and make sure that the family members cannot reach them.

- The workshop leader then counts to 3, and on *'3'* each family member jumps up to grab a tennis ball.

In this exercise the tennis ball represents the amount of people that can get onto the boat. Getting on the boat is not a given. Families are constantly forced to split up when faced with conflicts and emergencies.

- Discuss the exercise and what it means to be a refugee and to leave one's family, home and friends behind. What can one bring in an emergency? What are you ready to leave behind? Family? Friends? Belongings? If you were to arrive in a new country, would you be able to accept the rules and laws, even if the laws were fuelled by an underlying institutional racism?

- Do the exercise again, but this time the tennis balls will represent residents in the host country.

- The workshop leader counts to 3, and on *'3'* each group member jumps up to grab a tennis ball.

Discuss the exercise again. How many are able to welcome the new arrivals to their home? Are you ready to open up your house? Are you ready to accept the luggage – both mental and physical – that the refugees bring with them? What are you prepared to do to welcome people even if you do not share their worldview?

The right to be a host — *Sandi Hilal*

When I was eighteen years old, I left Palestine to study architecture in Italy. I spent more than thirteen years there, but continued to be referred to as an *extracomunitari*, meaning someone from outside of the community of the European Union (EU). Over time, this term has acquired negative connotations in Italy. A person from Switzerland or from the United States will not be referred to as *extracomunitari*, even though they are non-EU citizens. After completing a PhD in Italian, I had arrived at a point where I spoke the language so well that one would need to speak with me for a long time to understand that I was an *extracomunitari*. I can still remember a very interesting moment in Rome when I was sitting on a bus with an older Italian lady. We got off the bus and she asked me if I could cross the bridge with her, I said of course, and we began walking together. When we reached the middle of the bridge I asked her why she had asked me to accompany her. I was curious to know what she was afraid of. She explained that she was afraid of the *extracomunitari*. I looked at her, smiled and said that you are crossing the bridge with an *extracomunitari*. Her immediate response was that I did not look like 'one of them'. What has stuck with me since was her usage of the terms *them* and *us*. Since then, I have often returned to this situation to address the complete lack of identification and empathy, and with the hope of finding possible strategies to break and challenge certain fixed and prescribed roles within society.

Twenty years later, in 2016, I was commissioned to do a public art project by the Public Art Agency in Sweden. The commission was to take place in Boden, in the North of Sweden. I did not realise that Boden would bring me back to that story on the bridge in Italy, and would offer me ways to understand how to overcome my fear of living in the condition of what Edward Said beautifully describes as being 'out of place', or of becoming an *extracomunitari* again. Living in Europe, I am constantly faced with and challenged by the description of integration, as if it is something that will arrive sooner or later. But, in my experience, the way integration is understood within the framework of European nation states is more like a race toward something; a perfection that few can ever attain. I came to realise that when I was asked to behave as a perfect guest in Europe, my power to ever become a host has been taken away. So, I decided I was no longer willing to accept the role of the eternal guest I had been assigned; I decided not to run that race. Instead, I want to explore other ways of understanding, defining, and practicing integration, and to look for alternatives to the binary of inclusion and exclusion, by questioning who has the right to host? Who is told that they need to behave as a perfect guest? How can we analyse the power of hosting as a means of becoming visible and demanding agency? How can we understand visibility as a precondition for political subjectivity? How can we understand participation in society from the position of the *extracomunitari* and displaced people, without waiting years, sometimes even generations? And how can we insist on creating a sense of belonging within the Swedish public sphere, to be an active participant among its norms and codes?

In order to understand fully what I am intending to share with you, I should tell you what happened after I had spent thirteen years of my life in Italy. My partner, Alessandro Petti and I decided to move back to Palestine when our first daughter was born. It was the place from where we wanted to orientate ourselves in order to better understand the world we are living in. In 2007 we established DAAR – Decolonizing

Architecture Art Residency – with Eyal Weizman. *Daar* means home in Arabic. We opened up our house and invited other scholars, architects, artists, and interested people to investigate colonialism and how we could decolonise our minds and selves, in order to inspire others to do the same. We knew that sometimes power structures are rooted in our heads, and it is difficult to distinguish between your own narration and what has been imposed on you. In other words, we hosted in our home a discourse that at that time, could not have been hosted within a public space at that particular historical moment in Palestine. We felt empowered by demanding our right to host a discourse that had no room outside of our own private walls.

We lived for more than ten years illegally in Palestine, in the town where my grandparents and parents have always lived. As a family we lived with a temporary status as my partner never obtained a family reunion visa from the bureaucratic machines of the Israeli occupation, instead he had to leave the country every three months to be able to return on his tourist visa. We lived for more than a decade like this, ready to be expelled at any moment from the home that we had both designed together for our family to live in. When the moment arrived for us to leave, I was not ready. I felt uprooted, eradicated, and partially lost. It was also the same moment that I was commissioned to develop a public art project in Boden.

I arrived in Boden in November 2016 with fear and anxiety. I doubted my ability to engage with such an unfamiliar place and landscape. What I was unable to realise back then was that this seeming lack of connection to Boden allowed me to engage with both the city and its inhabitants in a unique way. It also offered me the opportunity to reflect on my life and work in Palestine and Italy in a different way than I had been able to previously.

Boden was not my choice, it was part of a commissioning process that I happily accepted. I had never even heard of the city before, but I was excited about the invitation, it felt like a glow from the Northern Lights, giving some hope to my new Swedish life. I was worried that by leaving Palestine, and our long work at DAAR and within refugee camps, we were leaving the frontline and the internal drive of our practice. I was doubtful that it would be possible to feel the same intensity and meaning in our work in Sweden. The project in Boden was initiated by an open call from the Public Art Agency asking to hear from local partners who wanted to collaborate around the production of public art. In Boden, the art centre Havremagasinet and the municipal housing company BodenBo applied with the aim of producing an artwork in the area Prästholmen, where a refugee house – the *gula huset*

(Yellow House) – is located. Working with marginalised communities in Boden offered the possibility of finding other places from where to practice, while maintaining our integrity. I met with refugees in Boden who told me, they would arrive and realise that what they found was not what they had dreamed of. They would find themselves in this dark place, 30° Celsius below zero, in the middle of nowhere, and completely alone. A state of passivity would set in, as if they had lost their political agency, an agency which before had been so strong. Projecting themselves elsewhere, they would blame the city and convince themselves that Boden was not their final destination.

I was desperately looking for somebody who was planning to stay in Boden. If everyone is looking forward to leaving, then who are the 'new citizens' of this city? To my surprise, I found Yasmeen Mahmoud and Ibrahim Muhammad Haj Abdulla.[1] I visited their house for the first time with Joanna Zawieja and Marti Manen, the curators from the Public Art Agency in Sweden. The two young Syrian refugees greeted us with incredible warmth and hospitality. It felt almost surreal to me. The dynamic I had been wrestling with since my days in Italy had shifted. Yasmeen and Ibrahim had made themselves the hosts. They were hosting representatives of the Swedish state in their tiny living room, refusing to accept their assigned role as eternal guests.

I realised hospitality is what is at stake, and in that tiny living room in the house of Yasmine and Ibrahim I recognised that what I was afraid of losing by moving to Sweden was in fact my right to be a host, my power of hosting in the way we practiced it at DAAR. What encouraged me the most was the ability to reflect and understand my life and practice from that far-away place in the North. I was able to understand things in a way I had never managed to in Palestine, the place where I have always considered myself a local. Boden – 80 kilometres away from the Arctic Circle, a place that I thought had no connection with my story, where I would be destined to be an outsider, to be the one 'out of place' – was in fact where I learnt what a home means. This realisation was the beginning of a new trajectory in my practice and research.

After visiting Yasmeen and Ibrahim, I went to Bard College in upstate New York where I spent a year with my family, as my partner and I were recipients of the Keith Haring fellowship in art and activism. At Bard I spent a lot of time in the library

[1] Yasmeen Mahmoud and Ibrahim Muhammad Haj Abdulla are originally from Raqqa, Syria. Yasmeen Mahmoud obtained her degree in architecture a few months before arriving in Sweden.

and had amazing conversations with friends and colleagues. It happened frequently that when I mentioned I was working with the idea of hospitality, people would associate it with the work of the philosopher Jacques Derrida and his book with Anne Dufourmantelle entitled *Of Hospitality (Cultural Memory in the Present)*,[2] to a point that it felt that this book should be, without a doubt, the point of departure for anyone that is trying to think through the notion of hospitality today. I remember how it felt while reading the book, how the more I read the more I felt disturbed, yet I was unable to understand this feeling. Why was I disturbed by a philosopher who was proposing unconditional hospitality? Why would I be disturbed by a book that proposes to set the law of hospitality above all other laws? Why would I be disturbed by authors that refer to the hospitality found in the desert and in Arab culture as an example to look at and understand seriously?

It took me a while to grasp that the reason for my discomfort with Derrida and Dufourmantelle was that according to their philosophy there could only ever be one entitled host, that in order to maintain the host's moral integrity (and their existing power position) they needed to become an unconditional host. This book made me apprehend that the law of hospitality in the desert is placed on top of all other ethical codes, not because of moral obligation but because hospitality was a way of surviving in the desert, where one day you can be a host, and then another day you are a guest. For Derrida and Dufourmantelle, hospitality is an ethical path, but for people in the desert it is a matter of urgency and a practice of survival. If you are a guest you need to make sure that your host will protect you whatever the cost, but you know that you are also obliged to defend your guest when it is your time to be the host. It became clear that in privileged Western societies there is an inability to imagine oneself to one day be the guest, or, we could say, refugee. In Western logic the roles are always fixed; the European always inhabits the role of 'master host'. Derrida and Dufourmantelle do reflect on the impossibility of unconditional hospitality, yet assert it as the only conceivable path to include a foreigner. Highlighting for them that the primary reference remains the Western state and a sovereign power.

While still spending time in the library with the textbooks, I began to have a long written conversation with Yasmeen. We wrote to each other more than twice a week as a way to begin to learn things about each other. What became clear to me

[2] Jacques Derrida and Anne Dufourmantelle, *Of Hospitality (Cultural Memory in the Present)*, (California: Stanford University Press, 1st edition, 2000).

was that the project in Boden needed to build on what Yasmeen and Ibrahim did when they arrived there; their refusal to assume the role of the guest, and instead opening up their living room to host whoever, according to them, would accept their invitation. Yasmeen and Ibrahim told me that outside their guest room (in Arabic we call the living room the guest room) they felt invisible, represented only as a number within the refugee statistics, while inside their guest room they suddenly became visible, seen for who they are. I learnt that Yasmeen and Ibrahim began to build connections and a sense of belonging in Boden by exercising their right to be hosts, it is how they began to lay down roots in the city. I saw in Yasmeen and Ibrahim's activity what my partner and I found ourselves doing in DAAR when we felt we were unable to belong to the public space in Palestine in the way that it was proposed to us. It is such seemingly powerless individuals who are best placed to perform this, and in the process make their agency visible. This subversion positions the newcomer as the primary reference point from which to explore the possibility of 'unconditional hospitality'.

From this starting point, a long collaborative process developed, which led to BodenBo offering us a ground-floor apartment in the Yellow House. There we created a living room that Yasmeen could use to host and amplify the way in which her own living room had functioned as a public space.

The Yellow House was built as part of Sweden's *Miljonprogram* (Million Program), a 1960s public housing project that aimed to construct one million dwellings across Sweden between 1965 and 1974. BodenBo offered us the third floor to set up the work, *Al Madhafah – The Living Room* (The Living Room). From my previous experience I knew that a public living room would not operate if not positioned at the threshold between the public and the private space. I asked if we could have the apartment on the ground floor instead. Once we were inside we decided to tear down all the walls that were not load-bearing in order to create a more fluid space. To connect the apartment with the outside, we replaced the yellow walls outside the apartment with glass walls.

This semi-public aspect was crucial for how the space would operate. In the Arab world, having a public living room is nothing new, these public living rooms have various names and functions, including: *madhafah*, *diwans*, and *majles*. These collective gathering places have always been fundamental to the organisation of society, especially with the absence of strong nation states. The Living Room works as a local space for public representation and only functions if there is a person in the community who claims himself (mainly men do this) as the host of a particular place,

Sandi Hilal, *Al Madhafah – The Living Room*, 2018. Photo: Sandi Hilal.

and who would normally open up a part of his private home to turn it into a semi public space. The role of host is sometimes inherited through family lines, other times the living room is initiated by individuals who feel the need to run a semi-public space. The host has both the power and the responsibility of running the place.

In the case of Boden, Yasmeen became a host in collaboration with Ibrahim and with the involvement of her mother and children. We had an interesting discussion with the curator Joanna Zawieja about how to run the place. It took a long conversation to come to a common understanding. For me and Yasmeen, coming from places like Palestine and Syria, we had in mind the role and responsibility of the host as someone with the keys to the place and who can keep it open when needed. The host is as much a reference point as the place itself. From the Public Art Agency's perspective it was easier to imagine the living room functioning much more like the communal laundry room in Sweden, where people write their names on a list to arrange the time when they can use the room. This distinction brought much to light about the differences in the idea and methods of hosting, and how public and private space are organised. We agreed to begin to operate slowly and organically by involving the inhabitants of the Yellow House first and then see where this led us. We adopted what Yasmeen and I later called the 'open-door policy' in which she would open up the space, prepare coffee and some sweets, and then sit down. This policy worked amazingly well with the Yellow House inhabitants. The house was always full of people who were coming and going. The next step was to think about how to encourage people from outside the Yellow House to become part of The Living Room. So, the Saturday rituals were created. The Saturday ritual begins with people meeting, and someone being assigned the role of head chef. They then take responsibility for the food that is to be prepared and explain to the others how to cook the meal. The food is then shared and eaten together, followed by coffee and accompanied by long conversations. Interest in the Saturday rituals has developed into a new lunch ritual in which refugees host politicians, instead of politicians always being positioned as the host of refugees. Here, the Yellow House becomes a place where people can experiment on their own terms with how to make a life in common with others.

I am not advocating that self-organisation outside of state institutions is better than state-led organising, but rather to recognise the power that comes with both conditions. Nor can I fool myself into thinking that, if I had gone to Boden alone as a single artist or architect, and met Yasmeen and Ibrahim to develop a socially engaged project independently, I would have obtained the same results. This was made apparent by the fact that the day after I arrived in Boden in order to develop The Living Room I was approached by a journalist because they wanted to meet the artist sent to Boden from Stockholm by the Public Art Agency in Sweden. There were expectations and an openness that permitted this project to take the course it has taken over the last three years. The Living Room is an example of how the Public Art Agency in Sweden opened a space for me to be able to exercise my right to be a host, and in turn I could pass on this same right to Yasmeen and Ibrahim in the Yellow House, and they are passing this right to be a host to other people in Boden. You could say that the Public Art Agency opened up a space for rethinking the normative relations between artists and art audiences. The approach was not focused on empowering marginalised people, but on giving them the chance to create their own living room on their own terms, where they became the host of a project not bent towards maximising audience figures or fitting into a predesigned structure.

The Living Room is a project that not only questions the role of the guest and the host, but it is also an attempt to challenge the separation between private and public spaces. In order to be a host you need to feel a certain kind of belonging, a sense of ownership towards the space where the hosting takes place. The challenge then is how to create this sense of ownership and right to participate as a host, not only in private spaces but also in public space. How can we set the conditions for alternative spaces that can generate a sense of ownership from within communities?

When thinking about the politics of hospitality it became imperative to think about the role of the institution, not only from its position as the only entitled host, but also its ability to rethink its relationship to the public; what are the implications of institutions becoming guests? To flip the institution-as-host that is required to empower its own guests. This question deals very much with power shifts and with the question of who has the power to host, and who is entitled to only participate as a guest.

The Living Room is not the only project that deals with these problems, but maybe it insists on understanding and acknowledging the positions and the power structures from where each of us operate. I can draw similar parallels with the experiment of the Research Station that began during Home Works at Konsthall C.[3] The first time I heard about the Research Station was after I had initiated The Living Room in Boden. It was through an invitation from Corina Oprea who, at the time, was the artistic director of Konsthall C. I distinctly remember how enthusiastic I was to learn about the project during the meeting. I was told that the Research Station was initiated because there was a need to host artists on site in the area of Konsthall C, and there was simply no place to do this. After a series of attempts, Anders Jacobson, the managing director of Konsthall C at that time, ended up signing an agreement to build a small house in a private garden of a local family. I understood that this semi-public room must not be more than twenty-five square metres in order to avoid the need for an official building application. The agreement between Konsthall C and the family was that the room could be used for eight years by Konsthall C, after which it would be gifted to the family.

What interests me about this experiment is the overlapping spheres of private and public space within a private garden in the neighbourhood where Konsthall C is located. Not only was the Research Station developed in order to address the urgent need for a space for hosting artists in the neighbourhood, but by creating it in a private garden more relations with the neighbours of the art space would be created. When I asked about the relation with the family that had accepted to share a piece of their garden I was told that they were an open-minded family engaged in neighbourhood

[3] The Research Station is a small house a few minutes walk from Konsthall C. It was completed in 2019 and operates as a site where artists, curators, researchers and activists embed themselves in the local community and work on issues regarding city planning, democracy and civil rights. The house functions as a satellite to Konsthall C, a residency for visiting artists and researchers, and a temporary space for exhibitions within the artist-in-residency program.

activities and that they were keen to open up their home and garden. It was noted that all they were hoping for was to be able to build relationships with the artists and the art community that was to be part of this eight-year co-existence experiment; and besides, in eight years they will find themselves with an additional home in their garden that they can use. It was definitely a win-win situation for both Konsthall C and the family. I was told that it had been a long negotiation. This family was not the initial family that Konsthall C had begun talking to about the project. Two previous families had withdrawn from the process before this third, successful attempt took place.

In 2019, I was invited to develop The Living Room by Mar Fjell and Malin Arnell as part of the exhibition *Circuit Training – A Retrospective in Becoming. Konsthall C 15 Years 2004–2019*, and we came to the conclusion that the Research Station would be the best context in which to host The Living Room. Besides the pleasing architecture, I felt that it was dealing with the same conditions of the threshold and semi-publicness as The Living Room. It was through the activation of The Living Room at the Research Station that I met with the family that owns the garden. We had a great conversation where they shared their doubts and excitement about what it means for them as a family (especially with having children at home) to open up their house to the unexpected. I was curious about the dynamics that were created and the agreement between the family and Konsthall C. Who becomes the host and when? Would Konsthall C contact them to ask permission each time they wanted to use the house? Who has the keys? Who manages the space? Who feels a sense of ownership for the space? Who is the host: Konsthall C or the family? How does living in close proximity and as neighbours work? Was the family able to use this house or would it be exclusively used by Konsthall C's visiting artists? Is the relation between the family and Konsthall C determined by a contract or by human relations which go beyond what is written on paper? If the contract needs to be questioned, how can this be dealt with in a flexible and productive way?

All these questions and more required that both the family and Konsthall C accepted a certain level of vulnerability in developing their conditions of collaboration and finding out how to work through these unknowns together. This is exactly where I see space for creating new practices; practices that search for new conditions that are not predetermined by a very safe and clear institutional trajectory.

How to speak about Home Works?

There has been a growing emphasis on the communication work involved in running an art space that, sadly, often reduces this highly important job of connecting and engaging with audiences to an act of branding and marketing. As a result, there is pressure for hits on social media platforms and large parts of budgets are spent on general advertising, rather than meaningful face-to-face encounters that could lead to new acquaintances and encourage discussion. The communication work of Home Works aimed to resist the pressure placed on art spaces for quantitative models of evaluation and assessment (often cheered on by funders) where the success of the exhibition or the space is measured according to audience numbers and website visits.

The communication work of Home Works was not about reaching out to as many people as possible, or crafting attractive press releases that would swoop up media attention. Instead, the programme wanted to see whether an art space could create a conversation with its public that was a two-way exchange. Hence, the Home Works 'communication plan' was based on one-to-one encounters with local people and drew on conversations with local associations, neighbours, artists and institutions to help shape the focus of the programme. Hosting and making visitors and participants feel invited was key to all activities.

While Home Works strived to make visitors feel welcome, it also wanted to create a place that made it possible for others to host events, or take ownership of situations independently. To have the opportunity to host is to acknowledge that you have a certain agency in a given situation *(see The right to be a host ↪ p. 185)*. For example, the host decides how to accommodate the guest, what will we eat? What will we do? How will we meet? And so on. The aim of Home Works was to encourage guests to also become hosts, so that the programme could be responsive and open to changes and unplanned suggestions.

With that said, it is important to acknowledge that some people were designated to take responsibility for the space, therefore, attempts were made to open up hosting in a way that did not mean that responsibility for the practical management of the space was deferred. It became part of the experimental nature of the programme to shift the conventional roles and relations between the visitor and the art space.

Communication was a key tool in working towards this intention, breaking down the often cold and objective language that art institutions use when addressing their visitors. Word of mouth, knocking on doors, hosting screenings in housing associations, organising reading groups at neighbours' apartments and discussing face-to-face were ways of building intimate networks that connected communities of mutual interest through the programme. This in turn was an attempt to create an art space that could provide the foundations for a public home and emphasise the care work that goes into running an art space *(see How to create a public home ↪ p. 239)*.

Ingredients

- A desire to meet people, and a creativity towards how to find ways to encounter people you do not already know
- A desire to communicate in multiple languages
- A desire to mediate an exhibition or an artwork in multiple ways
- An attentiveness towards the use of academic language
- An attention and playfulness towards visual material

Method

- Understanding how to speak is equally about understanding how to listen, so it was important for the Home Works programme to create frameworks that made it possible to listen to other voices, from visitors, new acquaintances and people in the neighbourhood. It is crucial also to listen to what is not spoken, to someone's body lanugage, what someone does not feel able to say, as well as, of course, what voices are not in the room.

- Welcome visitors when they arrive at the art space. Offering tea and coffee is nice (especially in Winter months). Always offer a tour of the art space and exhibition. This can help make people feel at home, to demonstrate that the space also belongs to them and is theirs to use. How can exhibitions and artistic research become dialogues rather than monologues?

- Try to find personal perspectives around the thematics of the exhibitions and the programme. One method can be through the written language of the exhibition handouts, and the way you communicate. Try and find a vocabulary that uses an everyday language. There can be a tendency to assume that this method might entail simplifying ideas or patronising your audience, assuming they might be unable to understand certain concepts. Leave this myth behind. Rather, stick to thinking about how you have discussed the exhibition with the artist(s). What anecdotes and personal connections can you bring to the exhibition that might build a path for others to experience the work? Are there references that might be nice to share with the visitor, that can act as further resources to support the work? Can these be available in the exhibition or at events?

- The aim to be as clear as possible was important in speaking about Home Works. Debunk the idea that art is smarter than other disciplines. Be sharper and make people feel connected and welcomed.

- Reaching out and getting to know people can be a difficult endeavour. Rather than using depersonalised communication devices, social media or advertisements, Home Works wanted to insist on artistic methods as a communication strategy. We did this, for example through screen printing, which is a great way to get to know people, as it takes a collective effort to push the ink through the mesh.

  During the summer, it might be possible to set up a small improvised print workshop at your local centre and invite passers-by to make prints with you.

  Other ways you can meet new people, is for example through handing out flyers at gatherings of local associations or unions, holding your weekly staff meetings at different organisations locally, or initiating reading groups in people's homes.

- How often does an exhibition text feel impersonal and alienating, using words with ambiguous meaning?

  Experimenting with tone and using everyday language was key for Home Works. Ask yourself: what kind of text (if it is a text), or image, or response, will help to mediate the programme? Maybe it is the last dish the artist(s) cooked, or the radio station they listen to. Break down the formats!

- Visual communication materials. How can you make exhibition handouts and other communication material speak to visitors in a playful way? How can the material look fun? Surprise the visitor, change their expectations of the art space. If there is material to take away, make it something you would want to look at over breakfast or share with your friends, children or grandparents. Make sure it is readable. It can be frustrating if the designer renders a text illegible, this includes within website design.

- Include directions to the art space or the site where the event or exhibition will take place so it is clear how to get there and what kind of access is available. Avoid holding exhibitions or events in spaces that are not accessible by wheelchair.

- Take responsibility for the material you have made. Sign it off with the names of those who helped make it. Break down the opacity of the organisation with names and faces, allowing visitors to understand who is involved.

- Reverse the order. If people do not come to you, you might need to go to them. One way Home Works tried to do this was through Gunilla Lundahl's research into the home care system. After interviewing 15 people who were receiving assistance about what it means to not be able to leave your home and how home care transforms the home from a private dwelling to a workspace for care staff, she compiled the material into a portable exhibition that was presented at the care company's office. Home Works' intention was always to find the most relevant situations for the artworks and exhibitions. This allows the research to reach outside the walls of the art space, to listen to the effects the work has within specific contexts.

- Make sure that the research is transparent, open, accessible, local and fun.

Some of the things that this recipe has developed in the past

- Laughter
- A new approach to writing and producing text
- Another way of developing new relationships within your neighbourhood and with a wider public
- New perspectives on what materials can support an exhibition or event
- Approachability. Organisations are made up of people not brands
- An emphasis on personal reflection to help the organisation to learn from its own work

Leftovers

Deletions and cuts from texts, drawings and diagrams can come in handy later when you want to follow the story of the mediation material. We often overwork, so things you have cut out may be important or usable, or recyclable and used in another text or exhibition handout.

This approach to communication builds a network of friends and allies who can help share the programme widely. It will also expand how it will develop beyond what you originally planned.

ARTIST
RUN
It's a fucking
Marathon!

Kitchen karaoke

Either your politics is liberating and that gives you joy, or there is something wrong with them.

— Silvia Federici[1]

The work of running a small artist-run organisation, can, as Nýló (The Living Art Museum) stated during a workshop with Ciara Phillips, 'feel like a fucking marathon'. Therefore it is important to incorporate moments of fun when you can let your hair down, hang out with friends, make new friends and enjoy the workplace, which can sometimes feel restrictive.

Silvia Federici tells us of the importance of joy in political work, a joy that keeps you

1 "Feeling Powers Growing: Interview with Silvia Federici" (2018) in *Joyful Militancy: thriving resistance in toxic times* https://joyfulmilitancy.com/2018/06/03/feeling-powers-growing-an-interview-with-silvia-federici/ (Accessed 1 March 2020).

going and makes you feel alive. The kitchen/office of Home Works was often transformed into a karaoke club during the programme. Karaoke can sometimes mean one person on stage with others listening, but during Home Works it was very much a collective effort. The inability to actually sing can help create suitable hosts, and make getting up to sing songs by Cher or 'What's Up?' by the 4 Non Blondes a nerve-wracking experience. However, with others in the kitchen/office behind you (literally) it can be a warm and energising cacophony which might compel other not-so-confident performers to get up on the kitchen stage and join the singing!

Ingredients

- A kitchen
- A projector and screen
- Someone with a computer and internet connection so that you can access youtube.com or other streaming channels with karaoke songs
- As many microphones as you can get hold of
- A speaker which you can plug your microphone into
- A disco ball
- Food to cook together
- Something to drink

Method

- Invite your friends and the public to a 'Kitchen karaoke' event *(see How to speak about Home Works? ↝ p. 195).*
- Stop working.
- Turn off the lights, turn on a revolving disco ball and aim a lamp at it.
- 'Let your hair down'.
- Turn on a projector and direct it at a screen.
- Set up speakers and microphones.
- As people arrive to make food, put on your favourite tunes. As if by magic the kitchen that is an office becomes a karaoke party *(see Recipes from the public kitchen ↝ p. 145).*
- Encourage people to sing in groups.
- When someone is ready to sing, find the song on the computer and sing together!
- If you do not want to use the microphones you can just sing in the crowd.
- Do not stop until you can sing no more.
- Before everyone leaves, ask for help in clearing up and returning the room to a kitchen/office.

Extra

Ice can be good for sore throats.

Leftovers

Great memories, great photos, a potential addiction to karaoke as well as new friends!

Part 4. Cleaning Up

(The leftovers of collaborative work)

> **The emotion work of enhancing the status and well-being of others is a form of what Ivan Illich has called 'shadow labour', an unseen effort, which, like housework, does not quite count as labour but is nevertheless crucial to getting other things done. As with doing the housework well, the trick is to erase any evidence of effort, to offer only the clean house and the welcoming smile.**
>
> — **Arlie Hochschild**[1]

If we assume that cleaning is a labour that removes the evidence of our hard work, how then can we think about cleaning differently? Rather than wiping away the evidence of our effort, our eating, our emotions, we aimed to reposition cleaning to be understood as the next step in the cooking process. This extended cleaning-cooking might involve saving leftovers for another recipe, or a washing up conversation where you learn every detail of the meal that has just been cooked, or the chance to compost waste in order to nourish the soil and encourage new growth. In this version of cleaning, emotional or material leftovers are starting points to be built upon, to be reincorporated into new recipes, rich with new learning.

[1] Arlie Hochschild, *The Managed Heart*, (California, University of California Press, 1983), p. 167.

What is required in this cleaning process is time for reflection. Time before the water and soap is mixed in the sink to survey the leftovers and see what traces of learning can be found? Time to search for the hidden emotions that we are taught to clean away, which might be brought to the surface with a gentle wash – a cleaning process that is altogether at odds with the expectations of 'good housework'.

Part 4. maps out some of the reflections that have been boiled down from ruminations at the kitchen sink; recipes and texts that share some of the traces and leftovers that were discovered during the clean-ups of Home Works; leftovers that informed how we collectively organised and connected Home Works to political struggles. A Home Works clean-up is to make visible leftovers that are to be composted and built upon. A clean up that can be served with a discussion on the political tactics that give weight to the emotional labour embedded within housework.

A recipe for working with art and social organising

For the original Women's Day Off in Iceland in 1975, a large copy of Ásmundur Sveinsson's sculpture, *Vatnsberinn* (Water Carrier), was crafted and collectively carried through the capital during the demonstration. The sculpture was also used on the poster for the event. The Water Carrier depicts a woman on her way to the river to wash clothes. When we first encountered the sculpture, we misinterpreted it as a person struggling to walk home with heavy shopping bags. Both readings, however, unequivocally point to the continued weight of gendered domestic labour and strategies to express the importance of valuing this work.

POWER of WOMEN

MAGAZINE OF THE INTERNATIONAL WAGES FOR HOUSEWORK CAMPAIGN No.5 15p/50c

ICELAND, OCT 24, 1975—GENERAL STRIKE OF WOMEN. Full-time housewives, factory workers, teachers, typists, actresses, childminders, telephonists, prostitutes, bank clerks, school girls, mothers, grandmothers. Some businessmen took their children to work. 90% of industry ground to a halt. *Meals not cooked. Shopping* not done. Floors not swept. Of 60,000 women in all Iceland, 25,000 at mass meeting in the capital, Reykjavik. Women struck to show their power—and did! *(More news and pictures inside.)*

What are the leftovers of the Women's Day Off and how might we remake or compost them for reuse? What parts of this struggle do we not want to reproduce today? It is important first to question what it means to organise under the term 'woman' when it has and continues to be a source of exclusion for so many. The struggles of today's trans movement against the gender binary regime and all of its oppressions, offer inspiring and important lessons to learn from. How to develop a feminist movement that fights for the liberation of all? These questions and discussions informed the feminist politics the Home Works programme developed and invested itself in, and were key concerns when researching the Women's Day Off.

The recipe below shares some of the ingredients and methods that were learnt through this research that can hopefully help you organise a collective 'day off', exposing the precarious work of cooking, cleaning and caring that society as a whole relies on.

Ingredients

- A desire to change society
- The courage to speak to people you do not know about your desires and see if they want to join you in your vision
- A desire to act
- Accepting that you might fail
- Accepting that you may not be able to change society
- A key aim
- History – learn from the past. How did people mobilise? What was the context? What can be learnt from past protests in order to mobilise a new movement? For example: What can the Women's Day Off and the International Wages for Housework Campaign teach us today?
- An intersectional approach to your struggle, how does power affect people in different ways?
- A bunch of creativity
- A scoop of joy
- Solidarity with other struggles
- A pinch of communication and flexibility
- Translation of communications, if you are working in multiple languages

Method

Grass-roots politics can take time and requires a lot of conversation and face-to-face meetings. Share your ideas with other people and see if they share your concerns. Share them at work, at home and with friends. Read into the social, economic and political history of how this situation is constructed and why it is reproduced. How have people addressed it in the past? Find a way of communicating your ideas for others to understand. This might involve working with a group or someone who is able to visualise your struggle and communicate the ideas clearly.

For example, try to transform your struggle into a stage play and use this as a way to publicise a meeting to discuss your concern and see who joins *(see How to make political theatre? ↷ p. 93)*. From this meeting, figure out collectively how to continue to address the issue. During the workshops with Stephan Dillemuth, the group learnt that when the first volume of Karl Marx's *Das Kapital* (Capital) was published in 1867, J.B. von Schweitzer studied it thoroughly and published the results in a newspaper. In order to make the book's more difficult ideas comprehensible to the readers, he used the form of a dialogue between two characters, not a far cry from Hildur Hákonardóttir's method of illustrating the story of the Women's Day Off *(see Yes, I dare, can and will ↷ p. 215)*. To J.B. von Schweitzer, the dialogue was not intended for the stage or as a live performance. Nevertheless, it began to be performed here and there in German *Arbeitsklubs* (workers' clubs). Until 1878, this was one of only a few attempts to share the relevance of Karl Marx's economic theory with workers. *Das Kapital* sold badly in the beginning, in 1867 only one hundred copies had been ordered, although four years later, most of the first edition had been sold. By that time, the J.B. von Schweitzer version had been performed at least fifteen times. Consequently, about two thousand people had learnt about Karl Marx's labour theory of value through performance. While these performances were often developed through workers' clubs and unions, today, resources for workers to unionise and have space to meet has dramatically dwindled. The struggle to find free space to meet is something an art space can help with, and by doing so support local organising. Offering a free, safe space for groups to meet during Home Works was an important part of the programme and many different groups were given the key to the art space.

When planning a gathering, flexibility in terms of time and meeting place can be key to ensuring that as many people as possible can join. Think about what time you would like to meet, is the space accessible and do you need to arrange support for people, such as childcare, so that people will be able to attend? If you cannot find a free space, ask around, and try to and avoid places where you have to pay. Some may not be able to afford it.

Using multiple approaches has in the past helped political campaigns. This means working both to address politicians in power, but also holding public demonstrations and talks that highlight concerns and empower yourselves and others. For example, in the International Wages for Housework Campaign it was important that domestic work was shared during meetings. This was a method of learning about the politics of domestic work by doing it together.[1]

It can sometimes be difficult to understand how much space you take up in meetings, check your blind spots. Who talks the most? What tools do you have to enable people to feel welcome, participate and be heard? One way Home Works dealt with this was to ask people to introduce themselves at the start of the meeting. It is also important to ask which pronoun people prefer, so that people can be addressed as they desire. The workshop would then conclude each discussion with a round where everyone was given the opportunity to talk and share their thoughts if they wanted to.

In Home Works it was important to think about who our work addressed. Language and translation are important to consider so that both visitors and staff have access to information *(see How to speak about Home Works? → p. 195)*.

Remember to have fun when organising. Politics can at times be hard work, painful and full of conflict, but it should always be joyful. If it is not joyful it can become too hard to carry out, and the movement that you are trying to mobilise can lose momentum. Do not forget to party! Political parties and movements can be born through parties! *(See Kitchen karaoke → p. 200)*.

Leftovers

The Women's Day Off formed a historical backbone to our research. We see ripples of the Women's Day Off in today's International Women's Strike,[2] which was formed in 2017 and has proved successful in overthrowing anti-abortion campaigns in European countries such as Ireland and Poland and constantly exerts pressure across large parts of Latin America in fighting gendered violence.

1 Silvia Federici in conversation with writers, (2020).

2 'The Women's Strike is a strike for solidarity between women – women of colour, indigenous, working class, disabled, migrant, Muslim, lesbian, queer and trans women.' See https://womenstrike.org.uk/about/ (Accessed 20 March, 2020).

Revolutionary threads — *Halla Þórlaug Óskarsdóttir and Hildur Hákonardóttir*

Hildur Hákonardóttir was part of the Home Works exhibition *Expansions of Homecraft* where she showed works made between 1970–1980, including a series of forty illustrations *(see Yes, I dare, can and will* *→ p. 215)*. The illustrations were instructions for how to start a revolution, because as Hákonardóttir says, 'in my opinion, the Women's Day Off was truly a revolution'. Here, she speaks to journalist and artist Halla Þórlaug Óskarsdóttir.

Halla Þórlaug Óskarsdóttir(HÞ): You have said that this revolution was a dream of many nations at that time, but Iceland was the only place this dream came true. Why do you think this was the case?

> Hildur Hákonardóttir (HH): I think one of the reasons was the size of our community. Jared Diamond talks about this in his book *Collapse*.[1] He studied societies on islands in the South Pacific, with regard to their prosperity. If the island's population was too small, it was not strong enough to be self-sufficient and withstand pressure and changes. If it was too large it had a tendency to split up into sections that would compete against each other. But when the size was right, people could easily communicate and see the usefulness of working together. Iceland in 1975 was the right size. Another reason was most definitely the clarity of the goal. It was simple: to prove that women's contributions to the labour market was essential for the society to function.

HÞ: You told me that the main argument for gender inequality in industries in those days was that women's contribution was not seen as relevant.

> HH: Yes. Women's work outside the home was considered a hobby – so they could afford better holidays for the family – casual work that did not really matter for them or society. This was used systematically in order to hold women back in the labour market. That is why I call it a revolution. Because after this day, you never heard this argument again.

HÞ: The Women's Day Off is a day women in Iceland still remember and celebrate, most recently on 24 October 2016, when thousands of women, all over the country went on strike at 2.38 pm and gathered to protest the wage gap, a gap that the government still does not seem to take too much notice of. What was your demand then?

> HH: Our demand was simply that the importance of our contribution should be acknowledged.

[1] Jared Diamond, *Collapse: How Societies Choose to Fail or Succeed*, (London: Penguin Books, 2005).

HÞ: In relation to this, how do you see women's contributions acknowledged in the art field? Do you follow women's art in particular?

HH: I guess I have not followed the general art scene enough over the years. It is only now that I am picking up the threads and looking at what is going on. Women's art does not interest me, per se, but rather rebel art and political art. That is what I mostly relate to.

HÞ: How was your political art received back in the 1970s?

HH: Rather awfully. Very awfully, even. I was told that politics and direct connections to what is going on in the outside world were inappropriate for the art world. The art scene should be a temple, subject to different laws. But this has changed drastically. Today I enjoy the fact that you cannot walk into a big museum without there being at least one exhibition that reflects contemporary political issues.

HÞ: Do you think that people's ideas of art have changed? That viewers interpret art in a more political way than before?

HH: I do not know if it came from the viewers, but the artists' perspective has changed, because of what today's world has come to be, you cannot be doodling in your own aesthetic corner. It does not work that way.

I am a tapestry weaver, and the discipline of the loom taught me how to structure things, which proved useful when dealing with political actions. When organising a loom, one needs to know how the threads work together, the difference between warp and weft, how to keep the tension even and to be able to visualise the outcome before you start. The same goes for politics. In that way weaving taught me how to organise and how to mobilise. This model came in handy when we were organising the Women's Day Off.

Hildur Hákonardóttir, *Ísland í NATO*, 1974. Courtesy of Listasafni Íslands. Part of *Expansions of Homecraft*. Konsthall C, 2016.

Yes, I dare, can and will

by Hildur Hákonardóttir

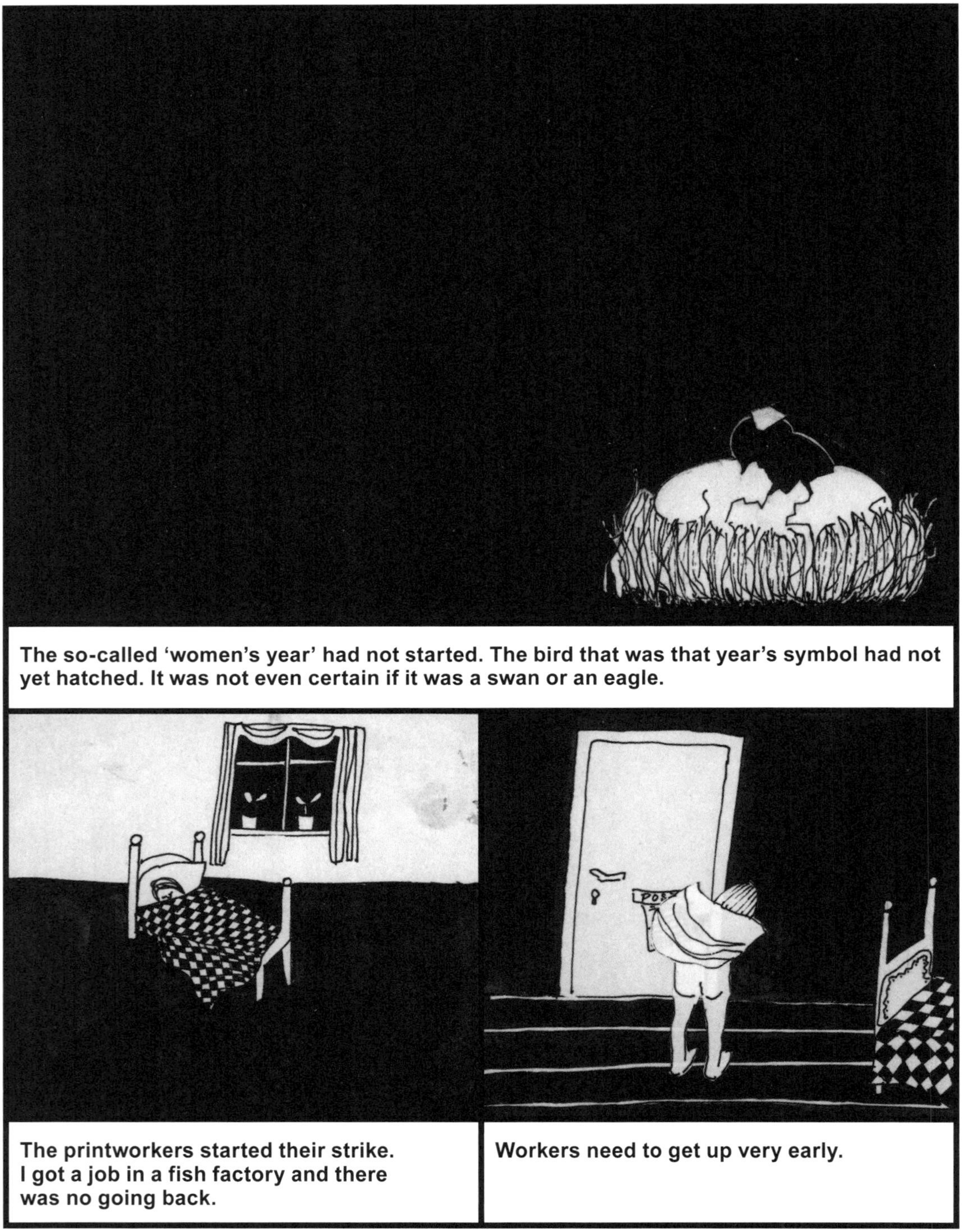
The so-called ‘women’s year’ had not started. The bird that was that year’s symbol had not yet hatched. It was not even certain if it was a swan or an eagle.
The printworkers started their strike. I got a job in a fish factory and there was no going back.
Workers need to get up very early.

I went down towards the Granda fish factory.
The sun was just beginning to rise.
When I spoke with the manager, the other women had already started filleting the fish.
They taught me their techniques and methods.

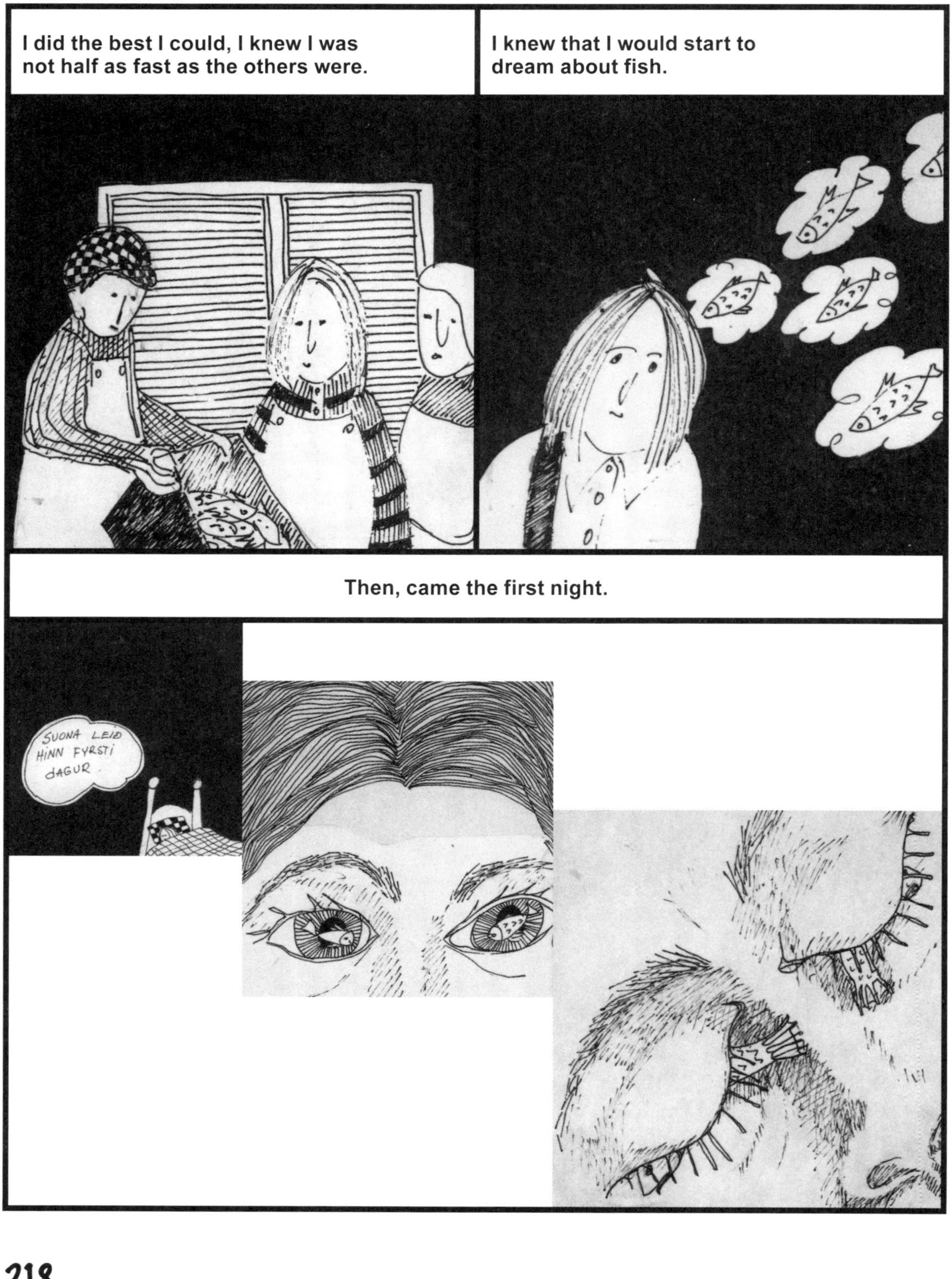
I did the best I could, I knew I was not half as fast as the others were.
I knew that I would start to dream about fish.
Then, came the first night.
SUONA LEID HINN FYRSTI dAGUR

The next day, during the coffee break the women talked about their working conditions. 'We get the same wage for the same work. But the male workers get a bonus and they know they will have steady work all the time.'

'It is only fair for us to get more money because we are the breadwinners.'

After work...

We work for our homes, our husbands and children as best we can. We also try to help each other.

We come home and more work awaits us.

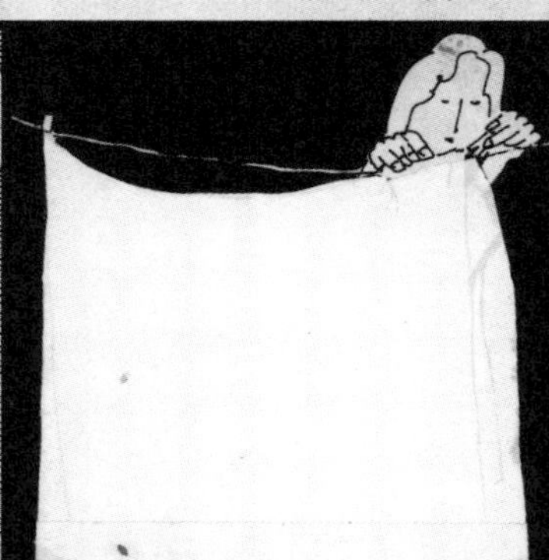

'Then there is too little time to read or go to meetings. We are lucky if we get enough sleep.'

'We also need security, wage security and overtime pay. The regular pay is not enough for a decent living, even if you live in rental apartments and try to save.'

Their story moved me deeply. There are so few conversations about the conditions working class women live under.

I thought a lot...

I stopped working in the fish factory and started back at the newspaper again.
ÉG HÆTTI OG FÓR AFTUR AÐ VINNA Á BLAÐINU. OG ENN VAR ÉG AÐ HUGSA.
I thought all the time about whether it was possible to use the International Women's Year to change something...
JAN. 1975
mér fannst ég þyrfti að tala við einhvern......
I decided I needed to speak with someone.
ÉG HRINGDI Í VINKONU MÍNA HJÁ RAUÐSOKKUNUM OG SAGÐI HENNI FRÁ KONUNUM .....
FRYSTIHÚSINU OG AÐ VIÐ ÆTTUM AÐ FÁ ÞÆR TIL AÐ KOMA Á FUND OG SEGJA OKKUR FRÁ VINNU SINNI.
I rang my friend in the Red Stockings group and told her about the women.

'Let's also ask other women from low paid sectors. Seamstresses, cleaning ladies, preschool carers, shop assistants and clerks. But that would be too many for one meeting.'

'GREAT! Better do something properly that is noticed during the women's year'.

'It will turn into a mighty conference.'

The Red Stockings worked fast. The low-wage conference in Lindarbæ started to take shape.

We rang some women we knew and asked them to talk at the conference.

To start with, the working women we contacted were doubtful.

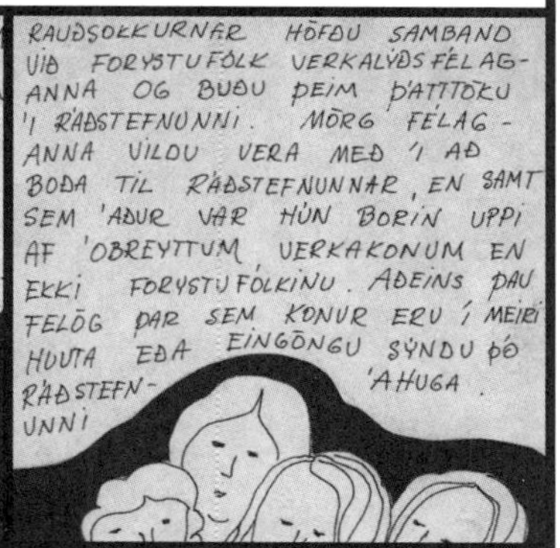

'Everyone is scared to speak publicly for the first time.'

'Do not worry, we do not want you to give a speech. Just tell us about your work day, your working conditions and pay. We will help you with everything you need. This will get easier once it gets going.'

The Red Stockings contacted the union leaders and invited them to the conference. Many associates wanted to be invited. But the conference was for working women, not the union leaders. Only unions with women members or where women were in a majority could join.

'Your voice becomes loud and you can feel alone.'

'Dear conference guests.'

'Here we are together, working women from diverse areas of work.'

'We cannot under-value the work we do despite our exposure to inequalities.'

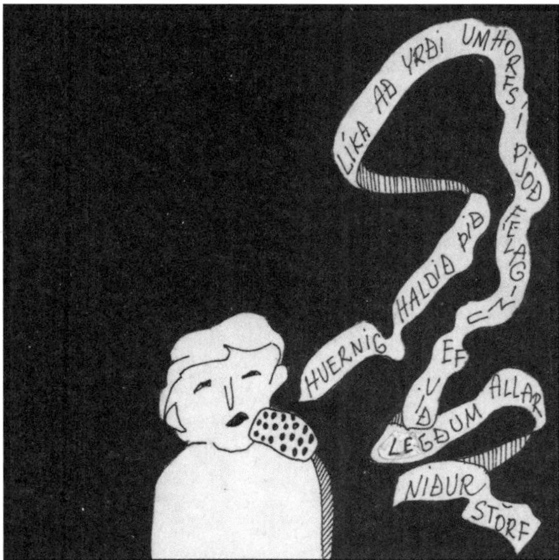

'What do you think society would look like if we stopped working?'

We show unity for one day during the International Women's Year.

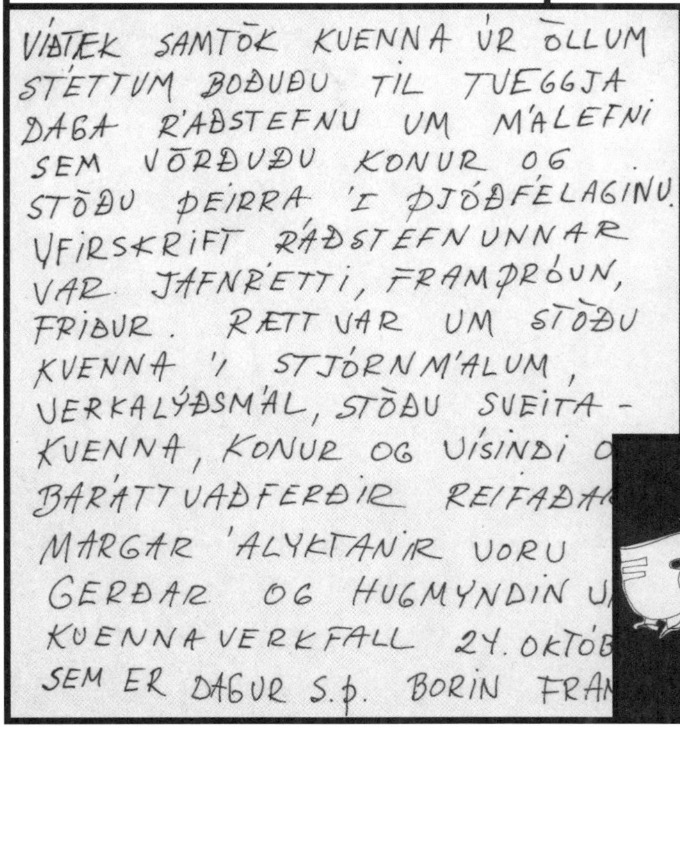

Many women organisations, even if they came from the countryside or belonged to a specific class, met for two days to discuss how equality could be achieved: in politics, union work, science and education along with how to take the struggle further.

After long discussions it was decided the women would take a day off to coincide with the UN Women's Day on 24 October.

Spring came.

'A strike means a battle and we do not want discussions like that at this conference.'

'What does it mean to talk about inequality if we do not fight for equality. Do you believe that we will get equality served on a silver platter.'

'To strike is a violation of the law ... it will intimidate the men.'

'If the word strike is what you are afraid of, we can call the 'strike', a 'day off'.

'Yes, we will call it a "day off!"'

It was apparent from the beginning that the women needed to meet on the Women's Day Off day.

The preparation committee needed to do two things, get everyone together and plan the meeting and gathering in Reykjavik on 24th of October.

Different points of view came forward. Some wanted the action to be only a part of the day, but in the end it was decided that it would be a whole day off.

VÆRI EKKI FLOTTAST AÐ FÁ RÁÐHERRA-FRÚ TIL AÐ TALA 'A FUNDINUM.
Would it not be amazing to get the wife of a minister to speak at the meeting?
PRUMP! ÞAÐ VERÐUR EKKI TEKIÐ MARK 'A NEINNI NEMA KONU 'UR VERKALÝÐS-STÉTT.
People will not take a working class woman seriously.
ÞIÐ GETIÐ EKKI FARIÐ AÐ TROÐA UPP MEÐ ÞETTA GAUL YKKAR. ÞAÐ VERÐA SKO AÐ VERA EKTA SÖNGKONUR.
'You cannot perform with this kind of screeching, it must be like a real choir.'
GASALEGAR KELLINGAR ERUÐ ÞIÐ. OG NENNIÐ EKKI AÐ LÆRA EITT EINASTA NÝTT OG SKEMMTILEGT LAG.
'You did not even bother to learn a new and fun song.'
VIÐ ERUM AÐ REYNA AÐ HALDA FLOKKS-PÓLITÍKINNI ÚT ÚR ÞESSU. EN SAMT GÆTU ÞÆR EYÐILAGT ALLA STEMN-INGU MEÐ ÞURR PÍPUHÆTTI OG FREKJU.
We try to keep party politics outside of this. Speeches about principles will spoil the atmosphere.

Even though people were not in agreement on every detail,
everyone supported the basic idea.
EN ÞÓTT EINING RÍKTI EKKI UM EIN-
STÖK ATRIÐI VORU ALLAR ÁKVEÐNAR
Í AÐ STYÐJA MÁLEFNIÐ.
The little bird,
the symbol of the Women's Year
had now become a full grown sea eagle.

From welfare to housekeeping — *Samira Ariadad*

The underpinning of Home Works with historical research into the Icelandic Women's Day Off called into question the changes around domestic labour in Sweden today. How is domestic work organised informally at home and by the state? And how does this organising continue to reproduce gendered, racialised and classed relations? Samira Ariadad researches the question of paid domestic labour in Sweden and what norms and exploitation it is founded upon and furthers.

This text was originally published in *Kvinnoledighetsdagen – Domestic Labour, Collectivity, Feminism and Migration*, eds. Jenny Richards and Jens Strandberg, (Sweden: Konsthall C, 2017).

> It is never worth fighting over cleaning but since you are the one suffering from the mess and your family members are not, either you have to stand alone with the work or with the whip. That is not reasonable, buy the service! It will make your life quality much better, it is not luxurious or overclass, just prioritising your own time!
>
> **— Blog comment from a post about home cleaning**

The quote above not only concludes the reasoning of many Swedish, middle-class women, it also indicates some of the key elements of the unequal situation women have met historically and are still facing today. The thought that only she is suffering from the mess, or is the only one who cares about cleanliness; the problem of housework only being hers, thus, puts the weight of the solution on her shoulders.

Instead of agreeing on what is necessary and what common preferences the family has, and dividing the work equally, she is left with the whip. The alternative is prioritising her time and instead hiring cleaning and other domestic services. The latter is not an alternative being discussed widely without pretext. In Sweden it is a tax deductible solution, promoted and paid for partially by the state, a scheme that has been in operation for the last ten years.

The question of the housemaid has resurfaced, due to migratory patterns, the diminishing of the welfare state and ongoing feminist discussions on women's work. It has taken a new turn and become even more important with the increase of domestic services in Sweden since the 1990s, and the tax deduction system introduced in 2007 called *rengöring, underhåll* and *tvätt* (cleaning, maintenance and washing), known as 'RUT'. Former feminist struggles are now in the shadow of the market economy and neoliberal politics; the women's struggles that gave us qualitative and public childcare, elderly care and a working public sector now have to fit the new conditions.

While public services took unwaged labour and made it a collectively (public) waged service, the patriarchy of uneven work distribution prevailed. This is seen both in the maintained low status of public care services, where workers are often paid low salaries, and recently, care services working under even more pressure as cuts in staff and resources are implemented through the methods of new public management.[1] The prevailing patriarchal structure of an uneven workload also manifested itself in

[1] See for example H M Dahl, "New Public Management, Care and Struggles about Recognition". *Critical Social Policy 4* (2009): 634–654.

women's unwaged work in their own households. Reports from the Swedish State Statistics Bureau have shown women doing around 60 percent of the domestic labour and men around 40 percent. It has also shown that the decrease in women's labour is not principally due to men taking more responsibility, but is rather because women have refused to do it, hence families are living in dirtier homes.

The strategies and victories over reproductive work take many forms, but the statistics also reflect the collective initiatives, politics and premises under which these inequalities become consolidated or resisted. Essentialist arguments and gender roles, wage differences and a conservative feminist backlash all boosted in a capitalist society, tie women once again to reproductive labour. The European Agency for Fundamental Rights declared that domestic labour has one of the highest risks of severe labour exploitation in the European Union (EU). Aching necks and shoulders, fed up workers, overworked and underpaid; domestic labour is perceived as one of the most precarious working sectors, involving, at its worst, trafficking and sexual harassment.

What can be common for the domestic workers in Sweden is isolation, a lack of knowledge about their rights, low levels of trade union membership, and a high number of workplace-related injuries. Cleaners in Sweden have the highest amount of long-term sick leave, over 90 days per year, and over two thirds of female cleaners stated that the work is gruelling and exhausting. The risks reported also include repetitive work, heavy-lifting, stress and excessive work-rates. As the site of work is the private household, it comes with power structures that must be negotiated and as the majority of the workers are working from a precarious position this gives rise to the risk of heavy exploitation. It is connected to the globalised patterns of migration, where women today are migrating to the same extent as men.

Women are ending up as domestic workers as a means to (sometimes) getting an EU work permit, and so they can send money back to their home country and be able to secure the lives of the family they have left behind. The exploitation of female domestic workers who have migrated is frequently manifested in the absence of any formal contract, contracts that do not correspond to the real tasks performed, low pay, irregular payment or often even no pay, excessively long working hours, no leave, and sexual, racial and/or sexist abuse. The initiatives aiming to tackle the conditions of domestic workers within the EU and in Sweden lack efficacy, since strategies like the RUT tax deduction scheme in Sweden are only helping to widen the market – they are not solving the problem. While both the EU and Sweden are promoting efforts to regulate the unregulated market of domestic services, the Swedish tax deduction system has not ended undeclared work or the risks associated with domestic service. Overall, power structures, migrant rights, education and the inspection of working conditions are just a few elements that need to be addressed.

Since the 1990s, cuts in public spending and the privatisation of care services were part of a neoliberal solution proposed by the right-wing coalition government that once again took power in 2006. When the tax deduction of domestic services, RUT (for domestic services) and ROT (for construction services)[2] was introduced, the conscience and energy of middle-class women who had suffered for a long time because of the unwaged reproductive work they performed, cracked, and they found a relatively easy way out. RUT offered a way to push the problem onto someone else while arguing that you are doing domestic workers a favour by providing them with work. As the quote at the beginning indicates, over ten years later, it is now not only seen as a last resort or luxury, it is seen as a right. The labour policy stating that job opportunities are crucial and meaningful in themselves, no matter what the job is, or dictating the working conditions and wages, has put its mark on the minds of citizens. Middle-class families and older people are now arguing that receiving private domestic services is a help for themselves, helps them keep peace within the family, and helps the Swedish economy by creating job opportunities.

Whether spoken by conservatives, neoliberals or contemporary social democrats, gender equality has been one of the liberal feminist arguments promoting this tax deduction. The argument is that by creating job opportunities it is regulating undeclared work. Yet, figures from 2013 show that only 10 percent of undeclared cleaning jobs have become declared and taxed. The undocumented market for domestic labour prevails. What has been created instead is the popularity and the expansion of the domestic labour market in general. Statistics from 2016 show that over 700,000 people are buying deductible domestic and care work for an amount of over 3.6 billion Swedish krona. In comparison to 2011, that is an increase of over 300,000 people. Since the tax deduction was introduced in June 2007, the amount of companies focusing on domestic labour has rocketed; 17,000 new companies have been created since the reform was introduced in 2007. While internationally, at least 80 percent of domestic workers are women, in Sweden women account for 63 percent. Every third domestic worker is born outside of Sweden, most commonly in Poland, Serbia, Croatia,

[2] ROT stands for *reparation, ombyggnad* and *tillbyggnad* (repairs, maintenance and rebuilding).

Bosnia and Finland which is much higher than the national average for migratory labour in other sectors. The legislation around domestic work is different from the labour market in general in terms of regulation of working hours and inspections. Working hours are more flexible, which means that an au pair, for example, is able to work 52 hours in a row. Inspections can be made if any of the parties – employer, customer or employee demand it, or in special cases. However, support for education around an individual's working rights through trade union membership is rare, which is down to a number of different factors. As domestic work is precarious and temporary it is often that the worker believes that they have a better bargaining position without the union. This unawareness of rights is not being addressed by the trade unions. As a result, workplace inspections are rarely made, and working conditions are much worse than they should be.

So, if welfare was an outcome of political uprisings and a realisation by politicians that creating a welfare industry for the population increased productivity and profit, it seems that now, in times of fewer political protests, capital and the state have come to the conclusion that welfare might not be needed at all. The reproductive work that welfare supports can be done for free by female relatives and the family, to the benefit of both capital and men. By creating a new sector for domestic labour, the rest can get this reproductive labour cheaply. Profits are to be made from the domestic worker, both through her work, but also by having her see to the care of her family in the *leisure time* she has left over.

More than ten years has passed since the beginning of this scheme, and the total deductible amount for housework has decreased from 50,000 to 25,000 Swedish krona, however this is not the case for people over 65 years of age. Sweden has a growing population of older people, similar to the rest of the EU. 20 percent of the European population is over 65 and the estimation is that this rate will reach 25 percent by 2050. Yet, despite this knowledge, about 80 percent of the time required to care for older people, that is several days a week or every day, is still covered by informal and/or family carers. And despite the growing number of carers in the EU, informal care is mostly provided by women (usually spouses, or middle-aged daughters or daughters-in-law).

The problematic approach to *creating job opportunities* and commercialising care and cleaning services is evident when looking at the work itself and at who does it. Consolidating low-skill work on an already racist and discriminatory labour market makes the situation worse. Women of colour working for the right for leisure time for white women (and their families) produces an isolated *solution* based on the exploitation of domestic workers, and is only available for those who can afford it. A new low-skill job market is created, where most workers are not organised in trade unions and are unaware of their working rights. Domestic labourers are among the hardest workforce to organise, in part due to migrant workers' fear of losing their work permit, the lack of common spaces to meet other labourers in the same field of work, temporary contracts and other precarious working conditions, but, critically, it is also due to a lack of knowledge of their fundamental rights; that they are entitled to a good working environment, paid damages for work-related injuries and more. Patriarchy and capitalism coexist, making the lives of some middle-class women easier, and some corporations more wealthy. Not only are working-class women left behind, but older individuals are left without the service they require if they are not able to pay for them.

Cuts in public care and cleaning services for those who require it, has created a greater need where the private sector can step in and fill the gaps left by dwindling welfare services. While commercial housework may be one way to go to decrease the amount of unwaged care work done by relatives, it is clearly only one of two ways. The public sector, nuanced by taxes is still paying for housework, but instead of having it in the form of a relatively effective public service, available for all, regardless of an individual's income, it has become a possible solution for those that can afford it. The problems do not end there. By making housework into a private, commercial service, heavy and exhausting jobs are created for a migratory workforce of working-class women, making it possible for an increasing number of middle-class women to develop their own careers. Studies have shown that the higher the income, the more of the maximum tax deduction through schemes like RUT are used. While regulatory initiatives like RUT are described, both nationally and within the EU as feminist initiatives, it is obviously a liberal feminist initiative, not only failing to make the lives of working-class women better, but moving the work from the shoulders of white women to a working class, many of whom are migrants overeducated for the job. It is the opposite of progress, which consolidates the lack of social mobility and increases the wage gap between the white and the migrant population. Working-class women are once again becoming the private servants of those more fortunate than themselves.

Storage matters

In the exhibition *Open House*, the artist Anna Ihle displayed a black carpet that was two by six metres and woven from clothes she no longer used, wanted or desired.[1] Anna Ihle's discarded clothing was not thrown away, but shredded and then woven into a tapestry layered with stories and histories.

The tapestry was like a clothing compost, teaching us a lesson in the creative act of reusing discarded material that we are encouraged to clean out, throw away and discard. Clearing out and cleaning does not have to mean completely getting rid of the 'mess'. Instead, it can be a process in which

1 Anna Ihle, *Clothes I Cannot Keep*, 2011.

materials are reused, becoming support structures for other situations like in the case of Anna Ihle's tapestry. In the running of a small art space a creative approach to cleaning can be essential. It enables materials to play different and multiple roles, which can help when finances are tight and in reducing the accumulation of waste, something many art spaces and art practices are prone to.

The reusing of sculptures and exhibition materials continued throughout the Home Works programme. This recycling practice required access to a good space for storing objects and materials, which is often overlooked in an art space. The storage room was an important factor for Home Works, as the space that enabled us to build many of the sculptures and materials for exhibitions prior to the event.

The storage space had to move three times during the Home Works programme. The landlord was at the time, focusing on how to commercially rent out the property. While it was possible to secure a free storage space with them, it also meant there was an expectation to be flexible with where that storage space was located. Moving storage space takes a lot of effort and time. Effort that can push a small art space like Konsthall C to breaking point. The third and final storeroom was a run-down space at the back of the building. It was ideal, as there was enough room to build sculptures, plinths and wall structures prior to exhibition openings. This gave the programme more time to prepare for the intense installation period. Stress is unfortunately a major part of exhibition installation, and that generally left the storage space in a mess. Hence, central to this recipe is creatively cleaning and tidying the storage, as that is an important factor in its continued functioning.

Ingredients

- A space (preferably where you can set up a wood-working workshop)
- A large table
- Equipment
- Shelving

Method

- Work as a team and make sure everyone understands the conditions for making.

- Building and preparing exhibitions prior to openings keeps time frames more flexible and installations less stressed.

- Placing an importance on the making of materials can offer new ways to learn about and rethink methods of display and installation.

- If you want the storage space to be shared and used by artists or other people in need of a workshop, make sure that tools and equipment are put back in their correct place.

- Have fun! Working during exhibition installations is often very stressful and having fun is key to making it a pleasurable experience.

- Clean, clean and clean some more. Make space to have at least two or three days off from office work after an exhibition opening (and some real days off too). Spend that time in the storeroom, see what leftovers can be reused in other unexpected ways. Putting tools and other materials back in their designated places. A storage space is like a kitchen, strict organisation might sound terrible but makes it much easier for others to use.

Leftovers

Sawdust, friends, pierced skin, blood stains and laughter. Objects that can be used in surprising ways.

How to create a public home

One answer to the perennial debate on art's autonomy is the possibility that it can be produced independently of art institutions, whether state or private. In the contemporary conjecture, the self-negation essential to art's development happens outside institutional practices. As a public form of the unfolding of each person's creative potential, the place of art during moments of revolutionary struggle has always been and always will be in the thick of events, on the squares and in the communes. At such moments, art takes the form of street theatre, posters, actions, graffiti, grassroots cinema, poetry and music.

— Chto Delat[1]

1 Chto Delat, "A Declaration on Politics, Knowledge and Art", 2008. See https://chtodelat.org/b5-announcements/a-6/a-declaration-on-politics-knowledge-and-art-4/ (Accessed December 2019).

The concept of a 'public home' developed throughout Home Works. It evolved from questions concerning the role of a publicly funded art organisation today. If we want to take Chto Delat's declaration on the previous page seriously, the art institution inhibits not only broad and diverse audiences from experiencing and engaging with exhibitions and events, but also the artists' ability to develop politically engaged work within the thick of social struggle. If the main platforms for artists to produce work are so severely limited and irrelevant – not to mention entwined with a colonial and patriarchal history that deems some art worthy and some art audiences worth speaking too – how can we re-think these spaces and re-orientate their focus without dismantling these art spaces altogether?

The Home Works programme wanted to build another type of art space that was relevant and embedded in the local struggles, whether localised campaigns concerning support for home care workers, or the global struggle of migrants. We mixed inspiration from the Swedish *Folkets hus* (People's House) movement with the notion of 'home' as a contested space between comfort, refuge and shelter, and added to the mix the construction of a space where it is possible for arguments to take place and expectations to be aired and debated.[2] Instead of building a public space for consensual discussion, Home Works' public home hoped to highlight the importance of difference and disaccord *(see Not knowing your home → p. 123)*.

The words *public* and *home* can be described as oppositional. In her book *The Human Condition*, Hannah Arendt discusses the division between 'public' and 'private/home'. She describes this division as highly policed in Western democracy, which legitimises some as political subjects who can act in the public sphere and others who are relegated to the domestic realm of privacy and invisibility, incapable of political agency.[3] Placing 'public' and 'home' together was for the Home Works programme a way of disregarding this division and, by extension, the Western epistemology that constructs the divide. Instead, it wanted to contest the separation and marginalisation of the home, and insist on the home as a site for exercising the agency of political subjects.

The political debate around public space in the city of Stockholm is ever-growing. The privatisation of public space, housing and infrastructure, as well as the dismantling of the People's House movement in Sweden, has led to an urgent need for spaces that are free for people to meet, organise and spend time in. Rather than concede that the city provides public spaces, Home Works' public home wanted to question the publicness of the city's public space and examine in what way they play into processes of democratisation and political subjectivity.

One of the things that Home Works wanted to do was to investigate what publicness might mean for a local art space. This desire was informed by understanding cities and urban centres across Europe and the United States as sites of growing inequality. Financialisation of land and property in city centres means that the well-off are able to occupy and commandeer public and private space while working-class people, often disproportionality made up of racialised and migrant communities, are redirected to the periphery. This process is often administered through large-scale gentrification projects disguised as 'urban renewal' that forces people out of their homes and neighbourhoods. Squares and public spaces are, at the same time, increasingly privatised. Social services are often moved out in order to make way for commercial interests. The Stockholm-based collective

2 The People's House is historically associated with organisations affiliated with the Swedish labour movement and was a space for workers to meet, learn and organise.

3 Hannah Arendt, *The Human Condition*, (Chicago: University of Chicago, 1958).

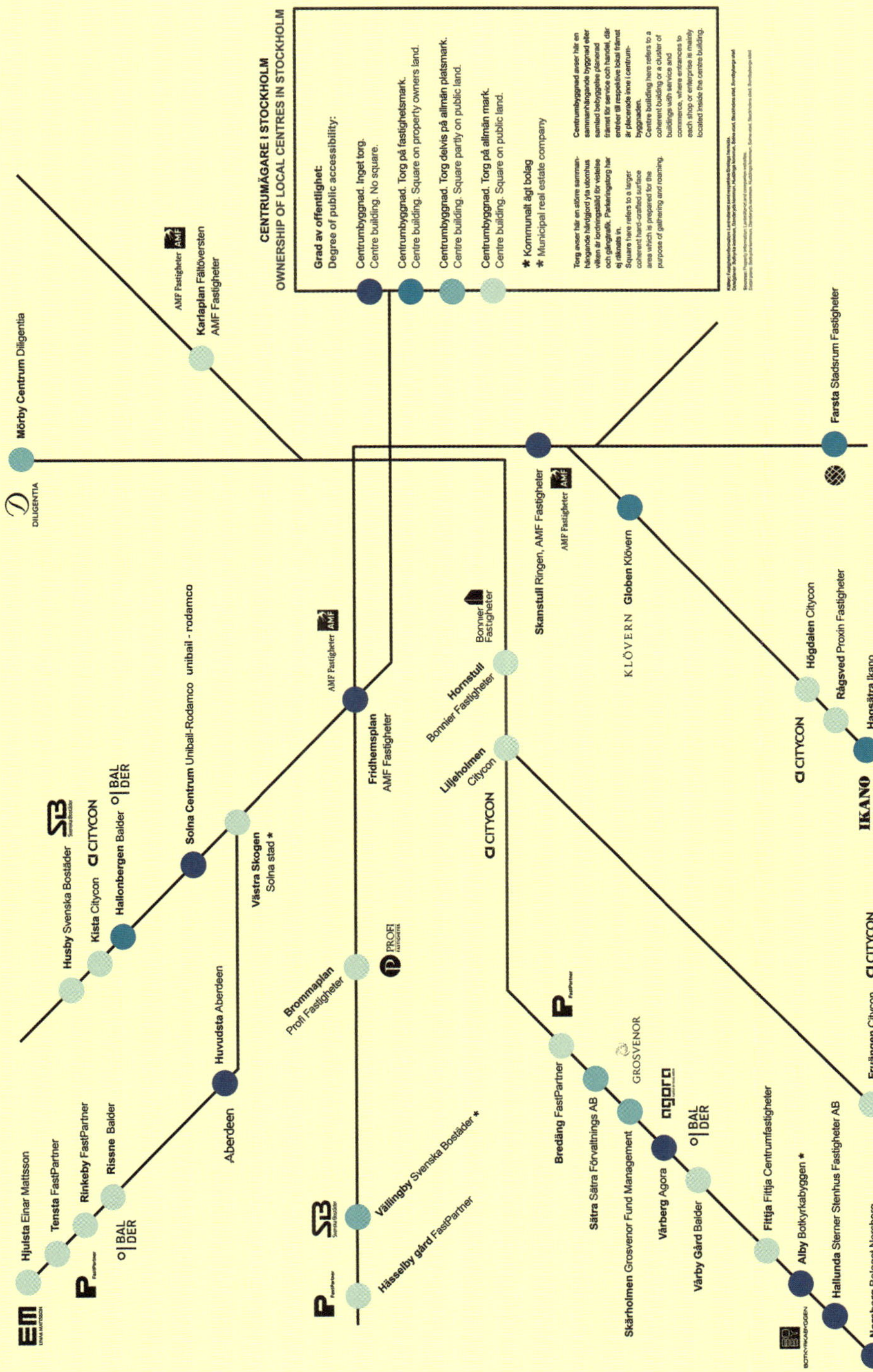
CENTRUMÄGARE I STOCKHOLM
OWNERSHIP OF LOCAL CENTRES IN STOCKHOLM
Grad av offentlighet:
Degree of public accessibility:
Centrumbyggnad. Inget torg.
Centre building. No square.
Centrumbyggnad. Torg på fastighetsmark.
Centre building. Square on property owners land.
Centrumbyggnad. Torg delvis på allmän platsmark.
Centre building. Square partly on public land.
Centrumbyggnad. Torg på allmän mark.
Centre building. Square on public land.
* Kommunalt ägt bolag
* Municipal real estate company
Mörby Centrum Diligentia
Karlaplan Fältöversten AMF Fastigheter
Farsta Stadsrum Fastigheter
Skanstull Ringen, AMF Fastigheter
Globen Klövern
Högdalen Citycon
Rågsved Proxin Fastigheter
Hagsätra Ikano
Hornstull Bonnier Fastigheter
Liljeholmen Citycon
Fridhemsplan AMF Fastigheter
Solna Centrum Unibail-Rodamco
Västra Skogen Solna stad *
Hallonbergen Balder
Kista Citycon
Husby Svenska Bostäder
Huvudsta Aberdeen
Rissne Balder
Rinkeby FastPartner
Tensta FastPartner
Hjulsta Einar Mattsson
Brommaplan Profi Fastigheter
Vällingby Svenska Bostäder *
Hässelby gård FastPartner
Fruängen Citycon
Bredäng FastPartner
Sätra Sätra Förvaltnings AB
Skärholmen Grosvenor Fund Management
Vårberg Agora
Vårby Gård Balder
Fittja Fittja Centrumfastigheter
Alby Botkyrkabyggen *
Hallunda Sterner Stenhus Fastigheter AB
Norsborg Bolaget Norsborg

Mapping the Unjust City[4] draw attention to these developments in a subway map diagram of Stockholm, noting the expanding privatisation of suburban centres often made invisible to the public.

Almost exclusively owned by private companies, these public spaces, which are still referred to as such, are undergoing a slow process of enclosure, where publicness is prohibited and profited from. The spaces shift from gathering points to places where the main purpose is consumption.

However, whether privately owned or not, we should understand public spaces in the city not as neutral spaces accessible to all, but, as Nancy Fraser argues, as sites of structural exclusion that reflect wider societal divisions. If public spaces need to be challenged on their publicness, how could spaces like the Home Works public home, provide training grounds for building a public that could undo the structural exclusion within their own construction?

The vision of Home Works' public home was to create a publicness that questioned and contested the dominant public we find in the city today, which are formed through a similarity of class, gender, job role and so on. And in contrast support a process of building diverse public communities through the active participation of people based on their difference, and with that difference, a diversity of perspectives, knowledge and experiences.[5]

Home Works' public home was, in this way, an attempt to rethink the purpose of the art space; from a space where you see art, to a pedagogical terrain for participating and practicing art and politics. A space that plays a social, aesthetic and political role for a community.

Ingredients

- Physical space
- Openness for not knowing
- Playfulness

Cooking time

Let the public home simmer for as long as possible. A home becomes homely over time and allows more people to be part of making the homeliness. Therefore, do not force the results but let it grow over time.

Method

All ingredients are mixed at the same time and will generate different results depending on the situation and the people involved.

SPACE
Finding a space can be hard, particularly if you are looking for something central. The Home Works programme had the advantage of taking over Konsthall C and transforming it into a public home. While this can pose many challenges and problems to be overcome, it can also be easier to work with an already existing space, but do not be afraid of starting from scratch.

BE TRANSPARENT
ABOUT YOUR CONDITIONS
What are the conditions of your public home? Does it have cooking facilities? How many people can it seat? How are the buildings/ rooms laid out? Is it accessible to those with diverse functionality? These are some of the questions that can be good to discuss in order to understand what conditions you are working with, and the physical, social and economic infrastructures that make the public home possible.

[4] Mapping the Unjust City / Vem äger staden is an interdisciplinary collective based in Stockholm, Sweden, formed in 2015, with members working in the fields of art, design, architecture and aesthetics. See http://www.mdgh.se/ (Accessed 20 March 2020).

[5] Nancy Fraser, "Rethinking the Public Sphere: A Contribution to the Critique of Actually Existing Democracy", *Social Text* No. 25/26, (1990): 56–80.

For example, Konsthall C is a publicly funded art space. The rent is waived by the landlord, Stockholmshem *(see Collaborators and other chefs → p. 10)*. Konsthall C did not have a rental agreement when Home Works moved in. It worked on an informal agreement with the company in which cultural capital was exchanged for space. Not paying rent was a critical factor that allowed Home Works and Konsthall C to keep its doors open. This agreement between Konsthall C and Stockholmshem was formalised during Home Works, which secured a five-plus-five-year rent-free contract. This was key for Home Works in ensuring that a space for meeting and experimentation was not at the mercy of market rates and changes, and that a notion of permanence and organisational stability could be established in a space that had been consistently driven by precarity, from its funding to how people were employed. The rent-free contract was one of the support structures of the Home Works public home that allowed time and focus to further think on how this home could be hosted through social relations. It is this inquiry that led the Home Works programme to explore questions of hospitality within the arts and how underlying contracts should be transparent and clear, in order for participants to understand the conditions of the space they were entering.

OPEN DOORS
Invite people and reach out to those beyond your existing networks. Bringing people together can be difficult in a city where people are far apart, stressed from work and life and scattered around the city. Therefore, cooking and eating together is a way of taking care and looking after yourself and your community.

LISTEN TO YOUR COMMUNITY
What do you choose to hear and how can you hear what is not heard? Listen to the things you did not expect to hear, the sentiment, the emotions or the silences.

PLAY WITH FORMATS
What is home to you? How is a home created? And how would a public home differ from the home you are used to? Who owns the space you are in? These are some of the questions that inform the structure of a public home.

Choral cleaning, with Nathalie Wuerth

A collaboration with Nathalie Wuerth began when she joined Stephan Dillemuth's open workshops on the preparation of *Workers' Variety Show Looks for Members!* Spending time together was an opportunity to learn about her practice and develop a collaboration for the Home Works programme. Nathalie Wuerth shared methods with Stephan Dillemuth's practice and also wanted to create a series of workshops. She wanted to explore people's relationship to domestic labour and try to understand how this work is devalued and hidden, as well as how much time is spent on this type of labour. The workshops invited former collaborators involved in Home Works and new friends. A score was produced, a choral transcription of all the vacuuming, feeding, tidying, coffee making and more. The mapping of these tasks formed the basis for

a collective performance, which was presented in the kitchen/office in 2016.

The work that Nathalie Wuerth developed was concerned with the devaluation of domestic work and how technologies have been invented to aid domestic work, but have also individualised these tasks and isolated those who perform them within the home. The creation of domestic appliances such as the dishwasher, the vacuum cleaner, the microwave, were supposed to reduce the time spent on the necessary tasks of everyday life. However, research has shown that new domestic technologies contribute to the expansion of work within and outside of the domestic sphere with extra work necessary to pay for these appliances.[1]

The question of cleaning in private homes cannot be discussed in Sweden without mentioning the controversial RUT system,[2] which provides tax breaks for those who can afford to pay for someone else (often a migrant worker) to clean (often middle class) people's homes *(see From welfare to housekeeping ↝ p. 231)*. RUT is a system that encourages the logic that those who are well-off should not in fact do their own dirty work. Rather, the Swedish middle class is able to receive public funds in the form of tax breaks to pay someone else a low wage to do it. A study of the RUT system by IMPact[3] revealed that in 2014 the government spent 20 billion Swedish krona on RUT tax breaks; approximately €214.6 million and 0.5 percent of Sweden's gross domestic product. RUT shows how public funds are used to support the maintenance of a wealthy class, and rather than changing the conditions or valuing of domestic work, ensures the continued devaluation of this labour.

Discussions on the politics of RUT and who performs domestic labour were fed into the workshops and the performance that was inaugurated in the kitchen/office of Home Works. Taking these discussions further, the work later transformed into a cleaning company – a choir of vacuum cleaners, dishwashers and tumble dryers that, in their collectivity, sought to socialise our often isolated domestic labour.

Participants

Sol Andersson, Sara Campanella Franceschi, Karin Ekholm, Annika Forell Pattocchio, Holly Keasey, Anna Kinbom, Vilda Kvist, Carolina Nylund, Jimmy Offesson, Jenny Richards, Jens Strandberg, John Söderberg, Sebastian Wahlforss, Nathalie Wuerth

Ingredients

- A place to meet and discuss domestic work
- Time to develop vocal skills
- Paper and pens for drawing a collective score
- Refreshments to provide energy for working together

Collaborators

- A voice coach

1 'As the German sociologist Otto Ullrich wrote, only modern technology's capacity to transfer its costs over considerable times and spaces and our consequent inability to see the suffering caused by our daily usage of technological devices allows the myth that technology generates prosperity to persist.' "Re-enchanting the World: Technology, the Body and the Construction of the Commons", Silvia Federici *Re-enchanting the World*, (New York: PM Press, 2019), p. 190.

2 RUT stands for *rengöring, underhåll* and *tvätt* (cleaning, maintenance and washing), a tax deduction law for domestic services that has been in force since 2007.

3 "Sweden – ROT och RUT avdrag", *PHS policies - Implementation and Monitoring Guide* (2020), published online at: http://impact-phs.eu/national-practices/sweden-rot-rut-avdrag/ (Accessed 2 March 2020).

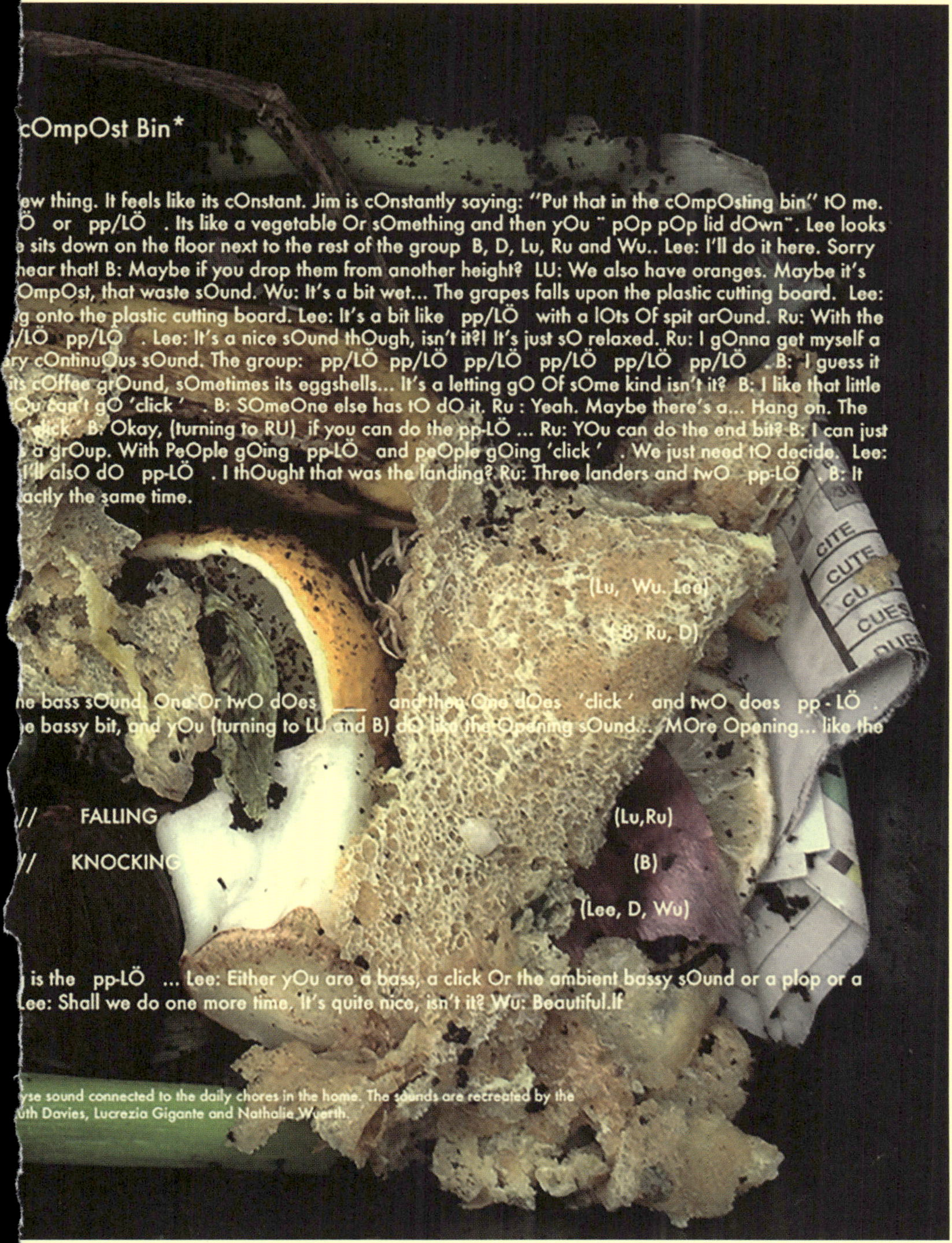
cOmpOst Bin*
ew thing. It feels like its cOnstant. Jim is cOnstantly saying: "Put that in the cOmpOsting bin" tO me.
Ö or pp/LÖ . Its like a vegetable Or sOmething and then yOu " pOp pOp lid dOwn". Lee looks
e sits down on the floor next to the rest of the group B, D, Lu, Ru and Wu.. Lee: I'll do it here. Sorry
hear that! B: Maybe if you drop them from another height? LU: We also have oranges. Maybe it's
OmpOst, that waste sOund. Wu: It's a bit wet... The grapes falls upon the plastic cutting board. Lee:
g onto the plastic cutting board. Lee: It's a bit like pp/LÖ with a lOts Of spit arOund. Ru: With the
/LÖ pp/LÖ . Lee: It's a nice sOund thOugh, isn't it?! It's just sO relaxed. Ru: I gOnna get myself a
ry cOntinuOus sOund. The group: pp/LÖ pp/LÖ pp/LÖ pp/LÖ pp/LÖ pp/LÖ . B: I guess it
its cOffee grOund, sOmetimes its eggshells... It's a letting gO Of sOme kind isn't it? B: I like that little
Ou can't gO 'click ' . B: SOmeOne else has tO dO it. Ru : Yeah. Maybe there's a... Hang on. The
click ' B: Okay, (turning to RU) if you can do the pp-LÖ ... Ru: YOu can do the end bit? B: I can just
a grOup. With PeOple gOing pp-LÖ and peOple gOing 'click ' . We just need tO decide. Lee:
I'll alsO dO pp-LÖ . I thOught that was the landing? Ru: Three landers and twO pp-LÖ . B: It
actly the same time.
(Lu, Wu, Lee)
(B, Ru, D)
he bass sOund. One Or twO dOes ___ and then One dOes 'click ' and twO does pp - LÖ .
e bassy bit, and yOu (turning to LU and B) dO like the Opening sOund... MOre Opening... like the
// FALLING (Lu,Ru)
// KNOCKING (B)
(Lee, D, Wu)
is the pp-LÖ ... Lee: Either yOu are a bass, a click Or the ambient bassy sOund or a plop or a
Lee: Shall we do one more time. It's quite nice, isn't it? Wu: Beautiful.If
yse sound connected to the daily chores in the home. The sounds are recreated by the
uth Davies, Lucrezia Gigante and Nathalie Wuerth.

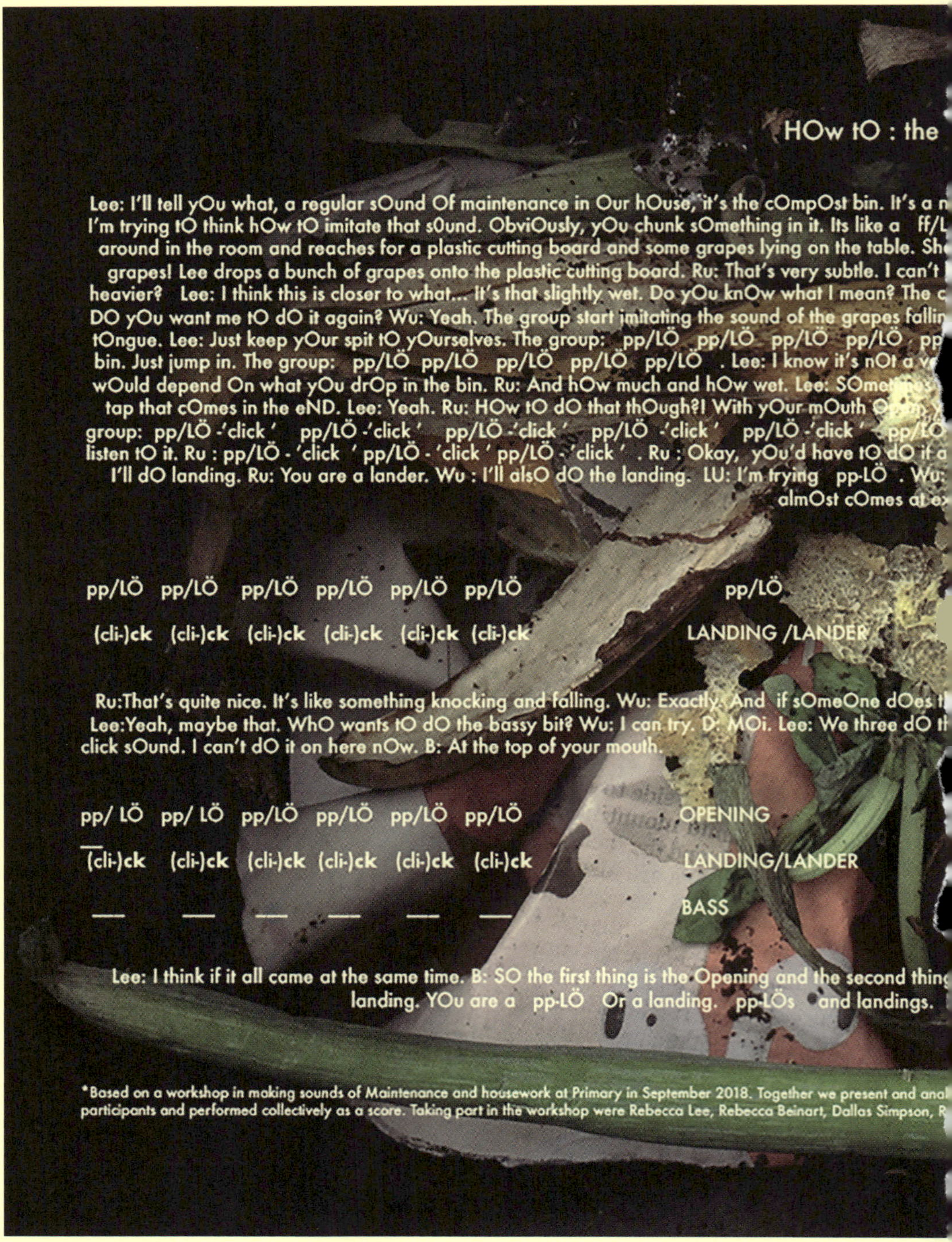

To Compose the Compost, by Nathalie Wuerth, 2019.

Method

- Find a time to meet with others for around two hours to talk about your domestic work, how you categorise it and when it happens throughout the day.

- Using a piece of paper, draw a clock and detail your domestic work routines. Share with the group. Look for differences and similarities in how people understand their domestic chores and how this helps you understand and value this aspect of everyday life.

- As a group, think about how you could bring together your different daily routines into a collective score that includes all of the different work done over a 24-hour period. At key moments during the day, such as getting up, there may be many different types of domestic work happening at about the same time. Depending on your group, there may be fewer tasks at night.

- Meet again and invite a voice coach or someone who knows how to help train your voice. Do a series of voice exercises to loosen up the body and extend the vocal range.

- In smaller groups, test how you would vocalise some of the domestic chores detailed in the earlier workshop. What would a coffee boiler sound like? How could you impersonate a vacuum cleaner? Practise these sounds together, help one another experiment with ways to make sounds with your voice and mouth.

- Using the score as a guide, start developing particular sounds related to the score and see how these can work in unison.

- Practice these together until you have found a way to vocalise the score. How long the score is, is up to you.

- Advertise the cleaning choir in your local neighbourhood. Invite people to book a vocal cleaning of their home.

Leftovers

You might want to set up other cleaning choirs to see what the different range of domestic work is like among people with different experiences. What can this tell us about the different ways domestic work is devalued? After a number of home cleaning chores you might want to find out how the home felt after the performance? What are the effects of collective choral cleaning? Rather than follow the domestic routines of the group, you might decide as a choir to focus on one type of domestic work, rather like today's cleaning companies.

Cleaning continues — *Gunilla Lundahl*

Looking back at all the responses that the questions generated over the two years, you can see how they interweave with each other *(see This is how it began → p. 39).* You can sense the way they came alive when they were combined, how they gathered meaning and fed from each other. And also, how unexpected learning was formed that could be developed in new contexts. The wish to create a considered dialogue with the locality and new strategies in response to the community's needs was kept alive from the viewpoint of the home. Is a home no more than a shelter and only for survival? Or is it a place dreamt of, absent, split, outsourced or forever coming into being?

Exhibition view: Mierle Laderman Ukeles, *Touch Sanitation*, 2015.

The starting point was the work *Touch Sanitation* by Mierle Laderman Ukeles from 1977–1980. With an outstretched hand and a *thank you* to all those who clean the dirt, slush and overflow from all the wear and tear of public environments, for their invisible work that is often cleaned away. An artwork that made visible the work that allows the city to shine and gleam and lets ourselves believe that we are civilised when we are not drowning in our own waste. Work that normally happens in the background, in the shadows, in the alleys, in the hidden spaces. Work that allows us to keep our own self-respect without needing to respect the bodies that serve us. Cleaning and clearing, organising the city. This is a labour that is as invisible on the large scale as it is on the small. A work that is seldom reached by an outstretched hand like Ukeles'. Her artwork provided a perfect beginning for the coming research in Home Works.

Many of the exhibitions during the programme moved in and out of the sphere of the home. In *Open House*, the third exhibition that took place in the old laundry, there were three distinct speculations revolving around what home can mean in a wider context.

Anna Ihle had listened to the washing conversations that took place in the part of the building that still operates as a laundry, where not only the washing was mulled over but also private comments between neighbours and trivial problems were aired. Chats that were illustrated by filming the washing tumbling around behind the machine door. The video reminded us of how practical functions in the home easily flow over into the public, which at the same time serves as a kind of glue between the inhabitants, and then how these chats disappear into the private. A loss for casual solidarity and recognition, and a meaningful space for ventilation and a quarrel is closed. Ihle supplemented her work with a huge, heavy, dark and impressive textile, woven from her used clothes. Clothes that she no longer desired or could keep. A tapestry that also embraced the perspective that clothes represent the most wasteful components within society *(see Storage matters ↝ p. 237)*.

Hiwa K's remarkable hybrid of a desert lodge and a one-room apartment built in concrete offered a playful and ironic commentary on the housing culture of the West, set in contrast to forms of co-living in families or groups, common in other parts of the world. Living conditions in Western cultures tend to concentrate on the individual, and separate or isolate people. Hiwa K's work brings the colonial eye into focus. He helps us question the Swedish living culture that was moulded in concrete during the 1960s and 1970s, and is now falling to pieces. With no new contract in sight, Swedish social welfare is privatised. Council housing is being sold off.

Home care was the third theme that examined the porous walls of the home. This time made visible through the practice of Bolaget *(see Who needs an umbrella when you cannot leave your home?* *p. 135)*. It was a cooperation established between the artist Lilian Lindblad Domec and Thomas Gilek. They met through the home care system, when Lindblad Domec needed help. Their cooperation was problematic in relation to the rules and forms of the home care system in Stockholm. A system that operated under the presumption that it should only serve a technical function, not be an act of friendship and reciprocal giving and taking. This artwork also provided an opportunity to include more actors with responsibility and work in home care. For instance, the trade unions, activists and the social commissioner in Stockholm were offered a platform for political action and discussion. The exhibition also followed the branches of the home care service near to Konsthall C, by giving voice to fifteen residents who received assistance from the service. Giving them a channel to reflect on how they can defend their integrity and the power over their private home.

Exhibition view: *Open House*, 2015.
Photo: Ola Bergengren.

A section of the exhibition was revived at a few more locations in the area in order to give more space to the local aspect. The presentation of Lindblad Domec's films also inspired the Home Works programme to make a link to Lars Gustaf Andersson's and John Sundholm's research on early immigrant filmmakers in Sweden, who witnessed and wanted to document how Swedish doors were shut for refugees. This collaboration later became the subject of another part of the programme.
With Ciara Phillips the exhibition space became light and unrestricted with a large

open floor and work tables, and an invitation to visitors to join a workshop. Come and create the material! Use words and pictures as starting points for dialogue and togetherness.

Konsthall C was included in the housing policy programme that was inaugurated in the 1940s, which was first put into practice in the area. At that time it was evident that the creation of a democratic society had to include access to communal spaces for different cultural activities, meetings, weaving, carpentry and hobbies. This was included in the rent. The home was more than just an apartment. What was then seen as a public utility is now given to the market; the body of the community is homeless.

Exhibition view: Ciara Phillips, *Warm Friends, Cold Cash*, 2015–2016. Photo: Ola Bergengren.

With Phillips this vision of a democratic society was paid another visit. Creativity was centred as the irreplaceable resource for the survival of democracy. Neighbours and distant guests, old and young, pros and amateurs were invited to a programme of workshops. With aprons, big cans of paint and silkscreen frames, she encouraged visitors to take charge of their world with the help of hand-printed words and images. To produce posters and prints that respected a word's ambiguity and strength, and using techniques that emphasised these words visually, vividly and effectively in this public room. Techniques, possibilities and inspiration were introduced through her own work, which was pasted up on the walls, before it was covered by investigations of power and possibilities offered by the visitors' creations. A demonstration of the strength embedded in a room for collective thought. A project made both for local empowerment and for building wider networks between suburbs. Could we reclaim the Swedish social welfare vision of democracy through housing that included workshops such as this?

What represents the content of work done at home? When domestic work was subjected to rationalisation and commercialisation, the idea of the housewife as a productive person was transformed into the figure of a consumer and she lost control of the necessary work in her home. The market took over. This shift was questioned by Kristina Schultz in her graduation exhibition at Konstfack University

Exhibition view: *Expansions of Homecraft*, 2016. Photo: Ola Bergengren.

Exhibition view: *Back to the Future Part 2*, 2016.

of Arts, Crafts and Design. How can you bring back the production of necessities to the home? She transformed her three-person household by removing everything it contained and began to produce these necessary objects herself. She managed fairly well with the acceptance of her family, and the process was documented through photos and presented as part of Home Works. Schultz could argue with confidence for the statement that there is much to learn when we delve into the foundations of our real needs. Schultz's revolution was both drastic and cosy. A provocation formulated against the mechanisation of the kitchen *(see 100 days of need and greed, and a potential recipe for change ➝ p. 61).*

But where are the children? Who listens to them? Where are they allowed to be? *Back to the Future* was an exhibition with a past at Konsthall C. Jenny Berntsson and Seçil Yaylali took their starting point from a question concerning the role that children are allowed to play in today's society. They worked between direct action and art as their form of research. During the exhibition period in spring 2016, they invited 500 children from preschools in the area to visit Konsthall C in small groups. They were made welcome and given the right to cross the threshold into this world of art. Yaylali and Berntsson had prepared the ground for the exhibition when, earlier that winter, they met with the children's teachers at their preschools. Together they held a three-day workshop and seminar on the idea of the preschool as a place for children to work together on their own experiences of home and to explore the political meaning of home from their point of view. The children's book *Katitzi* written by Katarina Taikon[1] about her childhood experiences in a Roma community, was presented as an underlying narrative with room for empathy and insight. In addition, the teachers were offered tools to encourage the children's exploration and help them build a dream of their own home using colour and form. They made objects that they could bring to the art space together with their thoughts, which they could share with friends and parents

Exhibition view: Joanna Lombard, *The Room is the Third Pedagogue*, 2016.
Photo: Ola Bergengren.

[1] Katarina Taikon, Katitzi, (1969), (Stockholm: Natur & Kultur Allmänlitteratur, 2015).

(see A real sourdough → p. 114). The project was an expression of respect for children and their capacity to create ideas for the future. It was also a visualisation of the responsibility invested in preschools to pursue a dialogue with children about the idea of the world rooted in the home.

Since spring 2016, respect for children as responsible opinion builders has taken unforeseen proportions. One aspect of this is the idea of learning and getting an education for a world to come. This topic is also handled by Fridays for Future[2] in an interesting way. They are taking their education into their own hands to a significant extent. Perhaps the time for a discussion around alternative pedagogies is now? It is a topic that disappeared with the discussion on free schools. Where is the freedom in pedagogy?

Pedagogy is a more or less a straightforward form of execution of power. Children's liberation process is the essence in most writings about alternative pedagogies during the 20th century. Some of it has penetrated into the school system today, but the overall discussion – including society, the idea of humanity, freedom and utopias – has not appeared on the horizon as anything more than words.

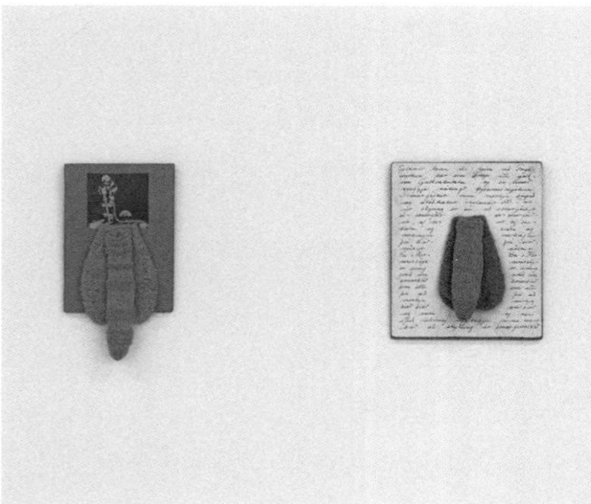

Hildur Hákonardóttir, *Úr sögu mannsins / From the History of Man*, 1971. Part of *Expansions of Homecraft*. Konsthall C, 2016. Photo: Ola Bergengren.

The priority of this discussion was clarified by Joanna Lombard through her cooperation with children from Martinskolan, a Rudolf Steiner school near to Konsthall C. Their clear, happy voices were sounding against the darkness of Lombard's personal background. Is there a pedagogical approach that is good for everyone? How can the closed doors of schools be opened?

The possibilities for the co-housing projects to reshape housework and broaden the responsibility for these tasks was never a topic for an exhibition in Home Works. Other perspectives came

[2] 'Fridays for Future is a global movement that began in August 2018, when 15-year-old Greta Thunberg and other young activists sat in front of the Swedish parliament every school day for three weeks, to protest against the lack of action on the climate crisis ... soon it went viral.' Published online at: https://fridaysforfuture.org/ (Accessed 2 May 2020).

to the fore. Research from the Women's Day Off in Iceland in 1975 offered working material and documents for an ongoing dialogue on feminist strategies to make work at home more tangible and thus recognised. The seminars, publications, films, dinners and walks were all equally important to the programme, with the touch of improvisation that was key to handling it.

Attention was also paid to the perspective of comfort as an element in the Home Works programme. Following the backlash against feminism in the 1980s, some could find solace in a growing interest in gardening, cultivation and craft. Hildur Hákonardóttir, an artist from Iceland, has come to represent this with her collection of documents from the Women's Day Off and textile art she made during the feminist uprising of the 1970s. She is one of Iceland's most renowned artists who brought the gender struggle of the Women's Day Off to the fore with the help of the 1,000-year-old tradition of weaving *(see Revolutionary threads → p. 211)*. Her practice focused on the awareness of the contributions of women to society and then moved on to questions of sustainability, and what our earth can bear. Her concern is now directed towards the most pressing issue. How will we access food? Who is responsible not only for the way it is cultivated but also for how we consume it at home?

The persistence of society was illuminated in many ways through the exhibitions and meetings. For example, inspiration came from Casco Art Institute and the Dutch artist group ASK! (*Actie Schone Kunsten*), with their attempt to form a 'household commons'.[3] Dady de Maximo presented a luxury fashion show with clothes created from life vests that symbolised those who had drowned in the Mediterranean Sea. Migration politics were also raised in the practice of Trampoline House[4] and their work developing a space for being together that was set up by migrants and activists from Copenhagen who were trying to create forms of asylum for refugees outside their closed camps *(see Listening to the sea → p. 183)*.

A course and historical reminder of artistic methods with the aim of investigating terms of work was offered by Stephan Dillemuth in his workshop *Workers' Variety Show Looks for Members!* It was the background for an exhibition that exposed a body dissected by work, the same work that appears both in the factory and the home.

3 Binna Choi and Maiko Tanaka, eds. *Grand Domestic Revolution Handbook*, (Utrecht: Casco and Valiz, 2014).

4 Trampoline House, works to ensure an integration that is sustainable – economically, democratically and socially. Published online at: https://www.trampolinehouse.dk/ (Accessed 2 May 2020).

Exhibition view: Stephan Dillemuth, *Workers' Variety Show Looks for Members!*, 2016.

Towards the end of the programme, students from the Royal Institute of Technology presented a study on a potential city planning process for the area; an exploration that over the next few years developed into a new research project: *Bomassan*.[5] It focused on the district as a place for solidarity and construction of a society based on the needs of everyday life.

The outside world flooded into Konsthall C during the two years Home Works lasted. Through exhibitions and events, a world was gently and imaginatively assembled and cared for by Jenny Richards and Jens Strandberg in collaboration with Anna Ahlstrand. My expectations were exceeded. Both in terms of content and the methods employed to make the questions I had initially posed come to life. Reliance and hope. A wonderful adventure.

[5] Bomassan is a research project exploring questions around city planning, densification, local democracy, neighbourhood engagement and social art practices. Published online at: http://www.bomassan.org (Accessed 3 May 2020).

The ongoing maintenance of Home Works — *Jenny Richards and Jens Strandberg*

When we return to Konsthall C, some years after the conclusion of the Home Works programme, the space still holds a sense of familiarity. The tiled floored with undulations your feet can remember. The low concrete plinth where washing machines once rested. The stains on the office tables, relics of Ciara Phillips' screen printing workshop, where you can still make out the words 'Home Works Is Also Work'.

The sliding glass door to the kitchen/office, where you can always find smudges of dirty hand prints from visitors and staff. As we wander through the space we are reminded of Konsthall C's history, its past exhibitions, but also the cracks, holes and precarity that the organisation has had to navigate over the years.

In 2010, when Anna Ahlstrand and Kim Einarsson took over Konsthall C, they felt excited. They wandered through the building, opening rooms that led onto others. The building felt like a space filled with possibilities. Disused rooms were waiting to be recycled, reused and inhabited. Ahlstrand, who continued to work at Konsthall C and who collaborated with us during Home Works, told us that by the time Home Works began, these rooms had started to be closed off. The spaces that she and Einarsson had uncovered were once again locked away. It was not just the unused spaces that had been rearranged. The communal laundry next to the art space had also undergone changes. The space where numerous machines once stood in a row were now individualised and closed off in separate rooms, accessible through a booking system by means of a digital key-tag. Even our storage room had been closed off and relocated. Yet, while the building's architecture had been exposed to changes, co-opted, and individualised, it still provided a stage for temporary gatherings and for moments of collectivity. A place where exhibitions and events could unfold.

Walking through the space we are reminded of writing funding applications, stringing together small budgets and exhibition installations. We are reminded of late night sessions of fixing, washing and cleaning the space. The labour of running the Home Works programme that was constantly reflected in the large mirror installed in the ceiling of the art space. The mirror, produced years before by the Malmö Free Women's University (MFK),[1] has become a permanent fixture in the art space. It has moulded itself into the existing architecture, mirroring the dirty, grey and white tiles of the floor. In these reflections, the mirror reminds both visitors and staff of Konsthall C's history and of the maintenance labour that is often swept away and hidden in art spaces. (Conveniently, it also covers up some large holes in the ceiling.)

Returning to Konsthall C in the years after we inhabited the space can feel like something of a homecoming. But what critical and meaningful reflections can be discerned in this homecoming? How did Home Works reflect the societal structures that it intended to alter? What traces of the Home Works programme can be found today, alongside Ciara Phillips' stained tables? What are the leftovers from

[1] See http://mfkuniversitet.blogspot.com (Accessed March 2020).

the collective work and can these intangible traces be detected? Or are they forever embedded in the infrastructure and invisible to visitors? Konsthall C's organisational model sees an artistic director limited to two years of employment in order to provide a platform for new directions and experimentation. With this in mind, should there be leftovers from one artistic programme to the next? Is it fair to expect leftovers from one programme to still be taken care of when you leave?

Looking up at MFK's large mirror, this text intends to reflect on this past home and grasp some of the lessons we learnt during the Home Works programme; lessons that, like the recipes in this Cooking Book, do not need to be tied to their site of germination.

Curatorial cooking

> The thinking of the International Wages for Housework Campaign is of course the idea that you have to turn the table, instead of reproducing capital you are reproducing the struggle, and instead of cooking for yourself, you cook for the struggle.
>
> **— Silvia Federici, in conversation with writers, Stockholm, 2020.**

We like to think of our approach to Home Works as a practice of curatorial cooking, as it was a process of experimenting with and mixing together diverse elements in order to produce forms of nourishment. These were then collectively tasted and explored with a particular focus on the reproductive side of curating and exhibition making. This means focusing on the labour that can often be hard to exhibit or present, but through which all public activities are made possible. It is the work of many people, based on temporary social relations. For example, home visits and conversations with artists, cooking for openings, valuing the playfulness and care that were involved in our relationships with collaborators. Numerous workshops also took place behind closed doors, as well as the administrative work to fundraise, budget and secure the future of the programme and art space. We worked on exploring how Home Works could embody feminist ideas of revalorising this reproductive labour within the programme. What was the invisible labour of producing and maintaining Home Works at Konsthall C and can this book contribute to critically articulating and reflecting it?

The recipes presented here should be read as tools for reproducing more sustainable art spaces, socially, emotionally and economically. Instead of emphasising the exhibitions and the capital (both symbolic and economic) that the programme garnered, we hope this Cooking Book shows other strategies born from artistic processes that evolve without a predefined outcome.

When reflecting on this method of curatorial cooking, we have found Bojana Kunst's questioning of 'art projects' helpful. In her writing she stresses the importance of creating art that works without an already determined goal. Projects, she says, work towards a 'retrospective future'. It needs to be planned in advance and therefore can only reach an 'already-projected future'. Projects work with 'a horizon of expectation, with a lot of possibilities but no actual change.'[2] Rather than a project being located in the present, it needs to look towards (or project) its future conclusion, and is born with an inherent mortal deadline. The end needs to be projected as a chronological continuity from its beginning point.[3]

Since the Home Works programme thematically focused on reproductive labour, which is often described as work without end, we wanted to encourage art production that also questioned a project-oriented structure. Instead of working towards a predetermined end, we encouraged artists to trust the process and the intangible, unknown possibilities and relations that a processual focus might open up. In many cases the collaborations and artistic productions that were generated happened in a spontaneous way without prior knowledge of what the outcome (if any) might be.

However, the conflict in the Home Works programme was that process-led modes of collaboration and production, do not suit the way funding structures work. Funders often require artists and producers to describe the perceived outcome of their research in the application. While believing in the transformative and pedagogical potential of our way of working, one of the challenges we faced was to square this with raising the funding necessary for our survival. This is a struggle we still experience today. Funders and funding structures have done little to move towards a more long-term, process-led funding structure. Many funding bodies in Sweden and elsewhere, operate within a logic that includes concrete outcomes and short-term results.

That said, Home Works was temporarily sitting within the structure of Konsthall C, where artistic programmes are limited to a two-year period. While we could have tried to secure open ended possibilities for our commissions and

2 Bojana Kunst, "The Project Horizon: On the Temporality of Making", *Le Journal des Laboratoires*, (2011). Published online at: http://www.leslaboratoires.org/en/ctxnode/636/all, (Accessed 1 March 2020).

3 Ibid.

collaborations, they were enclosed within an overarching structure that was limited. The temporality of the programme was mirrored in the employment structure that consisted of short-term contracts. Anna Ahlstrand who had worked as a producer for seven years prior to our beginning still lacked job security, an appropriate job title for the work she was doing and a wage that reflected her work of maintaining and running the art space.

Initially, in order to literally draw out some of these multiple expectations and the reality of the working conditions, we collaborated with the designers Maryam Fanni and Rikard Heberling to develop a visual profile for the Home Works programme. We discussed how to create a visual language that would communicate our activities and at the same time clearly convey that Home Works was a temporary guest at Konsthall C. We were keen to use our visual communication to try and point towards the complex and entwined relationship of temporality and continuity. Together, they developed a graphic profile and a logo that used the original design of Konsthall C; the same typeface, font size and style, but with the title of the programme, *Home Works*, within brackets, pointing towards the temporality of the programme. Brackets indicate a side note to the main point, that may not fit the dominant logic of the sentence (or in this case art space). Moreover, the bracketed logo of the Home Works programme also pointed towards the position of housework within capitalist society; a type of *bracketed labour* that is never fully valued as 'real' work.

Hospitality

> Hospitality, on the other hand, requires long-term practices that allow for an alternative give and take. Would this imply that we should work towards conditions that allow our guests to be able to invite us (back)? And what if the guests want to stay?
> **— Ruth Sonderegger[4]**

> The real question – one that [Charles] Esche asks indirectly when he reflects on the capacities institutions can offer and whether an institution can encourage the guest (the Other) to ask questions that

[4] Ruth Sonderegger, "Curatorial Hospitality?", *Cultures of the Curatorial 3: Hospitality: Hosting Relations in Exhibitions*, eds. Beatrice von Bismarck and Benjamin Meyer-Krahmer (Berlin: Sternberg Press, 2015), pp. 19–27.

> match the resources – is whose requests and whose desires are
> being considered?
> **— Maja Ćirić**[5]

Sandi Hilal's text in this Cooking Book describes how hospitality can have political and transformative potential when the roles of guest and host are not fixed. Instead, she calls for hosting where the roles can be switched and exchanged. Within the Home Works programme, we were constantly learning new things about the agency of the guest and of the host. For us, these roles were shifting positions, which was made clear in the beginning of the programme; as we were invited to be the guest directors of Konsthall C, while at the same time becoming the hosts of the institution and consequently the public faces of the organisation.

The role of the host is often assumed to be the curator, the person who decides who shall be the guest. This type of host has also been known as a sort of gatekeeper. A person that decides who gets to exhibit and who does not. It was important for us to see how we could rethink hospitality and address the power of the curator within the institution.

When reflecting on our roles, Anthony Huberman's writing has been useful, as he envisages a different role for curators. Instead of the curator being a host or gatekeeper in the art world, he contends that curators are not hosts at all, but should always be guests within an artist's practice. The curators are guests for example, at the artist's studio and in the artist's practice in developing their work. The transformation of curators from hosts to guests allows for new perspectives and insights into how curatorial and artistic practices can find different ways of working and learning from each other; ways that do not reproduce the power dynamics of the curator as the decisive host and the artist as a grateful guest. Weibke Gronemeyer continues this argument by asking how these shifts in power and roles can be extended to exhibitions.[6] She calls for exhibitions that produce situations of hospitality in which the artist and curator can escape the hospitable condition and instead join in the learning and sharing experiences of a guest.[7]

5 Maja Ćirić, "The (Un)spoken Abuse: Curatorial Hospitality through the Lens of Criticality", *Cultures of the Curatorial 3: Hospitality: Hosting Relations in Exhibitions*, eds. Beatrice von Bismarck and Benjamin Meyer-Krahmer (Berlin: Sternberg Press, 2015), pp. 205–206.

6 Weibke Gronemeyer, "Competing Agencies", in *Curatorial 3: Hospitality: Hosting Relations in Exhibitions*, eds. Beatrice von Bismarck and Benjamin Meyer-Krahmer (Berlin: Sternberg Press, 2015), p. 91.

7 Ibid. p. 91.

Throughout Home Works we tried to inhabit the role of curators as temporary guests in artistic practices, drawing on our own training as artists and our experience of community organising. We wanted the programme to facilitate the shifting of roles so that staff and visitors could move between host, guest and collaborator. Whereas curators commonly position themselves outside the artwork or the artist's practice, we wanted to find ways to dive right into it, often performing within works or building a sculpture as per the specifications of the artist.

This desire to push beyond dual relationships refers back to our introduction and reference to David Harvey's work around the concept of the 'right to the city', which insists on the vital importance of a communal right to access and contribute to the ways in which an (art) space develops and for whom it is intended. Through the Home Works programme we continuously wanted to consider the possibilities for building communities in which everyone has the right to occupy a variety of roles and contribute in different ways. We see these changing roles as part of a symbiotic relationship where the artist's practice influenced how we developed the programme, and the collaborators and public involved in the artist's commission shaped the way they developed their work.

One key critique of hospitality as exercised within art institutions relates to what happens when the exhibition or collaboration is over. Curator and critic Maja Ćirić contends that within hospitality a form of

> invisible abuse comes after the curatorial project has expired and the hospitable situation is over: when the guests are sent away from the hegemonic centre without resources to exploit their newly acquired symbolic capital. This is exactly how hospitality (is) employed in … exhibitions – to confirm existing territory by keeping the potential enemy under control.
>
> **— Maja Ćirić**[8]

Looking back on Home Works, there are many moments when hosting and hospitality could have been pushed further. One way we tried to work against the violence of

[8] Maja Ćirić, "The (Un)spoken Abuse: Curatorial Hospitality through the Lens of Criticality", *Cultures of the Curatorial 3: Hospitality: Hosting Relations in Exhibitions*, eds. Beatrice von Bismarck and Benjamin Meyer-Krahmer (Berlin: Sternberg Press, 2015).

hospitality that is encouraged and promoted through short-term project funding was to insist on hospitality not ending after the programme had finished. We worked on securing a rent-free contract, and on developing Ahlstrand's position from a producer to a managing director – a permanent position that would act as an artistic facilitator for the multiple hosts, actors and communities involved within Konsthall C *(see How to create a public home ↝ p. 239)*. Her role was concerned with maintaining, caring and nourishing the social relations of Konsthall C and the surrounding community, beyond limited artistic programmes and directions. Rather than operating as a singular host, we hoped that her role would facilitate and support the multiplication of hosts at Konsthall C. In practice, this meant exploring how to create an infrastructure that would allow people to come together not just as guests in a temporary programme, but by hosting, self-organising and influencing the organisation. This is something both ourselves and Ahlstrand have continued to work with; investigating in what ways grass-roots organising can shift and change institutional structures.

Dishwasher

> To be against forms of power and violence that are concealed under signs of happiness does not necessarily mean becoming unhappy, even if it does mean refusing to go along with things by showing signs of getting along. It is striking that Shulamith Firestone's 'dream action' for the women's liberation movement is 'a smile boycott', at which declaration, all women would instantly abandon their 'pleasing' smiles, henceforth only smiling when something pleased them'. To refuse the promise of happiness is to refuse the demand that you show signs of happiness. For Firestone, this means a shift of orientation; it means changing one's bodily habits: 'In my own case, I had to train myself out of the phony smile, which is like a nervous tic on every teenage girl'.
>
> **— Sarah Ahmed[9]**

When looking around Konsthall C for physical evidence of our habitation, verification

9 Sarah Ahmed, *The Promise of Happiness*, (Durham: Duke University Press, 2010), p. 69.

can be found in the kitchen and in the whirring dishwasher we bought during Home Works. On the front of it sits a sticker that reads 'The Revolution Begins at Home' encased in a small drawing of a figure that was used as the backdrop for the *Back to the Future* exhibition in 2016. Looking at the dishwasher brings back a feeling of success. It remained! It is still used and useful. It indicates a small tangible change. But, what is this desire to have tangible leftovers, like the dishwasher? Why can we not attribute similar feelings of accomplishment to the other more intangible side of our work? For example, the social relations and the reproductive labour we have so consistently emphasised. Is there something of a contradiction in our attempt to produce this book, which tries to create tangible traces from artworks that were all the more powerful because of their intangibility, because they boldly evaded normalised modes of exhibition presentation and dissemination? Modes that we believe fuel individualistic capitalist production and consumption of art. Modes that are reproduced by art institutions and their funders.

One way of moving beyond our inclination to look for concrete traces of our work, or force reductive outcomes onto complex processes, has been to think about the pedagogical emphasis throughout Home Works. We can see this perspective in line with a growing field of research into curatorial practices and art institutions that focus their attention on the pedagogical potential of their work. In 2010, Paul O'Neill and Mick Wilson edited the book *Curating and the Educational Turn*, which focused on art that views learning as an integral part of exhibition-making, rather than as a side product or afterthought. Throughout Home Works we tried to give space to practices that explored the potential of the art space as a site for learning. Through our collaborations we wanted to investigate the home which we see as our first site of schooling. We wanted to transform curating from an instrumental mode and instead focus on the learning processes it provides.[10] Irit Rogoff describes how these processual curatorial investigations often involve a 'low-key transformative process'.[11] The remnants or traces of these practices are often not easy to track down but can be described as situations where people are left with food for thought; new learning, knowledge, or unplanned discoveries. These intangible educational leftovers hold nutritious social value that at first might appear immaterial and hard to grasp. For us,

[10] Paul O'Neill and Mick Wilson, *Curating and the Educational Turn*, (London: Open Editions/de Appel, 2010), p. 18.

[11] Irit Rogoff "Turning" in *Curating and the Educational Turn* (London: Open Editions/de Appel, 2010), p. 39.

Home Works and the making of this Cooking Book has been a way to give weight to these vernacular learning processes. In contrast to academia or other formal learning situations, in which knowledge is an object to learn, we insisted on creating moments where people could value their own experiential knowledge and share their learning with others. In this way, we hope to show that learning and knowledge are indeed material, as they create social situations that bring bodies with different knowledge and experiences together in space.

Haunting /nostalgia

> Those who cannot remember the past are condemned to have it resold to them forever.
> **— Mark Fisher[12]**

While approaching the task of reflecting, it was suggested to us that we might be speaking nostalgically about the programme, for one's memory tends to highlight some connections and edit out others. But, if we take seriously that we can only ever inhabit our reflection as a form of nostalgia, does that disavow reflecting at all?

Svetlana Boym writes, 'Nostalgia is not only a longing for a lost time and lost home but also for friends who once inhabited it.'[13] Our attempts to research and question the home from political, cultural, social, aesthetic and economic perspectives, drew on our personal experiences of the home as a way to inform our ideas. Our lived experience could, in this way, be described as a form of nostalgia, or embodied knowledge, that informed our speculations on what a home might be, and what other ways of living we could imagine. This method of researching that begins with personal experiences was also extended to our collaborators and contributors so that the notion of the home could be reimagined and deconstructed from multiple and diverse perspectives. Reflecting back on this method requires us to pose the question: who was invited to contribute, and who was not? While wanting to deconstruct our understanding of the home, as informed by *Folkhemmet* (the People's Home), how much did we reproduce the same things we were trying to critique? What exclusions was the home of Home Works reproducing?

[12] Mark Fisher, *Ghosts of my Life*, (Winchester: Zero books, 2014), p. 25.
[13] Svetlana Boym, *The Future of Nostalgia*, (New York: Basic Books, 2001), p. 1.

We have referred to Home Works' inhabitation at Konsthall C as a 'public home', yet, during the programme we neglected defining what this actually meant *(see How to create a public home ↪ p. 239)*. It is only now, with an opportunity to reflect and learn, that we are starting to understand what principles and ideas this home consisted of, and how it might be a useful format for rethinking art spaces. In a way the public home could be described as a liminal place, neither a private nor a public dwelling, neither permanent nor temporary. Perhaps what we were trying to create was suffused with a nostalgic longing for a lost collective home, a common meeting place in a city which, over time, has been taken away, privatised, removed.

Leftovers

> The fact is that as I was trying to find the cause of my lack of joy ... What I missed was something which could positively generate emotions, a strong imaginary, which could open different scenarios. I needed to encounter other questions and new subjects, who desired and were able to effectively think a different world. Therefore, for part of the 80s I continued to wander around, from room to room, in the house of reproduction. Until, at a certain point, I saw the door to the garden, I saw the issue of the earth.
>
> **— Mariarosa Dalla Costa[14]**

While digesting Home Works, we thought of what to do with the remaining parts. What nourishment can we find in the leftovers of the leftovers? What other meals could be cooked with the remnants and who else could they be shared with? While cleaning up is often understood to include getting rid of leftovers, we wanted to try and save and take care of this material. Do we keep it? Are you sure you cannot eat any more? Shall I put them in the same bowl for your lunch tomorrow? The recipes in this book were conceived during this process of cleaning and organising, in the conversations over the kitchen sink. They are some of the leftovers of Home Works, of Konsthall C and of us. Leftovers from our curatorial cooking that

[14] Mariarosa Dalla Costa, "The Door to the Garden" (lecture), 2002. Published online at: https://www.generation-online.org/p/fpdallacosta1.htm (Accessed 1 March 2020).

we felt needed to be shared and composted. Much like cooking, composting involves mixing together ingredients and seeing what nutrients develop. The key difference is time, cooking can be a relatively short process with a plate filled with food in a matter of hours or minutes. Composting, on the other hand, needs a lot of time. It needs time for the material to slowly break down and form anew. In this sense, our composting has only just begun. Social value, like the nutritional value of compost, accrues over a long time. Time necessary to transform leftovers, by-products and unused materials and ideas into new soil. Included in these leftovers is the emotional labour of those that were a part of Home Works, the sleepless nights, the stressful times, and the domestic labour of maintaining the art space: the emotions, conflicts and reproductive labour that enabled us to produce the Home Works programme and reproduce ourselves. In this way the composting of these leftovers is a sort of breaking down of the breakdowns. Not so much as a way of making sense, but rather of dwelling on this material as an essential ingredient in all recipes. The usual side-products of daily life, rejections, devalorisations, grief, that are hidden away in order for other more affirmative parts to be visible. Reflecting back, Home Works was, in a way, an attempt to allow artists and participants to bring the struggles of everyday life, rejections, depressions and lack of money, into the art space. Our hope was to encourage artists to walk the line between life and art, in order to see if our individual struggles are in fact collective.

We wanted to encourage an art practice that saw the power in the powerlessness of this material. A practice that takes its lessons from the International Wages for Housework Movement and the women in Iceland who in 1975 had a 'day off' just to prove the indispensability of their labour. A practice that does not hide the fact that it balances two to four part-time positions to make ends meet, or never has a secure housing situation. We wanted to encourage artists to acknowledge and draw from their daily reproductive struggles as the main material for their commissions. A material that we can both learn and create from. If this material was used more in the production of exhibitions what kind of soil, or foundation for an art space would these compost artworks and exhibitions generate?

Sifting through our leftovers, the gaps in our working and in this book become evidently clear. One critical area left unexplored within the Home Works programme concerns how we thought about the politics and economics of cooking and food production. As we have learnt from Indigenous struggles and the work of Vandava Shiva, Maria Mies and Ariel Salleh – key initiators of the ecofeminist movement – a feminist political struggle cannot be waged without questioning ecology, agriculture, seed sovereignty, and land rights. Concerns which feminist groups the world over are fighting urgent battles around, as food production is further industrialised, polluting our bodies and the soil.

It is here that we leave you, so that when you cook these recipes you might start to think with and beyond the focus outlined in this Cooking Book. Beyond *Preparing the Kitchen* and our labour conditions and art production. Beyond *Cooking* and its collective processes. Beyond *Eating* and communal ways of experiencing art. Beyond *Cleaning Up* and the composting of leftovers, to wider organising with art and domestic work.

In the introduction we describe what it is like to enter Konsthall C. Now, when it is time to exit, we wander around the art space, from room to room. Like Mariarosa Dalla Costa we are opening and closing doors in the house of reproduction, to look to the garden and realise the plight of the earth is central to our reproductive struggles.

TIMELINE

TOUCH SANITATION
an exhibition by Mierle Laderman Ukeles, and *Reproduction, Education and Black Milk* by Joanna Lombard

- SURR SURR: monthly film club
  - The Gleaners, Agnès Varda
  - Bieffekten, Tina-Marie Qwiberg, Mikael Qwiberg and Jean Fredric Axelsson
- FILM SCREENING: by Emma Hedditch and Marina Vishmidt of the London-based Cinenova working Group.
  - *Jeanne Dielman, 23 quai du Commerce, 1080 Bruxelles,* Chantal Ackerman
  - *Bred and Born,* Joanna Davis and Mary Pat Leech
  - *Die Allseitig reduzierte Persönlichkeit – Redupers,* Helke Sander
- Soapbox: Discussion evening at Marabouparken
- Two housewarming dinners
- A konstfika – gathering artists in the local area
- WORKSHOPS
  - Konstfack
  - Dance and Circus School
  - Stockholmsskolan
- Exhibition tour: Mierle Laderman Ukeles
- FILM SCREENING: *The Individual and Collective* by Ed Webb-Ingall and Rehana Zaman.
  - *Things that Mother Never Told Us!* Carry Gorney
  - *Some Women, Other Women and all the Bittermen*, Rehana Zaman
  - *Orbital Re-enactments*, Joanna Lombard
- *Horrible Mixtures* a performance and dinner by Stina Nyberg

BACK TO THE FUTURE PART 1
a collaboration with 500 preschool children

- Exhibition tour: Erika Stark
- Lecture/presentation: Moa Tunström
- Film screening: *U-Barn* by Öyvind Fahlström

OPEN HOUSE
an exhibition with Anna Ihle, Hiwa K, Gunilla Lundahl and Bolaget – Lilian Lindblad Domec and Thomas Gilek

- AIRBNB READING CIRCLE 1 at Moa Tunström home in the area:
  - Yvonne Hirdman's Utopia in the Home (1992)
  - Ragnar Thoursie's Sånger från äldreomsorgen (2009)
- Strike! Summer party at Konsthall C
- Film screening: Lilian Domec's 16mm-films hosted by John Sundholm and Lars Gustaf Andersson
- Airbnb reading circle 2 in collaboration with Emily Fahlén at Teresia Bergström's home in the area: Leela Gandhi's *Affective Communities* (2005)
- Film screening: *Factory Complex* by Im Heung Soon

WARM FRIENDS, COLD CASH
an exhibition by Ciara Phillips

- Workshops in collaboration with schools, activist groups, artists as well as passers by and members of the local community
- *Women's Day Off* symposium with speakers: Emma Tolander, Maiko Tanaka, Þorgerður Ólafsdóttir, Becky Forsythe, Heiðar Kari Rannversson, Kamilla Askholm and Dady de Maximo. Respondent: Gunilla Lundahl. Food: Hökarängen's Vegetarian Climate Smart Cooking Group
- Film screening: *Women in Red Stockings* by Halla Kristín Einarsdóttir

WORKERS' VARIETY SHOW LOOKS FOR MEMBERS!
an exhibition by Stephan Dillemuth

- Workshop and party with members of the *Workers' Variety Show Looks for Members!*
- Film screening: *Kuhle Wampe or Who Owns the World?* Bertolt Brecht and Ernst Ottwalt

BACK TO THE FUTURE PART 2
an exhibition by Jenny Berntsson and Seçil Yaylali and 500 preschools children

- Workshops with all of the local pedagogues working in preschools
- Presentation and workshop with Hans Calderas
- Surr surr, *Taikon*, Gellert Tamas and Lawen Mohtadi
- *Washing Time*, a podcast conversation with Mohamed El Abed and Anna Ihle

EXPANSION OF HOMECRAFT
an exhibition with Toncirkeln (Shida Shahabi, Anna Sóley Tryggvadóttir), Kristina Schultz and Hildur Hákonardóttir

- Workshop by Toncirkeln with Martinskolan
- The Home in Home Craft, a symposium with Shida Shahabi, Anna Sóley Tryggvadóttir, Hildur Hákonardóttir, Silvia Federici and Temi Odumosu. Respondents: Jacqueline Hoàng Nguyễn and Anneli Bäckman. Food: Hökarängen's Vegetarian Climate Smart Cooking Group
- Knitting workshop

IMMIGRANT FILMMAKERS
an exhibition by John Sundholm and Lars Gustaf Andersson

- FILM SCREENING:
    - *Jordmannen*, Muammer and Synnöve Özers
    - *Löftet*, Menelaos Carayannis
    - *Monos*, Tensta filmförening and Babis Tsokas
    - *Hägringen*, Cineco and Guillermo Alvarez

THE ROOM IS THE THIRD PEDAGOGUE
an exhibition by Joanna Lombard

- Workshop with Pipsvängens children's choir
- Performance: Pipsvängens children's choir
- Performance: *Mig äger ingen, inte ens jag själv – a Strictly Educational Endeavour*, with students at the Piet Zwart Institute
- Book release: *Ljusbacken*, Joanna Lombard

BOMASSAN
a research project

- SEMINARS
    - Bomassan <3 KTH with Gunilla Lundahl, Rutger Sjögrim, Håkan Forsell
    - Presentation of proposals at Hyresgästföreningen vävstolen

CLAIR THE EAR
an exhibition by Nathalie Wuerth

- Three workshops with a choir
- *Radio-C Dark Matter Broadcast*, Kevin Dooley and Stefan A. Pedersen

CENTRIFUG RELOADED
a group exhibition of artists who had signed up to be part of Centrifug during the Home Works programme

IF THE SEA COULD TALK
Workshops and a fashion show by Dady de Maximo

- Book launch of *Kvinnoledighetsdagen: Domestic Labour, Collectivity, Feminism and Migration*, eds. Jenny Richards and Jens Strandberg

IMAGE CREDITS

p. 8–11 Illustrations by Jenny Richards and Jens Strandberg
p. 12, 14 Konsthall C. Photo: Per Hasselberg
p. 16 Konsthall C entrance. Photo: Konsthall C
p. 22 Hökarängen's Archive, Konsthall C, 2016
p. 26 Women's Day Off Material, Women's History Archives, Iceland, 2016
p. 27 Illustration by Channa Bianca. Women's Day Off Material, Women's History Archives, Iceland, 2016
p. 30 Collage by Konsthall C. Illustration by Sigrún Eldjárn
p. 38 A diagram of Home Works' curatorial structure
p. 47 Ciara Phillips, *Warm Friends, Cold Cash*, 2015 Photo: Ola Bergengren
p. 51, 52 Workshop Photographs from Konsthall C, 2015
p. 62 Kristina Schultz, *100 Days of Need and Greed*, 2015. Photo: Kristina Schultz
p. 64 Kristina Schultz, *100 Days of Need and Greed*, 2015. Photo: Kristina Schultz
p. 88 Mierle Laderman Ukeles, *Touch Sanitation*, (1977–1980), Konsthall C, 2015
p. 94 From *Workers' Variety Show Looks for Members!* 2016. Photo: Stephan Dillemuth
p. 95 *Workers' Variety Show Looks for Members!* Exhibition Poster made during *Warm Friends, Cold Cash*, Stephan Dillemuth in collaboration with Ciara Philips, 2015/2016
p. 97, 98 From *Workers' Variety Show Looks for Members!* Workshops with Stephan Dillemuth, 2016
p. 99–102 From *Workers' Variety Show Looks for Members!* Jimmy Offesson, 2016
p. 104 Joanna Lombard, *The Room is the Third Pedagogue*, 2016
p. 106 Joanna Lombard, *The Room is the Third Pedagogue*, 2016
p. 107, 108 Joanna Lombard, *Parabola Formula*, 2020
p. 110 Joanna Lombard, *The Room is the Third Pedagogue*, 2016
p. 112, 113 Toncirkeln, workshop part of *Expansions of Homecraft*, 2016
p. 115, 116 Jenny Berntsson and Seçil Yaylali, *Back to the Future part 2*, 2016
p. 122 From *Open House*, 2015. Khasrow Hamid Othman with Hiwa K
p. 135 Illustrations by Lilian Lindblad Domec
p. 136 Bolaget (Lilian Lindblad Domec and Thomas Gilek) Photo: Karin van Dijk
p. 138 From Gunilla Lundahl in conversation with Clara Lindblom, part of *Open House*, 2015
p. 139, 140 Illustrations by Lilian Lindblad Domec
p. 141 Postcards by Bolaget (Lilian Lindblad Domec and Thomas Gilek)
p. 143 Gunilla Lundahl, research, part of *Open House*, 2015. Photo: Gunilla Lundahl
p. 147 Housewarming dinner, 2015
p. 149 Large communal macaroni pie. Photo: Jennifer Bailey and James N. Hutchinson
p. 151 Recipes from Hökarängens Vegetarian Climate Smart Cooking Group, 2015
p. 152 From *Warm Friends, Cold Cash* with Stephan Dillemuth and Ciara Phillips, 2015
p. 159–162 Ciara Phillips, *Macaroni with veggie sausages, peas and optional ketchup*, 2020
p. 163 Ciara Phillips, *Warm Friends, Cold Cash*, 2015 Photo: Ola Bergengren. *Warm Friends Cold Cash*, Matilda Flodmark and Sara Kaaman in collaboration with Ciara Phillps, 2015
p. 164 Ciara Phillips, *Warm Friends, Cold Cash*, 2015. Photo: Ola Bergengren

p. 165 Illustration by Channa Bianca
p. 196 Anna Ihle, *Laundry Hour*, a conversation with Mohamed El Abed, 2016
p. 198 Women's Day Off Symposium, 2015
Ciara Phillips, *Warm Friends, Cold Cash*, 2015. Photo: Ola Bergengren
p. 199 From *Warm Friends, Cold Cash*, Nýló in collaboration with Ciara Phillips, 2015
p. 202 Hildur Hákonardóttir in front of *Sunnlenskar konur mótmæla á Alþingi / Country women protesting at Althing*, 1974, during an exhibition tour. Part of *Expansions of Homecraft*. Konsthall C, 2016
p. 208 Magazine of the International Wages for Housework Campaign. Photo: courtesy of Mayday Rooms, London
p. 213 Illustration by Hildur Hákonardóttir
p. 215–229 Hildur Hákonardóttir, *Yes, I dare, can and will*, comic, 1975
p. 230 Women's Day Off Material, Women's History Archives, Iceland, 2016
p. 231 Illustration by Channa Bianca
p. 241 Mapping the Unjust City (Maryam Fanni, Elof Hellström, Åsa Johansson, Sarah Kim and Paula Urbano), *Centrumkartan*, 2020
p. 243 From *Migration Filmmakers*, Lars Gustaf Andersson and John Sundholm, 2016
p. 245, 246 Nathalie Wuerth, *To Compose the Compost*, 2019
p. 248 From *Clair the Ear*, Nathalie Wuerth, 2016
p. 272 The ongoing maintenance of Home Works

All collaged images printed in red throughout the book are created by Johnny Chang and Louise Khadjeh-Nassiri.

THANKS

A heartfelt thanks goes to all the artists and collaborators who created the Home Works programme, you know who you are, we have learnt and continue to learn so much from you!

Thank you to everyone that visited, participated in workshops, viewed and discussed exhibitions, helped us cook when our brains were fried and guided us when we lost track. You helped the programme become a collective pedagogical work and grow roots in Konsthall C and its surroundings.

Thanks to all who contributed to the making of this Cooking Book. Your contribution has been crucial to our thinking and learning. We feel lucky to have been able to share in your work and to share in cooking together, which nourished Home Works' public home and kept the kitchen full of potential. Your contributions taught us about the home, life, pleasure, work and labour, for which we are ever grateful.

The multiple workings of Home Works meant there was a lot of reorganising and reframing necessary in order to translate some of our learnings into this book. We are incredibly grateful for the opportunity to work with Johnny Chang and Louise Khadjeh-Nassiri and for all their hard work. They have playfully and poetically recooked the original design profile of the programme, made by Rikard Heberling and Maryam Fanni.

We would also like to thank Kevin Dooley who copy-edited and Katarina Trodden who proofread the manuscript, both of whom gave this Cooking Book much-needed clarity. We are grateful to Längmanska Culture Fund for funding the book, Anna-Karin Domfors from Interim kultur artist cooperative for administration and Freek Lomme from Onomatopee for his support.

The book would not have been possible without the support of our parents Susan and Martin, Ingegerd and Mats, helping with installing exhibitions or washing up at openings. They were the first in teaching us about the home and work and showed us the importance of cooking, cleaning and caring. A deep personal thanks goes to our other close chefs David Eckersley, Stina Nyberg, and Louise Shelley as well as the board of Hökarängens stadsdelsråd.

We are forever grateful to have had the chance to work with Joanna Lombard and Gunilla Lundahl. Their trust to go on our curatorial journey – while having no idea how it would end – is daring and inspiring. It was not always easy, sometimes our discussions were left behind, sometimes we could not find the funding to complete their ideas, but their thoughts and feedback were crucial for the outcome of the Home Works programme and have been with us ever since.

Sincere thanks to Konsthall C's wonderful staff and board for all their hard work, commitment and energy: Anna Ahlstrand, Maria (Mia) Andersson, Maria Bratt, Vanessa Ekedahl Longo, Sara Degerhammar, Christian Malmdin, Sophia Persson Persdotter, Joran Stamatakakos and Lisa Torgen Devgun. We also want to thank the install teams that made the exhibitions possible.

Anna Ahlstrand who collaborated with us for two years was fundamental for the Home Works programme. Her expertise of running Konsthall C since 2010 allowed the programme to embed itself locally and brought us in contact with so many inspiring artists, contributors and friends. Not only did she closely work on every aspect of Home Works while maintaining the art space, but she gave us both emotional and physical support as well as carefully questioning our thinking when needed, often by starting a sentence with 'the thing is', which became our entry point into rethinking and reflecting on our work together. Thank you Anna for all your brilliant ideas, support and care, without you we would still be lost in the laundry, spinning in the tumble dryer.

It is important to remember Home Works was only possible because of a huge amount of free labour from all those who were part of the programme (including ourselves). While we worked against the overwork embedded in the logic of cultural working, the challenge to work less continues to inform our ongoing struggle against the exploitation of cultural work and the devaluing of our reproductive labour.

There are many more to thank but the pages are enough, so in short thank you all!

/Jenny Richards and Jens Strandberg

CONTRIBUTORS

ANNA AHLSTRAND is a curator and exhibition producer. She has been involved in the running of Konsthall C (2010–2017), producing several separate projects and exhibitions at institutions such as the National Museum of Science and Technology, the Museum of Modern Art, Tensta konsthall and on a freelance basis. Ahlstrand currently works with art in the public realm at Haninge municipality.

SAMIRA ARIADAD is a freelance writer and lecturer in philosophy and politics. She has been active in Forum for women's politics, a group focused on women's reproductive labour. Currently she is a media activist in the anarchist magazine *Brand* and an active participant in political underground culture and hacker spaces.

BOLAGET is a collaboration between LILIAN LINDBLAD DOMEC and THOMAS GILEK. Lindblad Domec 1922–2017 attended The Royal Academy of Art, Stockholm, in the 1940s. Her work includes painting, drawing, film, animation, stage design, ceramics, embroidery. Gilek 1968–2016 studied literature at Uppsala University and History of Ideas at Stockholm University. He worked as an assistant to Lindblad Domec for eight years.

JONNA BORNEMARK is a professor of philosophy at The Center for Studies in Practical Knowledge. Her latest book is entitled *Det omätbaras renässans: en uppgörelse med pedanternas världsherravälde* (Volante, 2018). She is the editor of thirteen anthologies, most recently *Horsecultures in Transformation: The Ethical Question* (Routledge, 2019). She is also a frequent guest at Swedish radio shows and she contributes to Swedish daily newspapers.

JOHNNY CHANG is a Taiwanese-American multidisciplinary designer and artist. His practice is concerned with circumstances of distance and diaspora, politics of voice and listening, and examines processes of sense-making through the debris of language and images. MFA in Visual Communication from Konstfack 2019. From SF Bay Area, California, currently based in Stockholm.

STEPHAN DILLEMUTH lives in Bad Wiessee, Bavaria. He teaches at Munich's Academy of Fine Arts and is a member of the administrative council of the Academy of Fine Arts, Vienna.

MARIE EHRENBÅGE works as a cultural secretary at Farsta stadsdelsförvaltning (the local branch of Stockholm City Council), which among other things includes to plan and coordinate the annual art project for all council owned preschools in the area (approximately forty). Her main duties include facilitating children and young peoples' access to culture, and add social value in city-development processes.

MARYAM FANNI is a graphic designer with a degree from Konstfack University College of Arts, Crafts and Design. She is currently a PhD student in Design at HDK Academy of Arts and Design. She runs her own design studio focusing on printed matter for cultural and non-profit clients, and research-based collective, artistic practices. She is based in Hökarängen and has collaborated with Konsthall C on a variety of projects since 2013.

SILVIA FEDERICI is an Italian American scholar, teacher, and activist from the radical autonomist feminist Marxist tradition. She is co-founder of the International Wages for Housework Campaign.

AUÐUR HILDUR HÁKONARDÓTTIR worked with textiles between 1969 and 1990. Her work has been exhibited both locally and internationally. She was active in the SUM-artgroup in Iceland and the women's right movement. Hákonardóttir works are found in the collections of the major museums in Iceland and she was awarded the Icelandic Visual Arts medal of Honour in 2010. She is also known as a gardener and a writer.

RIKARD HEBERLING is a freelance graphic designer.

SANDI HILAL is an artist, architect, and researcher. She is currently Co-director of DAAR (Decolonizing Architecture Art Residency) co-founded with Alessandro Petti and Eyal Weizman. Hilal was the head of the Infrastructure and Camp Improvement Program in the West Bank at UNRWA (United Nations Relief and Works Agency for Palestine Refugees in the Near East) from 2008 to 2014. Together with Alessandro Petti, she founded Campus in Camps in 2007.

LOUISE KHADJEH-NASSIRI is a graphic designer (MFA, Konstfack) working predominantly with printed matter and in different collaborative constellations. Based in Malmö.

JOANNA LOMBARD was born in Algeria and lives in Sweden. Her work explores issues of language, identity, origin and exclusion. Her work has been exhibited in shows and biennials, including Children of the Children of the Revolution, Färgfabriken, Tunnel Vision! Momentum 8, and Ghosts, Spies and Grandmothers, the 8th Seoul Art Biennial, South Korea.

GUNILLA LUNDAHL is a writer and critic in the areas of architecture, design and art. She is one of the initiating members of the women's collective BIG (Bo i gemenskap) that since the 1970s has been researching co-housing processes. Lundahl has published a variety of books; *Leken och allvaret* (2017)

(Playful and Seriousness) attends to the designers Ulla and John Kandell practices, *Karaktär och känsla* (2001) (Character and Sensitivity) discusses a century of Swedish home craft. Lundahl lives and works in Stockholm.

DADY DE MAXIMO is an artist, fashion designer, journalist and activist based in Copenhagen. His practice is strongly characterised by activism and migration politics, which are informed by his upbringing in Rwanda in the 1980s and 1990s. He became a board member of CAMP in October 2015.

TEMI ODUMOSU is an art historian, curator and senior lecturer in cultural studies at Malmö University, Sweden. She is the author of the award-winning book: *Africans in English Caricature 1769–1819: Black Jokes White Humour* (2017). Her research and curatorial practices are concerned with visual coding, colonial archives/archiving, post-memorial art and performance, and ethics of care-in-representation. Overall, she focuses on the ways art can mediate social transformation and healing.

KHASROW HAMID OTHMAN is a civil engineer based in Stockholm. He was born in Erbil, the capital of the Kurdistan Region, in July 1945 and graduated from the University of Technology in Baghdad in 1969. He worked most of his life as an engineer but recently entered the world of writing, writing regularly in Arabic on the Al-Hiwar website.

CIARA PHILLIPS has exhibited widely in public galleries and museums in the United Kingdom and internationally. Her long-term artwork 'Workshop (2010–ongoing)' was nominated for the Turner Prize in 2014. Recent exhibitions of Phillips' work have been staged at: Kunsthall Stavanger; V&A Dundee; Benaki Museum, Athens; TATE Britain, London; Western Front, Vancouver; Konsthall C, Stockholm and The Showroom, London.

JENNY RICHARDS and JENS STRANDBERG know each other from Scotland. After losing contact, they met again in 2012, by coincidence on a street in New York, which was the beginning of their long friendship. Inspired by the International Wages for Housework Campaign and other feminist initiatives, they have developed a rampant joy towards challenging contemporary categorisations of labour and how some work (like domestic, school and artwork) is devalorised and unpaid. Instead of accepting this capitalist perspective, they have continuously encouraged collaborators, artists, students and domestic workers to unionise as a therapeutic act of empowerment in order to rethink societal structures and the politics of home. Since finishing Home Works, they have focused all their attention on climbing down the career ladder, throwing it away and joining the struggle.

KRISTINA SCHULTZ is a freelance designer who studied at Design Academy Eindhoven and Konstfack University of Arts, Craft and Design. *100 Days of Need and Greed* was her degree project for Konstfack in 2015. The project led to major conflicts in the Department of Industrial Design, and she has not yet had her degree approved.

HALLA ÞÓRLAUG ÓSKARSDÓTTIR works both in art and writing, in recent years she has focused on writing plays for stage and radio.

TONCIRKELN is a collaborative work by SHIDA SHAHABI and ANNA SÓLEY TRYGGVADÓTTIR. Shahabi (1989) graduated from the Royal Institute of Art in 2013 and has since worked in the field of music and performing arts. Sóley Tryggvadóttir (1984) is a composer and sound designer based in Stockholm. She graduated from the Stockholm Academy of Dramatic Arts in 2010.

NATHALIE WUERTH is an artist and care worker based in Stockholm, Sweden. In her work, the voice is used as a material, testing the limits of the body and its languages. Between pre-verbal states and noise, text and touch, citations and textures, the voice occupies another, that of a vacuum cleaner or an object-weave. Wuerth recently exhibited at Primary, United Kingdom and Error, Mexico.

(Home Works)

COLOPHON
Onomatopee #187
Cabinet project
www.onomatopee.net

ISBN: 978 94 93148 37 6

Home Works – A Cooking Book: Recipes for Organising with Art and Domestic Work has grown out of Home Works, Konsthall C, Stockholm, Sweden, (2015–2017)

Made possible thanks to the generous support of Längmanska Culture Fund

Administrated by Interim kultur artist cooperative

Part of Konstfack Artists' Book Collection 2. Konstfack, University of Arts, Crafts and Design, Stockholm, Sweden

EDITORS
Jenny Richards and Jens Strandberg

COPY EDITOR
Kevin Dooley

PROOFREADER
Katarina Trodden

GRAPHIC DESIGN
Johnny Chang and Louise Khadjeh-Nassiri, based on the Home Works graphic profile by Maryam Fanni and Rikard Heberling

TYPEFACE
Times New Roman, Arial, Courier, and Marker Felt

PRINTER
Printon, Tallinn, Estonia, 2020

We did our very best to credit everyone in this book appropriately. We apologise for any mistakes. Please contact us with any questions or concerns.

Konsthall C

Kulturföreningen Konsthall C
Cigarrvägen 16
123 57 Farsta, Sweden

www.konsthallc.se
info@konsthallc.se

ONOMATOPEE

Lucas Gasselstraat 2a
5613 LB Eindhoven
The Netherlands

www.onomatopee.net
info@onomatopee.net